Cormac McCarthy and Performance

Cormac McCarthy and Performance

PAGE, STAGE, SCREEN

Stacey Peebles

University of Texas Press   *Austin*

The author gratefully acknowledges permission to use excerpts from the following previously published material:

"Cormac McCarthy and Film." *The Cambridge Companion to Cormac McCarthy*. Ed. Steven Frye. New York: Cambridge UP, 2013. 162–174.
"Cormac McCarthy's Dramas and Screenplays." *Critical Insights: Cormac McCarthy*. Ed. David Cremean. Pasadena, CA: Salem Press, 2013. 161–178. Used by permission of EBSCO Information Services, Ipswich, MA.
"Hang and Rattle: John Grady Cole's Horsebreaking in Typescript, Novel, and Film." *Cormac McCarthy: All the Pretty Horses, No Country for Old Men, The Road*. Ed. Sara Spurgeon. London: Continuum, 2011. 43–57. By permission of Bloomsbury Publishing Plc.
"Hold Still": Models of Masculinity in the Coens' *No Country for Old Men.*" *No Country for Old Men: From Novel to Film*. Ed. Lynnea Chapman King, Rick Wallach, and Jim Welsh. Lanham, MD: The Scarecrow Press, 2009. 124–138.

Requests for permission to reproduce material from this work should be sent to:
Permissions
University of Texas Press
P.O. Box 7819
Austin, TX 78713-7819
http://utpress.utexas.edu/index.php/rp-form

♾ The paper used in this book meets the minimum requirements of
ANSI/NISO Z39.48-1992 (R1997) (Permanence of Paper).

LIBRARY OF CONGRESS CATALOGING-IN-PUBLICATION DATA
Names: Peebles, Stacey L. (Stacey Lyn), 1976–, author.
Title: Cormac McCarthy and performance : page, stage, screen / Stacey Peebles.
Description: First edition. | Austin : University of Texas Press, 2017. | Includes bibliographical references and index.
Identifiers: LCCN 2016035705
    ISBN 978-1-4773-1204-9 (cloth : alk. paper)
    ISBN 978-1-4773-1231-5 (pbk. : alk. paper)
    ISBN 978-1-4773-1205-6 (library e-book)
    ISBN 978-1-4773-1206-3 (non-library e-book)
Subjects: LCSH: McCarthy, Cormac, 1933—Criticism and interpretation. | Motion picture authorship—History and criticism. | Playwriting—History and criticism. | Authors, American—20th century—History and criticism. | Motion picture authorship.
Classification: LCC PS3563.C337 Z797 2017 | DDC 813/.54—dc23
LC record available at https://lccn.loc.gov/2016035705

doi:10.7560/312049

Contents

Acknowledgments

THANKS FIRST TO THE WONDERFUL STAFF OF THE BILL Wittliff Collections at Texas State University, where the Cormac McCarthy Papers are housed—Steve Davis, David Coleman, and above all the incomparable Katie Salzmann, who not only makes archive visits a delight but provides clarifications, advice about logistics, and lots of good humor. More generally, I am grateful to the Wittliff Collections for granting me permission to quote from material in the Cormac McCarthy Papers. Thanks also to Mr. Wittliff himself, who was gracious enough to speak with me about the subject of this book.

Many thanks to Silvia Erskine for granting me permission to quote from Albert Erskine's notes and correspondence, and also to Rebecca Tesich for permission to quote from Steve Tesich's unpublished screenplay adaptation of *Blood Meridian*.

My good friend Dianne Luce read all of my manuscript in draft, and I'm grateful, as I always am, for her excellent guidance and conversation. Steve Frye read portions of it and talked through most of the ideas with me, which is always as much fun as it is illuminating. Nick Lawrence, Dan Manheim, Scott Olsen, Steve Davis, and Dan Kirchner also read sections and gave me helpful comments. I'm grateful to them for their time and intellect, as I am to William Weber, Matthew Hallock, Danielle LaLonde, Shayna Sheinfeld, and Azita Onsaloo, who all helped me navigate areas of study that were relatively new to me, like conceptions of tragedy, theatrical history, apocalypticism, and recent theories of adaptation. Part of the fun in writing a book is the conversations and new friendships it leads you into, and this was no exception. Andy Ingalls was kind enough to get excited about every aspect of this project, and further to put me in touch with Austin Pendleton, who took time out of his superlatively busy schedule to talk to me about his experience with *The Sunset Limited*. Thanks to both of them for the good story-telling. I'm grateful as well to Dustin Anderson, who helped me come up with this book's title, and to Peter Josyph for sharing his own explorations of McCarthy and performance with me.

As was the case when I was writing my first book, I was lucky enough during the planning, writing, and revision of this one to have the feedback and support of a group of like-minded scholars: Danielle LaLonde, Robyn Cutright, Sara Egge, Kaelyn Wiles, Mary Daniels, KatieAnn Skogsberg, and Jenn Goetz. We may all work in different fields and in service of different disciplinary expectations, but nothing keeps the wheels turning like getting together to set goals, evaluate writing practices, and vent as needed.

Jim Burr's editorial guidance on the project, from start to finish, was impeccable and always good-natured. Kirk Curnutt once told me that being an editor means that you have the opportunity to ensure that "people are treated the right way," and Jim fits that bill to a tee. I'm also deeply grateful to James Cox, one of the readers Jim assigned who was, until recently, anonymous to me. Professor Cox read the manuscript through in two different iterations and provided ample and incisive commentary for each, undoubtedly making this book a better one.

Thanks finally to Cormac McCarthy, whose work has long thrilled and fascinated me, and to my family—especially Calliope, my own small, vivacious, verbally and physically gymnastic Muse.

Cormac McCarthy and Performance

Cormac McCarthy, Center Stage

"*T*ALK SHOW GODDESS MEETS MR. END OF THE WORLD." That's how one headline described the auspicious meeting between Oprah Winfrey and Cormac McCarthy that was broadcast on 5 June 2007 (Helm). Winfrey had selected the author's postapocalyptic novel *The Road* (2006) for her book club, and McCarthy, after many years of granting interviews very sparingly and those only in print, had agreed to a televised conversation with her. A few months earlier, *The Road* had won the Pulitzer Prize for fiction. At the ceremony, however, McCarthy wasn't present to accept the award—instead, Sonny Mehta, the editor in chief of McCarthy's publisher Alfred A. Knopf, accepted it on McCarthy's behalf ("2007 Pulitzer"). Throughout his long career, McCarthy had always made a point of keeping public statements about his work to a minimum, and even the Pulitzer ceremony was no exception. But suddenly he had agreed to appear on *The Oprah Winfrey Show*, a decision that would necessarily put the author and his writing center stage.

It was a moment that caught many off guard. McCarthy wasn't known for being particularly interested in media or popular culture figures like Winfrey, nor were audiences used to seeing him engage in public and publicized conversation. But as this book argues, conceiving of McCarthy as a reclusive, isolated author committed only to writing long fiction misses a great deal of his creative life and work. Winfrey's segment on McCarthy includes voice-over commentary that calls him the author of ten novels, and most people do know him for these books set in the American South or West that explore difficult questions about the seemingly endemic violence of the world, evinced in narratives that contrast sometimes terse regional dialect with highly elevated prose, creating what Dianne Luce has called an "oscillation between field and ground ... [and] the interplay between the realistic

1

and the philosophical" (*Reading* viii). Like McCarthy's "reclusiveness," however, these novels are really only half the story. Throughout McCarthy's career he has also been invested in writing for film and theater and so has been more engaged with media and performance than has been assumed. In addition to novels, he is the author of five screenplays and two works for theater, and he has been deeply involved with three of the seven film adaptations of his work. McCarthy is also more given to collaboration in his creative endeavors than has generally been recognized, as his work with people like editor Albert Erskine, director Richard Pearce, and whale biologist Roger Payne attests. A more complete consideration of McCarthy reveals that he has routinely welcomed others into his creative projects and, just as routinely, has demonstrated a keen interest in writing directly for film and theater as well as a desire to see how filmmakers would bring his writing to the screen.

McCarthy's interest in film dates back to the 1960s, when a number of production companies contacted Random House, his first publisher, about purchasing the rights to *The Orchard Keeper* (1965) and *Outer Dark* (1968). The 1960s also marked the beginning of McCarthy's relationship with Albert Erskine, his first editor, with whom he would have a decades-long partnership. Erskine undeniably helped shape his writing and career, and he accustomed McCarthy to working productively with others on later projects. One of those is 1977's *The Gardener's Son*, a screenplay based on an 1876 murder that he researched alongside director Richard Pearce and then further contributed to the production itself. Broadcast as part of PBS's *Visions* series, the film drew good ratings, accolades, and even two Emmy nominations.

That initial success was short-lived, however, as McCarthy wrote three screenplays in the 1970s and 1980s that were never produced or published in their original form. "El Paso/Juarez" (eventually retitled "Cities of the Plain") and "No Country for Old Men" were later reworked—the latter quite drastically—as novels, and "Whales and Men" reads like a workshop for McCarthy's ideas about ecology, language, and morality, especially as reflected in the Border Trilogy (*All the Pretty Horses* [1992], *The Crossing* [1994], and *Cities of the Plain* [1998]). Also in the 1980s, McCarthy wrote the first of his two works for theater, *The Stonemason* (1995). It has a troubled history, including accusations of racism and the unprecedented return of grant funding intended to aid in its production at the Arena Stage in Washington, DC; the full play remains unproduced. In contrast, *The Sunset Limited* (2006) has seen a number of successful productions both in the United States and abroad, beginning in Chicago with Steppenwolf Theatre Company's 2006 staging.

In 2000 the first big-budget film adaptation of a McCarthy novel hit screens when Billy Bob Thornton's *All the Pretty Horses* was released. Anticipation was high, but reviews and box-office receipts were lackluster, a disappointing reception that many attributed to conflict between Thornton and the studio, Miramax, over the film's running time. John Hillcoat's 2009 adaptation of *The Road* was the subject of similarly good press and even Oscar speculation during its production, but the film received mixed reviews upon its release. The risks inherent in adapting a popular novel paid off for the Coen brothers, however, when they brought *No Country for Old Men* to the screen in 2007, winning Oscars for Best Picture, Best Director, and Best Adapted Screenplay. Tommy Lee Jones, who plays Sheriff Ed Tom Bell in *No Country*, then had a more modest success with his adaptation of *The Sunset Limited* for HBO in 2011, which stars himself and Samuel L. Jackson.

The most recent films with a McCarthy pedigree are Ridley Scott's *The Counselor* (2013) and James Franco's *Child of God* (2014). The former is particularly notable because McCarthy wrote the screenplay, his first since *The Gardener's Son* to be produced, and he also served as an executive producer on the film. Finally, no consideration of McCarthy and performance would be complete without addressing *Blood Meridian* (1985) — McCarthy's sprawling, philosophical, and hyperbolically violent Western that's been tempting directors since at least the mid-1990s. Ridley Scott, Todd Field, Andrew Dominik, Tommy Lee Jones, John Hillcoat, and James Franco have all tried, with varying degrees of investment, to adapt the novel, and at least two full-length screenplays have been written, by Steve Tesich and William Monahan. None of them, however, has ever made it into production, fueling speculation that the novel may be unfilmable — though that speculation has been countered by McCarthy's own insistence that it could be done, and done well.

In one sense, the sections of this book dealing particularly with the film adaptations of McCarthy's novels may seem to fall prey to one of the dangers of adaptation studies: the automatic privileging of literature over film. "By organizing themselves around canonical authors," Thomas Leitch writes, such projects can run the risk of "establish[ing] a presumptive criterion for each new adaptation" and "establish[ing] literature as a proximate cause of adaptation that makes fidelity to the source text central to the field" (3). Certainly McCarthy is indeed the focus of this book, though I hope the study as a whole demonstrates and analyzes McCarthy's engagement *with* film throughout his career rather than simply using his work as a de facto measuring stick for those adaptations that were produced by others. And as Leitch does in his own study, I avoid using fidelity as a single criterion for judging those adaptations and instead discuss the variety of ways that fidelity has been a concern for the filmmakers themselves.

This book, then, is primarily an exploration of McCarthy's engagement with film and theater that uses correspondence, manuscript materials, interviews, and critical sources to tell this relatively unknown story of the author's work and its relation to the screen and stage. In addition, emerging from this story is the influence of tragedy on McCarthy's career. This is a fitting interest for an author invested in drama and performance as well as long fiction, though it also speaks to McCarthy's rich and various portrayal of violence and suffering in all of his work. McCarthy could well be said to have a tragic vision of the world, as he considers violence and suffering inevitable but places great weight on our human responses to them. These responses are enacted in moral choices, in physical labor, and in narrative—stories told by the characters as well as, of course, McCarthy himself.

Just as classical tragedy calls characters and audience to acknowledge and respond to the devastation at hand—"I'm at the edge of hearing horrors," says Oedipus on the cusp of his anagnorisis, or tragic recognition, "but I *must hear*"—McCarthy also emphasizes the role of the witness.[1] John Grady Cole and Llewelyn Moss are the heroes of two of McCarthy's most obviously tragic works, though Billy Parham and Ed Tom Bell, as witnesses to the violence that overcomes John Grady and Moss, are no less significant as characters, and perhaps more so. There is no shortage of other examples: the "chorus" of townspeople who offer their reflections on the life and death of Lester Ballard in *Child of God* (1973); the opening of *Blood Meridian*, which calls on the reader to "[s]ee the child" (not to mention the kid's own witnessing of the violence around him, as well as the judge's complex interrogation of witnessing as a fundamental human practice); and the opening of *Suttree* (1979), which also invites the reader to contemplate a *"world beyond all fantasy, malevolent and tactile and dissociate,"* a city *"beset by a thing unknown"* (4). The last paragraph of this italicized invocation frames the story to come as performance—perhaps as tragedy, or at least its aftermath: *"The rest indeed is silence,"* it begins, in a nod to Hamlet's last words. Then: *"A curtain is rising on the western world. A fine rain of soot, dead beetles, anonymous small bones. The audience sits webbed in dust. Within the gutted sockets of the interlocutor's skull a spider sleeps and the jointed ruins of the hanged fool dangle from the flies, bone pendulum in motley. Fourfooted shapes go to and fro over the boards. Ruder forms survive"* (5).

In an interview about *The Sunset Limited*, McCarthy remarked—summarily and without elaboration—that "literature is about tragedy" (Carr). Regardless of his reasons for making that association, the further considerations that his work encourages are all topics engaged by tragedy as well as by the genre's long line of theorists: the workings (or failings) of jus-tice; the nature of the divine; the effects of human choices in what can seem like a deterministic universe; the individual's place in society as well as the natural world; understandings of evil, love, and knowledge; and the charac-ter and function of representation itself. In the chapters that follow, I'll tell the story of McCarthy's work with film and theater while drawing out that work's tragic elements and implications, illuminated by readings of the texts and the performances themselves as well as by periodic references to the most influential of those tragic theorists.

The first in that long line of theorists is Aristotle. His understanding and framing of the dramatic form developed in fifth-century Athens emphasized plot and character—and more specifically, the importance of individual choice and action. "Men are the certain kinds of individuals they are as a result of their character," Aristotle wrote, "but they become happy or miser-able as a result of their actions" (13). In tragedy those actions lead to misery, a change of fortune that is most powerfully staged, according to Aristotle, in scenes of peripeteia, or reversal (when things go bad), and anagnorisis, or recognition (when the tragic hero recognizes how and why things have gone bad). That hero should be a kind of "man in the middle," or as Aris-totle put it, neither a person "superior in excellence and uprightness" nor one of "baseness and rascality" (24). He does what he does out of hamar-tia, a much-discussed term that has been translated in many different ways, most commonly as "tragic flaw," but also, as Julian Young notes, as "fault," "mistake," "fallibility," "frailty," and "error" (35). In other words, some have understood the events of tragedy to be a consequence of character, a "flaw" such as hubris in the hero himself that brings him down; others understand them as the result of a wrong choice, which could very well have been made in ignorance. Indeed, considering different tragedies and different interpre-tations of them can lead to any number of conclusions. Kathy Eden writes that perhaps the best way to think about hamartia is as "somewhere between an act that is fully intended and one that is completely unexpected"—that is, an act that is "not, strictly speaking, voluntary, in that the agent does not freely choose the act with full knowledge of its particulars, [and] neither is it, strictly speaking, involuntary, in that it is not wholly unforeseen" (46). As I discuss in chapter 5, Richard Gilmore has noted that hamartia is a Greek term derived from archery that means "off the mark," suggesting that "one's aim has been slightly off." This definition, Gilmore argues, is particularly apt for Llewelyn Moss in McCarthy's novel *No Country for Old Men*, who is first seen firing a shot using both caution and considerable skill but who is never-theless a bit off the mark. The devastating events of the narrative all follow from there (62).

McCarthy himself reflects a generally Aristotelean notion of tragedy in another interview, this one about the title character of his screenplay *The Counselor* (2013), whom he describes as "a decent guy who gets up one morning and decides to do something wrong." He then adds, "And that's all it takes"—for tragedy to ensue ("The Counselor" commentary). The counselor is "decent"—not base, but not particularly superior either—and his decision sets in motion a machinery that can only end badly. As I discuss in chapter 6, the counselor can be understood as an Aristotelean tragic hero, though McCarthy's screenplay also includes elements of Jacobean revenge tragedy, as Russell Hillier has noted. Those elements of revenge tragedy, however, are eliminated from Ridley Scott's film, an omission that has the effect of rendering a major female character less as an intelligent and motivated avenger (if an excessive one) and more as a sexualized monster, destroying everything around her with her unquenchable appetites.

McCarthy's most obviously tragic works—the screenplay of "Cities of the Plain" and the Border Trilogy as a whole, *No Country for Old Men* (2005), and *The Counselor*—can be generally understood in Aristotelean terms, though his work resonates with other theories of the genre as well. Aristotle's description of tragedy's structure and effects stands in opposition to his teacher Plato's views on poetry generally.[2] Aristotle believed that poetry (a category that includes tragedy) arises from humanity's "natural desire to imitate" and "universal enjoyment in imitations," a pleasure that was not merely idle but educational: "[A]s they contemplate reproductions of objects they find themselves gaining knowledge as they try to reason out what each thing is; for instance, that this man is such and such a person" (5–6). Plato, however, was suspicious of representations and worried about the influence of poetry in a number of his dialogues. He does so most famously in the *Republic*, in which Socrates and his interlocutors discuss how an ideal, just city would be constituted. In such a place it would be necessary to restrict or censor the poets, Plato writes, as they "composed false tales" and often offered portrayals of gods behaving badly, an inappropriate influence for the "thoughtless young things" in need of a strong moral education (55). But more broadly, in book 7 of the *Republic*, Plato suggests in his "Allegory of the Cave" that the way to true happiness is to free oneself from a fettered existence watching shadows dancing on a cave wall and move upwards toward the light—to go from watching shadows, or imitations of things, to seeing the things themselves in the daylight, and finally to contemplating the sun, or "the *idea* of the good … the cause of all that is right and fair in everything" (196). Those prisoners in the cave, watching shadows cast by "artifacts … statues of men and other animals wrought from stone, wood, and every kind of material," may be well entertained. They don't realize, however, that the images they see are shadows of imitations of material things and thus several levels removed from day-light, or the world of the Forms—the nonmaterial, causal, and higher level of reality. For Plato art can be diverting, but dangerously so—art distracts rather than illuminates.

Though McCarthy seems to follow Aristotle in his understanding of tragedy and is himself an artist—and thus someone who presumably believes that artistic illumination is indeed possible—his work often evinces both an appreciation of Plato as well as a suspicion of representation. Garry Wallace reported in 1992 that Irving Brown, a friend of McCarthy's and a professor of philosophy, believed that McCarthy "had over-read Plato," a statement that confirms the author's interest in Plato even if his interpretation was a matter of debate (135). *The Gardener's Son* and "Whales and Men" include characters wondering about the possibility of photographs or language to "replace the world," and the theme shows up in different ways in the Border Trilogy and *The Sunset Limited*. Dianne Luce has written about the influence of Plato on McCarthy's Southern work in particular in her book *Reading the World*, and in another article covering "Whales and Men" and *The Crossing* (1994) she writes that for McCarthy, "'the thing itself' carries connotations of truth, ultimate essence, the sacred heart of things that inspires reverence, and he implies that humans access the thing itself only by transcending the obstacles posed by artifact, language, and physical sense in moments of spiritual in-sight that constitute a direct and immediate apperception of the 'world as given'" ("Road and Matrix" 208–209).[3]

The Border Trilogy, which developed from McCarthy's original screenplay "Cities of the Plain," is very much concerned with this interplay of myth, language, dreams, and lived experience, all shot through with the inevitable presence of injury, pain, violence, and suffering. But the Border Trilogy also takes place in real locations and precisely situated historical contexts. As John Wegner has argued, for instance, John Grady Cole may not have fought in the Mexican Revolution, but it has everything to do with what happens to him.[4] And that relevance exists because he crosses a border and tries to make a life for himself in a different culture, one in which he is an admirably fluent speaker of the language but uncomprehending of other matters, like the intri-cacies of gender relations in a family and community. John Grady's conflicts with the dueña Alfonsa over his relationship with Alejandra and with the pimp Eduardo over Magdalena (and perhaps even with his beloveds them-selves, Alejandra and Magdalena) might seem an apt example of the way that Hegel understood tragedy. "The essence of tragedy," Hegel argued, "consists in the fact that, within conflict, each of the opposing sides has its *justifica-tion* while each can establish the true and positive content of its own aim and character only by denying and infringing the equally justified power of the other" (1196). Mark Roche puts it like this: "Tragedy arises, according to Hegel, when a hero courageously asserts a substantial and just position and so falls prey to a one-sidedness that is defined at one and the same time by greatness and by guilt.... [T]he conflict can be resolved only with the fall of the hero" (51–52). John Grady and the dueña could be understood as versions of Antigone and Creon: the former justifying his desire to be with Alejandra on the basis of love and his own hard work and good character, and the latter countering with points about cultural difference, gender roles, and familial expectations. Given their individual backgrounds, cultural knowledge, and current circumstances, they are both right.

David Williams argues for a reading of *Blood Meridian* that works similarly, claiming that the novel "[pits] irreconcilable metaphysical options against each other" (6) as represented by the kid and the judge (though Williams follows Charles Segal's understanding of tragedy more explicitly than he does Hegel's). Identifying these opposing justifications and ethical or even metaphysical systems is productive, I believe, in thinking about McCarthy's Western works in particular, though I would argue that the dueña in *All the Pretty Horses* is a more formidable opponent—one whose stance is quite reasonably defended—than, say, Eduardo in *Cities of the Plain*, whose ethical position is more difficult to justify. More broadly, however, Hegel's understanding of how tragedy works as "the dramatisation of historical forces and their casualties" (as Jennifer Wallace describes it) is different than the way that McCarthy has said he thinks about history (121). For Hegel, tragedy is a demonstration of the violent but inevitable progress of civilization: "The heart of Hegel's general philosophy," writes Julian Young, "is a telling of 'world' history (in practice, the history of the West) as a *Bildungsroman*, as a series of painful but productive conflicts through which 'world' or 'human spirit' educates itself by passing through a sequence of 'shapes of consciousness' (worldviews) where each 'shape' is more advanced, more 'rational,' than its predecessor" (111). McCarthy has been notably skeptical of that view. "There's no such thing as life without bloodshed," he told Richard Woodward in 1992. "I think the notion that the species can be improved in some way, that everyone could live in harmony, is a really dangerous idea. Those who are afflicted with this notion are the first one[s] to give up their souls, their freedom. Your desire that it be that way will enslave you and make your life vacuous." It's clear that McCarthy was familiar with Hegel at least in passing—a note in his manuscript materials reads, "Hegel says that man as a being alone before the universe is heroic"[5]—but where tragedy is concerned, McCarthy's work might be better illuminated by Hegel's notion of conflict rather than how Hegel framed the outcome of that conflict.

Nietzsche framed tragedy's central conflict differently, as an opposition between the Apollonian forces of reason, order, art, and individuality against the Dionysian forces of jubilation, intoxication, and "primordial unity." "We attempt to live necessarily in the world of Apollo," Jennifer Wallace explains, "by making representations to ourselves of the world, the gods, justice, reason, and so on." But then we discover the Dionysian world hidden behind those things. Often the devastation of tragedy and the annihilation of the tragic hero becomes "strangely the source of joy. [Nietzsche] relishes the tearing down of individualism back to the 'primordial oneness' because it involves a degree of self-abandonment and release" (125). William Quirk has written specifically about *The Sunset Limited* as a minimalist example of Nietzschean tragedy that pits the rational, individualist professor against his Coltrane-loving, soul-food-cooking savior, an unorthodox evangelist who preaches the brotherhood of all men, a unity accessible even without the knowledge of Christian sacred text. These two characters' rhetorical struggle reflects Nietzsche's framing of tragic conflict in many ways. More broadly, Nietzsche's notion of a communal understanding that transcends language echoes McCarthy's suspicion of representation as well as his fascination with the animal world. McCarthy often describes animals existing in a community bound by sense perception and instinctive understanding rather than language—since "[n]omenclature is the very soul of secondhandedness," as a character puts it in "Whales and Men" (57).

Nietzsche describes the tragic hero ultimately being forced out of his isolationism and back into the primal unity, while René Girard sees the opposite—the tragic hero is forced out of the community and into exile. Girard explains both religious practice and tragedy as rituals of sacrifice, in which a scapegoat figure is targeted in order to purge the community of an outbreak of chaotic violence and restore equilibrium. (Restore it, at least until the next outbreak.) A character like Oedipus, then, "becomes the repository of all the community's ills" (77). "Violence is not to be denied," explains Girard, "but it can be diverted to another object, something it can sink its teeth into" (4). The sacrifice "serves to protect the entire community from its own violence; it prompts the entire community to choose victims outside itself" (8)—or at least to choose victims it can claim are outsiders, different, "not like us." It's a description of culminating violence that resonates with McCarthy's portrayal of alienation and difference, of characters seeking, and often failing, to find communities of their own. McCarthy's first screenplay—which is also his first work written for performance of any kind—is *The Gardener's Son*, and though the reasons behind the protagonist's act of violence are left implicit, that character's sense of alienation can be understood as a significant factor in his murder of a textile mill owner. With his subsequent execution, the community perhaps hopes to staunch the violence of social change and industrialization, a misdirection that is convenient if not effective: in events like these, explains Girard, "society is seeking to deflect upon a relatively indifferent victim, a 'sacrificeable' victim, the violence that would otherwise be vented on its own members, the people it most desires to protect" (4). Arguably, Lester Ballard, the protagonist of *Child of God*, is similarly tragic, as his violent acts of necrophilia and murder as well as his subsequent institutionalization and death are the result of having been ostracized so completely by his community—his difference created by a community that had already labeled him as such, despite his status as "a child of God much like yourself perhaps" (4).

All of McCarthy's works are suffused with both human and natural violence. Set against that devastation are the human communities and ecological systems that McCarthy portrays as potentially sustaining forces. Various characters imagine that animals like whales, horses, and wolves have access to this kind of transcendent communion, though it's also evident in humans' acts of kindness toward one another. In the novel *Cities of the Plain*, Billy Parham insists on stopping to help a group of Mexican workers whose truck has a flat tire. "The hell with that," comments his friend Troy, but Billy expends considerable effort to get the tire patched and reinflated (30). By the time he finishes, night has fallen. When Troy later questions him about it and asks if Billy did it because of some sort of "religious thing," Billy responds by telling him a story (one that would be familiar to readers of *The Crossing*):

> No. It aint nothin like that. It's just that the worst day of my life was one time when I was seventeen years old and me and my bud—my brother—we was on the run and he was hurt and there was a truckload of Mexicans just about like them back yonder appeared out of nowhere and pulled our bacon out of the fire. I wasnt even sure their old truck could outrun a horse, but it did. They didnt have any reason to stop for us. But they did. I dont guess it would of even occurred to em not to. That's all. (36)

McCarthy celebrates moral action with or for other beings as, paradoxically, both a counter to and an inherent part of the tragic weight of his characters' experiences. And while McCarthy is a great portrayer of wordless action and the silent communion of shared labor, more often humans have to try to understand each other through language. That can be a source of great beauty and solace—Billy chooses to share this story with Troy, after all, rather than merely remember it—but it can also be the source of misunderstanding, misdirection, even loss of "the real," as many characters worry. For McCarthy, violence and the creation of community are the two poles of human existence, and tragedy is the shaping of language around those two experiences. In the best of circumstances, language (or representation gener-ally) is a way for characters to respond to devastation and move toward com-munity, though it can also be an obfuscating force. Thus the significance of the witness, often left behind after violence claims the tragic hero's life, de-ciding what story to tell in response.

BRINGING THE MYTH ONSTAGE

John-Pierre Vernant and Pierre Vidal-Naquet argue that tragedy in fifth-century Athens was spurred by a kind of historical collision: "On the way out was the old society which looked back to the heroic past, myths and belief in the gods; on the way in was a new secular society governed by law, logic and democratic practice" (Wallace 22). In other words, tragedy al-lowed the Greeks to reexamine their myths, and mythic heroes, in light of a new historical context and different cultural practices. Certainly many of McCarthy's narratives (from *The Orchard Keeper* onward) depict similar col-lisions between older values and a modernized landscape and society. For ex-ample, as I discuss in more detail in chapter 2, McCarthy describes his origi-nal screenplay "Cities of the Plain" as the story of "John Grady's romanticism and stubborn pride as emissary of the clearly defined values of the old west." Those values are "already well under siege" and ultimately bring him "to a confrontation that can be neither avoided or survived."[6]

And in some sense, when McCarthy himself appeared on *The Oprah Win-frey Show*, he allowed for a reexamination of the myths that had defined him as an author—that he is reclusive, isolated, staunchly traditionalist. His pres-ence on this public stage both reflected and subverted those notions. Oprah's first statement to McCarthy emphasized the rarity of seeing him in person: "Well, you look just like you do on the back of the cover." Though his re-spect for Winfrey is clear, McCarthy also seems a bit apprehensive as it be-gins. "This is a first for me," he acknowledges. Though McCarthy has been a published author since 1965, and by 2007 could call himself the winner of a MacArthur Fellowship, a National Book Award, and the Pulitzer Prize, among other accolades and a host of popular and critical acclaim, he had granted only two major interviews in all that time. Both were conducted by Richard Woodward, for the *New York Times* in 1992 and for *Vanity Fair* in 2005. (Garry Wallace's account of meeting McCarthy was published in 1992, and there are a smattering of short interviews in Tennessee newspapers from the 1960s and '70s ["Author"; "Gardner's Son"; Byrd; Jordan]. The Tennessee articles are brief, and the Wallace essay, though illuminating, is the story of a friendly encounter that happened three years previously; Wallace notes that it was "neither intended nor conducted as an interview," though he did ask McCarthy's permission to publish it [139].)

Seeking publicity, then, has not been a priority for McCarthy, and in a culture where some authors blog, Tweet, maintain Facebook pages, and otherwise promote themselves and their work, McCarthy's reluctance to do anything of the sort can be the subject of fascination. In the interview with Winfrey, for instance, she asks him about a story told by his second wife, Annie DeLisle, who said that at one point during their married life she and McCarthy were living in "total poverty" in a dairy barn near Knoxville. "Someone would call up and offer him $2,000 to come speak at a university about his books," she said. "And he would tell them that everything he had to say was there on the page. So we would eat beans for another week" (Woodward, "Venomous"). Anecdotes like this one have often been repeated in order to justify calling McCarthy stubborn, archaic, or even a hermit.

Winfrey chooses McCarthy's resistance to publicity as her entry point. "Why have you never done it before?" she asks, referring to the interview itself. "Well, I don't think it's good for your head," he responds, and a reaction shot of Winfrey shows her involuntary double take. "You spend a lot of time thinking about how to write a book," he elaborates, "you probably shouldn't be talking about it—you probably should be doing it." It's nothing against the press, he clarifies. "You work your side of the street and I'll work mine," he says, and laughs. Though McCarthy appears slightly impatient with questions about whether he has a writing schedule or is motivated by a "passion" for writing, he continues to engage with her on topics like his representation of women, how he became a parent at an older age, his vacillating belief in God and the importance of prayer, and the impact of 9/11 on a story like *The Road*. He takes Winfrey seriously, and the conversation is a substantial one rather than the stonewalling of someone uncomfortable with personal interaction. It's notable, too, that it took place at the Santa Fe Institute, a scientific research and education center where McCarthy maintains an office and enjoys the company and conversation of physicists, biologists, economists, and mathematicians, all of whom study complex systems.

As the conversation comes to a close, Winfrey asks him if he cares that his books are now read by millions rather than just a few thousand, as was the case for several decades of his career. "You know," he smiles, "in all honesty, I have to say that I really don't. I just don't. I mean, you would like for the people who'll appreciate the book to read it, but as far as many, many people reading it—so what?" It's not a sentiment that Winfrey is used to hearing. "You are a different kind of author," she marvels as the segment ends. McCarthy describes himself here as a writer uninterested in presenting himself to the public. He seems to have no desire to perform—he's certainly no

Norman Mailer or Truman Capote, who regularly put their outsized personalities on display on the talk show circuit. Yet here McCarthy is, doing *Oprah*.

And unlike true shunners of public recognition, such as J. D. Salinger or Thomas Pynchon, McCarthy also appears on the dust jackets of his books—which, as Winfrey mentioned, had previously been one of the only ways to get a look at him. Those photos reveal McCarthy in an impressive range of guises: as a nicely dressed young man with just a hint of a smile on the jacket of his first novel *The Orchard Keeper*; caught in the midst of speech on *Outer Dark*; as a mustachioed fellow in a wide-collared shirt on *Child of God*; denim-jacketed by the Tennessee River on *Suttree*; slouched casually in front of piles of books on *Blood Meridian*; looking serious and more professionally rendered on the jackets of the novels of the Border Trilogy; and in the same classic head shot for both *No Country for Old Men* and *The Road*. Especially on the jackets of his earlier novels, McCarthy appears relaxed and at ease with this form of self-presentation. And less than a year after McCarthy's *Oprah* appearance he showed up at the 2007 Academy Awards—the very temple of performance—cheering alongside his young son John Francis McCarthy as *No Country for Old Men*, the film adaptation of his novel, won four Oscars, including the one for Best Picture. Though McCarthy has largely avoided making public statements about his work, "recluse" is a misnomer—and a label for which reporter Richard Woodward is perhaps most responsible, as I discuss in chapter 1.

WHERE THE STORY TAKES YOU

In McCarthy's conversation with Winfrey, she asked him where his idea for the story of *The Road* came from—a book with an ending that, as I discuss in chapter 4, critics have alternately called both hopeful and devastating, happy and sad. When he started writing, Winfrey asked, did he know how the story would end? "No, I had no idea where it was going," he replied. "Some people say, do you plot everything out?" he elaborated. "And I say, no, no, that would be *death*." He laughed. "You can't plot things out. You just have to trust where it comes from."

That might seem like an odd statement from an author who has been so demonstrably interested in tragedy. Regardless of the particular combinations of story, implication, and affect that scholars have variously argued the genre demonstrates, everyone agrees that tragedies don't end happily. Jennifer Wallace aptly lists the genre's recurring features: "Many plays work up towards a particular crisis and explore the subsequent feeling of irreversibility. Many tragic plays dramatise loss, whether that be the loss of life or simply the loss of hope. Most plays include some elements of conflict, chiefly between one individual and the world, fate or the gods." But, she adds, "not all plays, which are universally regarded as tragedies, contain these features. And none of these plot features means anything if they do not stir emotion" (3). Steven Knepper has written specifically about McCarthy's screenplay *The Counselor* as tragedy and how a consideration of the play leads to further questions applicable to the genre overall:

> Is it more about the existential plight of a lone individual or the political crisis of a community? Is tragic recognition a matter of stoic acceptance or solidarity with the suffering? Does tragedy veil particular, contingent instances of loss and violence as immutable aspects of the human condition? Is true tragedy resolutely pessimistic? If so, is tragedy effectively dead in the modern West, which has inherited religions of messianic hope and mythologies of secular progress? Or do these currents open up the possibility of a new form of tragedy? *The Counselor* raises all of these questions. (38)

But Terry Eagleton puts it most succinctly in his defense of the relevance of tragedy against charges like those by Bertolt Brecht and George Steiner that it situates narratives transhistorically and thus fosters "political fatalism" (and which Knepper engages in his argument regarding *The Counselor*). Eagleton quite rightly notes that "no definition of tragedy more elaborate than 'very sad' has ever worked," at least not as a universal descriptor (3).

Although McCarthy often engages with the structures and thematic concerns of tragedy, he would seem to resist even that inevitability—that things will turn out badly. In his own work, things aren't "plotted out" in advance. Rather, he tries to "trust where it comes from," which is clearly not a set of narrative, stylistic, or thematic expectations. Even in McCarthy's fictional worlds, where violence is often endemic and suffering is unavoidable, one shouldn't make assumptions about the way things will turn out—failing to be open to possibility constitutes the worst kind of capitulation. This is, I think, a distinctive element of McCarthy's vision. In the viscerally dark world that he describes, some characters revel in that darkness, while others struggle, perhaps fruitlessly, toward some kind of illumination. Maybe things will indeed end in a way that is "very sad," and even tragic, but the characters keep struggling nonetheless. Who knows, after all, where the story will take you?

First Forays

*O*N 6 JANUARY 1977 THE NEWEST INSTALLMENT OF A television series called *Visions* premiered on PBS. The series ran from 1976 to 1980 and offered original dramas each week, many of which were historically based. That day's film was called *The Gardener's Son*, and it told the story of Robert McEvoy, who in 1876 had shot and killed textile mill owner James Gregg in Graniteville, South Carolina. The film was directed by Richard Pearce and starred recognizable faces like Brad Dourif as McEvoy, Ned Beatty, Kevin Conway, and Jerry Hardin. Most viewers wouldn't have heard of the screenwriter, a relatively unknown author named Cormac McCarthy.

Given that, they certainly wouldn't have noticed when the screenwriter himself made a small cameo in the film. Immediately before the tensions between McEvoy and Gregg flare into gunfire, Gregg leads a group of businessmen on a tour of his mill. They eye the clattering machinery and busy workers with solemn appreciation and shake Gregg's hand as they exit. One of them wears a dark suit and top hat and is noticeably younger than the others. It's McCarthy, portraying one of the class of industry bosses that so enrage his protagonist. The cameo is ironic and a bit Hitchcockian, surely a delight for this author making his debut into the world of cinema.

But this foray onscreen was neither the first nor the last example of McCarthy's interest in and involvement with film. Most people who have heard of McCarthy—and that's considerably more now than in 1977—think of him primarily as the author of award-winning novels like *All the Pretty Horses* and *The Road* and further as the kind of traditionalist who would likely scorn screenwriting as an artistic practice. American novelists who have turned to the movies have often belittled the work, even when it paid the bills. "I once tried to work seriously at my craft," said Nathanael West, referring to his first three novels, "but was absolutely unable to make even the beginning of a living" (Hamilton 165). So he went to Hollywood—to work less "seriously," but also to make decent money. F. Scott Fitzgerald made the same move in 1937 to write scripts for MGM, including some work on *Gone with the Wind*. He, too, saw the work as a necessity rather than a creative opportunity. "Listen, Nunally, get out of Hollywood," he told Nunally Johnson, another novelist who began writing screenplays. "It will ruin you. You have a talent—you'll kill it there" (Hamilton 188–189). William Faulkner considered writing for the movies to be a way of financing his novels—screenwriting was a somewhat dirty practice that nonetheless could enable you to do your real work. "The way I see it," he said, "it's like chopping cotton or picking potato bugs off plants; you know damn well it's not painting the Sistine Chapel or winning the Kentucky Derby. But a man likes the feel of some money in his pocket" (Fine 155–156).

Despite these negative attitudes toward Hollywood, as Mark Eaton points out, "nearly every major American writer of the modern period"—and here he's referring to the first half of the twentieth century—"either sold work to the studios or actually worked in them" (468). Even a partial list of those authors, he notes, would include

> not only [James M.] Cain, Fitzgerald, and West, but also Maxwell
> Anderson, Stephen Vincent Benét, Raymond Chandler, John Dos
> Passos, Theodore Dreiser, William Faulkner, Dashiell Hammett,
> Horace McKoy, Frank O'Hara, Dorothy Parker, Robert Sherwood,
> and Thornton Wilder, as well as British writers like Aldous Huxley,
> Christopher Isherwood, and Evelyn Waugh. (468)

Eaton goes on to argue that Hollywood has influenced modern American fiction in several ways: "as a conscious or unconscious pressure on literary form; as an influence on literary content; and as a major source of income for writers through selling screen rights to novels and stories as well as through screenwriting contracts" (472). Though many of the authors themselves may have dismissed their efforts as secondary or as a means to a financial end, the aggregate effect on American letters of all that thinking about movies is undeniable.

Despite McCarthy's own appreciative engagement with screenwriting and film production, his reputation has largely been that of an old-fashioned author who would likely disdain Hollywood at least as much as West, Fitzgerald, and Faulkner did. That reputation is due in large part to Richard Woodward, who interviewed McCarthy for the *New York Times* in 1992 and introduced the author to the general public for the first time. It was a more momentous introduction than most realized. *All the Pretty Horses* was about to be published and make McCarthy, at long last, a bestselling and critically acclaimed author, not to mention a winner of the National Book Award. But just as he didn't attend the ceremony to accept his 2007 Pulitzer Prize, neither did he turn up to accept that earlier award. And after Woodward, he didn't grant another interview for thirteen years. In the interim Woodward's article gained a great deal of retrospective weight and became the classic portrait of McCarthy, the only widely available resource during that time for people looking to find out more about this author, his life, and his creative work.

Woodward describes McCarthy as a warm storyteller who is eager to talk about his many interests, but as someone who is also, in his words, "hermitic" and "an obstinate loner." Echoing the characteristics he saw in many of McCarthy's protagonists, Woodward writes about a man who "has spent most of his adult life outside the ring of the campfire." It's a romantic portrayal, one of an author who has endured "neglect and hardship" in service to an uncompromising vision and whose status as "the kind of writer who has almost ceased to exist"—a true "writer's writer"—reflects his own "premodern" characters and their ideas of virtue.

Yet Woodward does mention McCarthy's friendships with people like director Richard Pearce, physicist Murray Gell-Mann, and whale biologist Roger Payne and, significantly, notes that his relationship with his longtime Random House editor Albert Erskine was the sort "that scarcely exists anymore in American publishing" because it was so close. "There is a father-son feeling," he quotes Erskine as saying, though he also adds Erskine's sheepish admission that despite the support, Random House never managed to sell very many of McCarthy's books. Woodward also makes passing reference to an old screenplay that would be the basis of the Border Trilogy's third novel. Woodward doesn't give a title, but this is "Cities of the Plain," which McCarthy was indeed working on as early as 1978.

Details like these, however, are overshadowed by the more striking image of the solitary novelist pounding out stories of lonesome male heroes on an old typewriter. He works alone with nary a screen in sight—don't bother him, and don't ask him where he gets his ideas. But the reality is a bit different, and people like Erskine and Pearce are at the center of that difference. McCarthy worked closely with Erskine as he began his career as an author, and Erskine helped him negotiate a number of early queries about adapting his work for film. *The Gardener's Son*, however, was the first of McCarthy's works to appear onscreen, and McCarthy writes the historical story as a Southern Gothic tragedy that results in two deaths and the devastation of two families, but which is deliberately ambiguous about what individual or social forces cause the events to unfold as they do.

In July 1963 Cormac McCarthy was an unpublished author who had just completed the manuscript of his first book, an untitled work that would eventually become *The Orchard Keeper*. He was working with Lawrence Bensky, an editor at Random House; he had chosen to contact Random House about his book because, as he told Woodward almost thirty years later, it was the only press he had heard of. Bensky was pleased with the product and wrote to Albert Erskine, another editor at Random House, who had famously shepherded authors like Faulkner, Ralph Ellison, Eudora Welty, and Malcolm Lowry into publication. Bensky announced McCarthy's completion of the manuscript, adding that "[t]his is a writer of real talent with an unlimited future." In the upper right corner of the letter, there is a small notation, most likely made by Erskine before he filed the letter: "Film."[1]

One of Erskine's first thoughts about McCarthy, then, was the cinematic potential of his work. That potential would gather speed in the coming years, as production companies began to contact Random House and the author about film rights and adaptation possibilities. First, though, that book had to come out, and Erskine rolled up his sleeves to address the manuscript and its new, unknown author. It was fitting, especially at the outset of his career, that McCarthy ended up working with the former editor of both Faulkner and Welty, as his first four novels are all set in Tennessee and are firmly rooted in the Southern and, more particularly, Southern Gothic tradition associated with those authors as well as Flannery O'Connor, Erskine Caldwell, Carson McCullers, and Walker Percy. As it happened, however, Erskine would often push back against the modernist style and certain of the more grotesque narrative elements that McCarthy incorporated into his work and that constitute a significant reason why he has been associated with that tradition in the first place.

As *The Orchard Keeper* neared publication, Erskine and McCarthy shared an extended correspondence about elements of the novel that would later become McCarthy's style signatures, such as his refusal to enclose dialogue in quotation marks and his use (or lack thereof) of apostrophes and hyphens. Erskine initially objected to McCarthy's punctuation choices and pejoratively referred to those practices as "extend[ing] Faulkner's beachhead of unconventionality in several directions." When McCarthy responded with his own rationale—noting, for instance, that apostrophes are "superfluous in the uses discussed and an eyesore"—Erskine eventually relented, though he insisted upon better consistency in the nonstandard usages.[2]

The extensive and detailed exchange, with give and take on both sides, is not one we might expect from an author who has long been associated with his particular way of rendering language—and with solitary iconoclasm. During the 2007 interview with Oprah Winfrey, she asked him about how he developed his style, wondering if this was his "immediate style that just became a Cormac McCarthyism." McCarthy reiterated the views he expressed to Erskine all those years ago, responding that "there's no reason to blot the page up with weird little marks. . . . It's important to punctuate so that it makes it easy for people to read." But it's also notable that each time she asks him about style, he mentions an influence. Erskine's name doesn't come up, but he talks about several others. James Joyce is a good model, he says: "He keeps it to an absolute minimum." He explains a job he had while at the University of Tennessee, working for Professor Robert Daniel, who asked him to repunctuate a series of eighteenth-century English essays in order to make them more readable. And he mentions the novel *Andersonville* by MacKinlay Kantor, which doesn't incorporate quotation marks to separate dialogue from the rest of the text. He seems reluctant to call this kind of writing a "Cormac McCarthyism," as she puts it; for him, style doesn't spring up from an individual. It's the product of influence, reflection, and the ideas of others coupled with your own. After all, "books are made out of books," as he told Woodward. "The novel depends for its life on the novels that have been written." I won't be the first to note that McCarthy is well aware of the literary, historical, and philosophical traditions that he engages.

Erskine, then, was also an important catalyst in the development of McCarthy's style, though the two men's work together didn't come to an end once those initial decisions about punctuation were settled. In fact, they came to unprecedented loggerheads over *Suttree*, McCarthy's sprawling novel of 1950s Knoxville. Erskine found the manuscript objectionable on multiple levels: it was too long, too obscene, and featured a protagonist who was, for Erskine, entirely unsympathetic. In May 1977 Erskine spent several days writing a long letter to McCarthy about those objections, topped with an epigraph from Coleridge's *Biographia Literaria*: "[I]t is not possible to imitate truly a dull and garrulous discourser, without repeating the effects of dullness and garrulity." He finds the secondary characters "indistinguishable" and "equally boring." Then, in a section dated three days later, he interrogates the differences between the title character and a tragic hero like Hamlet—prompted, he says, by a television broadcast of Laurence Olivier's *Hamlet* (1948). "Both are fascinated by maggots, excrement, decay; but beyond fascination, Suttree seems to relish this constellation." In the end, however, Hamlet is heroic while Suttree is juvenile. "Hamlet is a tragic figure," Erskine writes, but "Suttree [is] only pitiful, and chiefly to himself." Erskine suggests that Hamlet is tragic, and therefore more interesting, because his attraction to the morbid or scatological is tempered with more elevated pursuits and traits, the kind of status that Aristotle found imperative for a tragic hero. But Suttree stays in the muck. Suttree, as seen in the finished novel, arguably does have more "elevated" characteristics, like his care for others and his validating acceptance of the transgender character Tripping Through the Dew. Critics have not often read the finished novel *Suttree* as tragic, generally noting how the considerable comedy balances devastating events like Wanda's death and finding the ending an affirmative one. Dianne Luce, however, has called Suttree a self-conscious Hamlet figure, grieving the loss of a son and seeing human life as "a series of stagings and restagings through the centuries of the same stories of passion and death" (*Reading* 212); Bryan Vescio has compared *Suttree* to *Huckleberry Finn* and called it a work of "tragic Humanism," following Leslie Fielder. In his reading, the novel "is tragic because it denies the possibility of transcendence in general, and it is humanist because it offers as consolation only the human community to check our loneliness momentarily" (62). As my readings of many of McCarthy's works will show, I agree with Vescio on his identification of McCarthy's humanism but argue that it is that very human (and, sometimes, human/animal) community that offers the possibility of transcendence even in the face of tragedy.

Erskine's reading of the draft of *Suttree* moves him to worry that the "tedious nonessentials" of the story mar the whole, which is "basically so good," making it unnecessarily vulnerable. (It's notable that this novel is the Southern grotesquerie that Erskine finds too extreme, despite having previously worked on *Outer Dark* and *Child of God*, which feature a child-murdering, cannibalistic trio and a homicidal necrophiliac, respectively.) Erskine ends the long, three-day letter graciously, noting that of course "you may be right and I may be wrong," despite his extreme misgivings.[3] In an article about the working relationship between McCarthy and Erskine, Dianne Luce notes the significance of this letter, and of McCarthy's response to that relationship:

> As a whole, Erskine's May 1977 memo is the sort of critical communication that might have presented a genuine challenge to the working relationship of the two men after fifteen years and three previous novels brought to publication. And McCarthy's response to it might have been an angry sticking to his guns, or despair at such a reception of the long novel that had taken him twenty years and many drafts to complete, especially from the editor who had championed him at Random House from the beginning of his career. In fact, his response was more complex than either of those extremes. Examination of the setting copy for *Suttree* reveals that, in response to his editor's serious reservations and confusions, McCarthy undertook another round of

carefully considered revisions over the next eight or nine months.... McCarthy's revisions addressed Erskine's complaints without sacrificing his own vision for the novel. ("McCarthy and Erskine" 323)

In the end, McCarthy did trim the manuscript, removing several lengthy episodes that contained sharply funny vignettes and character development but that did, the two decided, unnecessarily add to the story's length and distract from the focus on Suttree. He also, however, "performed substantive local rewriting of diverse passages," in Luce's words, rather than just cutting the manuscript's length (325). They effectively had "taught one another how to work together" (303).

In engaging McCarthy in an ongoing conversation about style and content during the development of all these early novels, Erskine obliged him to push back, to defend his choices, and at times to understand the need for changes. Though both regretted that the books hardly sold, neither doubted their quality, and Erskine remained McCarthy's involved editor and tireless champion until his retirement in 1987. *Blood Meridian* was the last book they worked on together before McCarthy moved to Knopf. (Erskine did make a few suggestions on an early draft of *All the Pretty Horses*, but as Luce reports, he was then ill with throat cancer that was diagnosed in 1987. Erskine died in February 1993 ["McCarthy and Erskine" 329].)

But Erskine had a hand in more than just McCarthy's literary production. As I noted, he may have been the first to think about film adaptation as a possibility, though McCarthy himself indicated an early interest in getting involved in the movies. In 1964, as he prepared to become a published author, he provided Random House with some information about himself in order to help them with marketing. The life he describes is a colorful one: he talks about "hustling pool for a living," hitchhiking, taking courses at the University of Tennessee with no other goal than to please himself, and working in an auto-parts warehouse. Currently, he writes, "I divide my time between walking, reading, and talking to strangers."[4] He emphasizes his lack of steady employment, and in another document that asks him about his occupations other than writing, he responds that he has held "all kinds of odd jobs," everything from "dishwashing to motionpicture acting."[5] It's not clear what movie or movies this might have been, but somewhere in the midst of all his wandering, McCarthy got an up-close look at the film industry. (And he may have remembered this "odd job" in 1977, appearing in front of the camera for *The Gardener's Son*.)

Erskine, in making that early note about this new author and erstwhile actor, was prescient. Just a few years later, in 1967, two people interested in pursuing film rights were in contact. Philip Berkley of Berkley Associates wrote to McCarthy via Random House and asked about representing him in the sale of the film rights to *The Orchard Keeper*.[6] Around the same time, Harrison Starr of Barnett Pictures called to ask about McCarthy's next work. That book only existed as a rough-draft manuscript at that time and didn't even have a title. (Eventually, it would become *Outer Dark*.) The interest was encouraging and indicated both that film players had their eye on McCarthy and that they didn't expect him to be a one-book wonder. Nonetheless, neither of these deals was pursued, and Random House denied Starr access to McCarthy's second novel before it was published.[7]

The next year, however, a more substantial offer appeared. In August 1968 a company called Parallel Productions contacted Howard Kaminsky at Random House about purchasing performance rights to *The Orchard Keeper* and *Outer Dark*. For a one-year option, they offered $250 for the first novel and $500 for the second, with an additional $500 for each for a second year. If the options were exercised for film, drama, or live television, Parallel would pay $12,500 for *The Orchard Keeper* and $17,500 for *Outer Dark*.[8] This was serious money, and it got the author's and his editor's attention. Erskine wrote McCarthy about the offer the next day, and McCarthy approved it by telephone.[9] In October, however, McCarthy wrote to Erskine, wondering what happened with "the movie people," and if he might expect a check sometime soon.[10] Erskine told him that the lawyers were examining the contract on both sides of the deal and that he would be in touch soon with more information.[11] Unfortunately, by October 1970 nothing had come of the deal, and after McCarthy prodded him in a letter, Erskine noted in December that the option had expired on 18 December.[12] It was a disappointment, not least because of the potential payoff that was lost.

There were a number of early queries and offers, but though interest seemed high, none of them came to fruition. In 1971 another company considered optioning *The Orchard Keeper*, and McCarthy asked about any progress in a letter to Erskine that he received on 20 May. Money was an ongoing concern; as the two discussed an advance for his third book, McCarthy noted that "[i]n order to get reasonably clear of debt, finish my house, and get ensconced somewhere for a year or so in the privacy I need to finish this book, I will have to have about fifteen thousand. I hope that doesnt sound like a lot of money to you because it aint."[13] Then in a letter to Erskine, received 1 December 1971, McCarthy makes reference to yet another film option, this one for *Outer Dark*, and says that he doesn't want his book advance paid for out of "movie money"—that is, he wants to keep the accounts separate.[14]

But neither the movies nor the money ever appeared, and McCarthy continued to scrape by with a bit of an advance here and the proceeds from an award or two there. His major windfall came in 1981 with the MacArthur

Foundation Fellowship, but even that had its limits. In 1985 he wrote to his friend Howard Woolmer and indicated that he was still looking to the film industry as a potential source of profit. "Mostly these days I'm trying to get a film script produced into a film," he said. "The MacArthur largess expires in a little over a year and I've gotten used to eating regularly and dont know what will happen when the money stops."[15] (I'll return to the fate of that particular script in chapter 2.)

And so when Richard Pearce approached McCarthy in 1975 about writing a screenplay for a film that Pearce would direct, McCarthy's close work with Erskine and his interest in bringing his writing to the screen made him amenable to the suggestion. Pearce wanted to work with historical material, the 1876 murder of James Gregg by Robert McEvoy in Graniteville, South Carolina, and produce an installment for PBS's *Visions* series. The story, a violent act committed in an era of rapid historical change in the South, was right in McCarthy's wheelhouse, though the form was an unfamiliar one. Up until this point, McCarthy had pursued arrangements in which his stories would have been adapted by others, and writing a screenplay himself was a little daunting. He told Pearce, in fact, that "he had never even seen, much less written" one before (Pearce, Foreword v–vi). Nonetheless, he was willing to try. Before he started writing the story proper, the two men engaged in a period of intensive research together, finding out more about the people involved in the murder, the town, the region, and the cultural and historical context of this event.

When they started work, the primary source for information about Graniteville and the textile mill was Broadus Mitchell's laudatory 1928 biography of William Gregg, patrician and patriarch. William, who dies in an early scene of *The Gardener's Son*, is the father of James Gregg—as well as, Mitchell writes, "the father of Graniteville" and of "the Southern cotton manufacture," and a man who dreamed of "whole social betterment ... [the] intelligent use of economic resources, and a fuller life for the average man" (258–259). In Mitchell's portrait, Gregg was a man of vision who saw that the only way out of the South's economic problems was to move from an agricultural society to an industrial one, which would have the effect of reducing poverty and increasing efficiency, profits, and the general welfare. Gregg was both a successful and a tragic figure, argues Mitchell, because he made his case both in his writings and in reality—in the form of the Graniteville mill—but he died before his ideas could spread, in "the dark days of after-war collapse, a generation before the fruition of his hopes" (ix). McCarthy and Pearce, however, had a different kind of tragedy in mind.

Gregg died in 1867 from an illness that developed after he pitched in to help repair a broken dam. Mitchell takes pains to note the gravity of his passing, reporting that "[e]very man, woman, and child of the village" came to the funeral (255). But he doesn't mar the biography with Gregg's son James's ignoble death. In the main text he notes that after the patriarch's funeral, his wife Mrs. Gregg whiled away her days as a "celebrated knitter of baby socks" for her great-grandchildren and adds: "Little remains to be told" (256). Only in the footnotes does he admit that "[t]he fate of James Gregg is properly a part of this story." That fate was delivered by Robert McEvoy, the "bad boy of the village" and an amputee who had lost a leg while playing on a freight car. One day in April 1876, he entered James's office at the mill and shot him—"nobody knows why." Though Gregg fired a shot in return, McEvoy escaped and, wearing a wig and women's clothing, boarded the train to Aiken. But an incautious remark from his sister—"Now be careful and don't let them catch you"—alerted the conductor, and McEvoy was arrested in Columbia, sent back to Graniteville, tried, and hanged. McEvoy's father buried the boy himself, "out of fear, so the story goes, that doctors would disinter [him] to dissect the brain," later moving the body once more to an unknown spot (327–328).

As Luce has noted, there are a few details here that don't show up in the screenplay for *The Gardener's Son* but rather resonate with details in *Child of God*: Lester Ballard dons a "frightwig and skirts" in the latter days of his flight from society and the law and indeed is "flayed, eviscerated, dissected" after his death, his head "sawed open and the brains removed" (*Child of God* 194; "First Screenplay" 73). Ballard's portrayal, like McEvoy's, is also the product of historical research, though less obviously. As Luce argues, McCarthy likely based aspects of the character on two murderers, James Blevins of north Georgia and Ed Gein of Plainfield, Wisconsin. (The latter was the model for Norman Bates in Robert Bloch's novel *Psycho* and Alfred Hitchcock's 1960 film; see Luce's chapter "The Cave of Oblivion" in *Reading the World* for the historical details here.) For both Ballard and McEvoy, motivation is an important question. Ballard may be a murderer, arsonist, and necrophiliac, but he's also a child of God—so why does he do those things? (If his dissected brains hold any secrets, McCarthy doesn't say.) McEvoy is similarly enigmatic, and the furthest Mitchell takes his speculation is that his murder of James Gregg was merely the act of a "bad boy" who acted for no apparent reason. Before seeking out McCarthy for the film project, Pearce had read *Child of God* and was intrigued by it, possibly noting these similarities to McEvoy's story. He particularly liked the author's approach to his subject matter: "By never presuming an author's license to enter the mind of his protagonist," he said, "McCarthy had been able to insure the almost complete inscrutability of his subject and subject matter, while at the same time thoroughly investigating it. Here was 'Negative Capability' of a very high order. I was hooked" (Foreword v).

As Pearce and McCarthy continued their research, they discovered accounts that cast a less flattering light on the Greggs and their textile kingdom than did the Broadus Mitchell biography. Tom Terrill, who at the time was working on a yet-unpublished article titled "Murder in Graniteville," shared some of his research with the two men (Luce, "First Screenplay" 72). Rather than describing a symbiosis between a benevolent patriarch and a grateful citizenry, Terrill traces the conflict between management and workers in this era of industrialization and documents considerable changes in labor, commerce, landscape, and class relations. In 1875 Graniteville workers had initiated a monthlong strike against the mill because of a wage cut, and in 1877, as McEvoy awaited his execution, several hundred people signed a petition asking the governor to commute his sentence (209, 212). After the unrest of the strike, Terrill notes that the petition gave people in Graniteville "an unusual opportunity to vent themselves about the factory, the village, and company officials" (212). Both the strike and the petition were ultimately unsuccessful, but they reveal the animus that locals—as well as McEvoy, possibly—felt toward the industrial capitalism and urbanization that the mill and the Greggs represented.

What, then, was the murder of James Gregg by Robert McEvoy? Together Pearce and McCarthy crafted a story, textually and then cinematically, that considers this question. What are the factors that contribute to a moment of violence that, in typically tragic fashion, undoes two families and a town? That McCarthy is writing for performance makes the tragic implications of the narrative more obvious—The Gardener's Son invites considerations of violent cause and effect, though it doesn't offer any clear anagnorisis, or sudden awareness of the forces at play, for either the protagonist or the audience. Broadus Mitchell explained the historical murder as a random act, the unthinking choice of the village "bad boy," while Tom Terrill considered it a class rebellion, a member of the alienated working class striking out against the patrician heir of wealth and power. The Gardener's Son incorporates both historical and psychological considerations in its fictionalized version of the story while ultimately resorting to neither as a final explanation—though the narrative does subtly emphasize McEvoy's sense of alienation as he moves through a rapidly changing environment. Thus not only did his experience with The Gardener's Son give McCarthy his first opportunity to write for film and stay involved in the production process—an experience he would repeat many years later with The Counselor—but the narrative itself engages themes and ideas that are echoed in many of McCarthy's other works.

Robert McEvoy's first line in the screenplay of *The Gardener's Son* is spoken offscreen, and it encapsulates the position he will take with regard to just about everyone and everything in the rest of the story. "No, damn you! No!" he is heard to say to the visiting Dr. Perceval, who presently enters the McEvoy kitchen and informs the family that the boy's injured leg is beyond mending and must be amputated. Mrs. McEvoy weakly objects, but the doctor is emphatic: "It is beset with rot" (13).[16] Mrs. Gregg, who encouraged the doctor to look in on the boy despite her own husband's grave illness, tries to speak to Robert and convince him of the necessity of the operation; when she walks into his bedroom and greets him, he doesn't answer, beginning a pattern of silence or withheld responses that will continue throughout the story (14).

McEvoy survives the removal of his leg, but William Gregg is not so lucky. His funeral occurs in the following scene, as McEvoy observes from a window; *"pale and wasted,"* the action description notes, *"he watches the funeral with no expression at all"* (18). McEvoy is alone, even when surrounded by those who would help him, and he watches the effects of another family's loss without apparent identification or sympathy. Though William Gregg only appears briefly in the screenplay as a mute, gravely ill old man, his life and death loom large, as he is understood as the driving force behind the mill and the "new Graniteville." At his funeral he is eulogized with great reverence, in a way that resonates with Mitchell's descriptions as the maker of a kind of utopia, one who refined the goods of the region: "To see what he has wrought," the preacher says, "the neat homes, the churches and schools, the gardens and the lovely grounds and last but not least the massive factory structure with its beautiful and perfect machinery, these things seem created almost by magic" (19). In this vision, Gregg was almost godlike, a man who could call into being a perfect union of the machine and the garden — a relationship that, as Leo Marx noted in the works of American Romantic writers like Melville, Hawthorne, Emerson, and Thoreau, usually appears as one of conflict or interruption. But William Gregg worked for everyone, the preacher emphasizes, and the industrial results are like well-sown seeds that "shall continue to bear fruit for generations after the first laborer himself has passed away" (19).

It's a lovely image of a town, its mill, and a great maker who drew it all together for the benefit of everyone. The screenplay, however, quickly undermines this ideal, situating the narrative more firmly in the tradition Marx identified. In the next scene, the mill comes to life at dawn, but instead of a pastoral image we get what is literally the underbelly of a great and malevolent beast. Inside, *"the great wheel that turns the spindles stirs sluggishly, the belts slither and turn, the overhead shafts begin to revolve, the spindles turn"* (19). There are no shepherds tending a "beautiful and perfect" flock of machines, but rather children toiling in noisy, unpleasant conditions while other poverty-stricken people, desperate for work, are brusquely turned away by James when they arrive on a train, looking for jobs. James, who has assumed his father's position as head of the mill, sees the workers not as people to be uplifted by the benefits of work but as irritants, an unfortunate necessity for product and profit—unless they are female, and attractive. When Martha McEvoy happens into James's office while seeking her brother, James's eyes open with real interest. He flirts openly with her, asking if she has a boyfriend and calling her "feisty" and "a handful" (26). Martha plays along, shyly and innocently, but when James puts a ten-dollar gold piece on the desk between them and asks, "Would you like to have that?," the full implications of their conversation and his intentions strike her, and she flees the office in fear.

In the screenplay Martha doesn't tell her brother about James's advance. This seems to be one of the few instances in which McCarthy alters the historical facts; the real-life McEvoy claimed that Gregg's sexual pursuit of his sister was the reason for the murder (Terrill 210). (He made that claim during the two-year gap between his conviction and execution, a time lapse that is condensed to a matter of days in the screenplay.) This would have been a simple explanation, and a sympathetic one as well, but *The Gardener's Son* deliberately avoids it. The reader may dislike James and his rude, entitled behavior, but it isn't presented as the sole root of McEvoy's animus. That, it seems, is deliberately left open to interpretation, though the screenplay does hint at McEvoy's dislike of the mill and what it represents.

McEvoy is never a part of the mill's culture. After his leg is amputated, he works there briefly tidying offices but disappears from the job almost as soon as he starts it. He seems to resent the new social hierarchy that the mill imposes on the town, asserting that people can't be truly known by their job titles, amount of wealth, or place in society. When his little sister says she wishes their family lived in a better house, he replies that it "wouldnt make you no better from what you are" (*Gardener's Son* 29). The quality of a house, he implies, is not a reflection of the quality of people who live there. Robert leaves town without giving notice at the mill and returns after a two-year absence, *"[a] solitary figure riding the last boxcar"* (32). He comes upon two gravediggers at the cemetery and discovers that his mother has died; he angrily shoos them off, telling them that she's not to be buried there, that "[s]he dont belong to the mill" (35). He wants to keep his mother away from the mill's sluggish, mechanical tentacles, in death if not in life. At the McEvoy house, his mother's body rests in its coffin as several women in mourning dress sit with her. He angrily ejects these people as well, telling them, "You all get out. I dont know you" (36). He doesn't know anyone, and no one knows him, either—not even his sister, to whom he says, "You dont know how I am. You dont know me." "You're still my brother," she replies, stating what for her is obvious, but his response reveals his intense disillusion: "The good book says all men are brothers but it dont seem to cut no ice, does it?" (39)

McEvoy then goes looking for his father, seeking him in several places: the old Gregg greenhouse, now decrepit and left to rot under James's leadership; an overgrown orchard that his father used to tend; a barn where a group of locals play cards, drink, and banter; and finally the mill and James Gregg's office. In that office, McEvoy will once again insist on his isolation—and thus, perhaps, on his status as an individual undefined by appearance or class. "I was huntin my father," he tells James. "He was the gardener." "I know who he was," James replies. "No you dont ... You might know his name is all," McEvoy retorts. People are not to be known by their occupation or social standing or even by their name. When James tries to dismiss him, saying that "[w]e dont need your kind here," he unwittingly plays precisely to McEvoy's anger, and it sets him off. "What do you mean my kind," he asks, adding, "You think you can say anything you want about people and they just have to put up with it ... You think people dont know what you are?" (54–55). When James flips a ten-dollar gold piece on the desk, just as he did with Martha, and tries to buy McEvoy's compliance, telling him to "[t]ake it and get out," McEvoy is infuriated. James realizes his mistake, blanching before reaching for the pistol in his desk. But McEvoy fires first, shooting James twice in the office and once outside, where James follows him, pistol in hand. When James finally falls, the moment is so significant that the constant clatter of the mill's machinery stops: "*There is an immense silence*" (57). McEvoy's action has stopped the heart of the new Graniteville just as it stopped Gregg's, indicating that, as McEvoy might have suspected, the continual forward progress of industry is not as necessary and unstoppable as it might have seemed. James's "better standing," after all, didn't protect him from a well-aimed bullet.

When McEvoy is tried for the crime, he does not testify on his own behalf; his lawyer insists that mentioning James's treatment of his female employees or the fact that James drew his pistol first would be seen as an attempt to "blacken the Gregg name," something that would be looked upon unfavorably by the jury (61). Thus he is convicted for murder "with malice aforethought," though by all indications this was not the case (68). Neither does he speak when asked by the judge if he can "show cause, if any thou hast, why execution of the judgement established by law for the state should not be passed upon thee" (69). Whatever motives he might have had—or felt he had—he keeps them to himself.

His father struggles to understand the catastrophic events, both how his son could do such a thing and how he will manage to bear the loss of two family members. The elder McEvoy tries to seek answers from Whipper, an African American lawyer assigned to the defense. But Whipper, in his way, seems as devoid of hope as Robert McEvoy. When Robert's father weakly asserts that "God is just," that justice must exist at the divine level if not at the human one, Whipper scoffs at the idea. "If men were no more just than God," he says, "there'd be no peace in the world. Everwhere I look I see men trying to set right the inequities that God's left them with" (67). Justice is elusive, in this world or beyond, and the elder McEvoy is left bereft by the chaos of it all.

Inequities, both Whipper and Robert McEvoy suggest, seem intractable, though each in his own way resists those divisions. After all, Whipper is an African American lawyer, and McEvoy has struck a defiant (if inarticulate) blow at the particular wheels of commerce and class division in Graniteville embodied in the figure of James Gregg. Luce has noted the similarities of his act to the murder in Camus's *The Stranger*: "In both works the 'murders' are existential acts of self-defense; in both the rebels stand in the dock for others: Meursault for his friend Raymond, whose fight he has taken up, and Robert for his sister, his father, and all the oppressed millworkers of Graniteville" (*Reading the World* 185). While it's not exactly clear what McEvoy is standing up for, he does stand up—though here, his action is both effect and cause of his ongoing isolation rather than a self-conscious act of solidarity. McEvoy meets his end—his final isolation—with apparent calm. In the hanging chamber, a priest helps him into a long white robe, *"McEvoy cooperating and serious, like a priest being dressed for a sacrament"* (84). He hands his crutch to the priest, refuses once again the opportunity to make a statement, and stands on one leg as he awaits the opening of the trap door. After he falls, the doctor and sheriff review the formalities of reporting his death, and McEvoy's life is officially over.

One wonders if his death might serve as a catalyst for some kind of resolution to the problem of people "not knowing" each other or reacting to one another on the basis of class hierarchy, or, as Terrill's historical research suggests, if it could draw some attention to the dehumanizing effects of industrialization, perhaps serving as one of the "tragic cataclysms" that Hegel argued move human history forward. But fittingly for McCarthy's views of history and progress, it seems to have the opposite effect. Before McEvoy is killed, Martha visits the home of Mrs. Gregg in order to apologize, to tell her that "your son never done nothin to me," and to "say I was sorry. Somebody had to" (72). The grieving Mrs. Gregg—who, like the elder McEvoy, has in short order lost both a spouse and a son—is moved, and remarks that in Martha's face she can see "nothing in you to do with death and murder" (74). Martha, in other words, doesn't bear her brother's guilt by virtue of association. But when Martha fumblingly tries to assure Mrs. Gregg of her son's innocence, that James's flirtation and offers of money just "sounded worse than what it was," Mrs. Gregg becomes angry and reverses her view. "Oh you are a little darling, arent you?" she says softly, assuming Martha is accusing her family rather than trying to comfort her (75). Any fragile connection the two had made is now severed, and Mrs. Gregg even regresses to James's open prejudice: "My son was right about you people," she says, implying that her husband's idealism was misplaced (76). McEvoy's death, then, only perpetuates this kind of fragmentation rather than resisting it.

In the end, McEvoy might spit at the reader the same thing he says to so many in the story: "You dont know me." And we don't, not really, although he's as defined by his isolation and silence as much as he would be by an eloquent closing monologue. He stands alone in every sense, even from the reader. The filmed version of *The Gardener's Son* retains this quality while also visually emphasizing McEvoy's status as a man in a changing world—a common characteristic for McCarthy's protagonists. Although McEvoy and *Blood Meridian*'s kid may be the least articulate characters in the author's fictional worlds, they share with others like Lester Ballard, John Grady Cole, and Ed Tom Bell a wary distance from the progress happening around them. What does it mean for a man to be evicted, disabled, disinherited, or just "overmatched," as Bell puts it? Of these characters, only Bell makes it to the end of the story alive—the others, willingly or no, leave the stage, and McEvoy's departure, on both page and screen, is one of the more enigmatic.

THE STORY ON SCREEN: "NO EASY PATIENT"
IN THE MIDST OF CHANGE

Once the screenplay of *The Gardener's Son* was written, Pearce and McCarthy began the work of bringing that departure to life onscreen and further delineating the absent-presence of Robert McEvoy. And they did work together—rather than turning in the screenplay and heading home, McCarthy continued to collaborate with Pearce on the creation of a shooting script and the casting of the film. In an undated letter from 1976, McCarthy writes to Pearce about his most recent draft of the screenplay, in which he has responded to suggestions from Pearce and also revised the story with the work of filming in mind. "I have worked out a shorter graveyard scene with James and Mrs Gregg," he notes, adding that it "could be shot in the graveyard the same day as the monument removal scene and would require no propwork or dressing and would simply entail five minutes of dialogue." In closing, he reminds Pearce that they "are going to have to spend some time together on the shooting script."[17] In another letter, he writes with a number of casting suggestions: Royal Dano for the doctor, Keenan Wynne [sic] for Patrick McEvoy, and "an actor with all his legs" but with one "strapped up behind him" for Robert McEvoy, among others.[18] And he didn't just make suggestions; Pearce has said that McCarthy came to every casting session, even those for extras, which amounted to seeing over a thousand people in South Carolina. He was there during filming as well, telling a reporter, "It's backbreaking work. On location for 30 days, and the last week we were working 16 to 18 hours a day. You've got to be some kind of weirdo to think that it's fun. But it sure kept my interest up—and writers are basically pretty lazy people" ("Gardner's [sic]").

McCarthy was so involved, in fact, that it delayed his work on *Suttree*. He wrote to Howard Woolmer late in 1976 and warned him not to expect the publication of that novel until he could review the manuscript one more time. He "got involved with the making of my film," he explained, and though the book was "essentially finished," it would have to wait a little longer.[19] It was still very much "his" film, even as the text gradually made its way into image and sound.

After the film's opening shots reveal the lush South Carolina landscape punctuated by the mill and its large smokestack, Robert McEvoy is introduced with the scene of his amputation. Mrs. Gregg (Nan Martin) has come to assist, even though her husband is on his deathbed. She is the voice of assured authority as she visits Robert's bedside and calmly tells him that what the doctor said is correct—he must have the operation to remove his leg. In contrast to her smoothly controlled presence, Robert himself looks wild and disheveled. He is played in the film by Brad Dourlf, most famous at the time for his role as another inarticulate, troubled young man, Billy Bibbit, in the adaptation of *One Flew Over the Cuckoo's Nest* (1975). As McEvoy resists Mrs. Gregg's dictate as he resisted the doctor—"He won't be no easy patient," his father had remarked—she insists and pulls back the covers to reveal a leg black with sepsis. He slumps back on the bed, defeated, and the final shot of the scene shows him framed diagonally in close-up, his sweaty face with wide-open eyes and dry lips staring sightlessly into the camera. It is not an auspicious beginning for this new time in his life, and the pain of this threshold is emphasized by close-up shots of the pans, chemicals, small tools, and finally the two saws that will help remove the rotted leg—which is carried down the stairs in a bloodstained sheet by the doctor's assistant once the procedure is completed. Even the practiced poise of Mrs. Gregg is shaken by the experience.

Shortly thereafter McEvoy sits in his room carving a wooden leg, using

Robert McEvoy (Brad Dourif) anticipates the amputation of his leg in an opening scene of Richard Pearce's The Gardener's Son *(PBS, 1977).*

his uninjured leg as a model, attempting to replicate what he lost as closely as possible. But the likeness doesn't help him much—the representation is no substitute for the real thing. When he arrives at the mill to begin work as an office boy, his figure is framed in the doorway, leaning on a crutch; his hair, though combed, still looks wild and ungroomed, and he chews on something as he gazes around the room, failing to properly greet Captain Giles, the mill's timekeeper. "I can do anything anybody else can," he assures Giles, though his awkwardness would seem to tell a different story. Those in charge at the mill fail to see such potential, with or without his injured leg.

The new leader, James Gregg, is first seen at his father's funeral, where his mother catches him impatiently looking at his watch during the proceedings. That unpleasant first impression is amplified when James rejects a group of families who have traveled to Graniteville looking for work, sending them back where they came from. In a scene that was added to the shooting script, he makes his class prejudices clear. He pauses with his mother in the grave-yard so that Mrs. Gregg can place flowers on her late husband's grave and by a headstone that just reads "The Little Boy/1855." She explains to James that the boy had been on the train, gotten sick, and was taken off the train and died in Graniteville, unknown and forlorn. Mrs. Gregg wonders "what God would mean by such a thing," but the boy's circumstances make James ruminate instead on the habits of indigent wanderers, "eat up with hookworm, God knows what else. Inbred. Their eyes grown together. Come down here expect us to put them to work." Mrs. Gregg chastises him and reminds him of the advantages he's had, but James is adamant in his assessment: "They say the Good Lord must have loved the poor because he made so many of them. I think he just kept trying to see if one of the squint-eyed sons of bitches wouldn't get off his ass and do some work." His mother, however, reflects her husband's utopian vision: "Your father put a good deal of store in the common people. They need this company. He believed that this place could be a garden. A garden of industry. That people only needed the opportunity to work." They disagree strongly about the character of the poor, though in the following scene, Martha stumbles upon him drinking in his office and his leering interest in purchasing her favors is obvious. "These people" may be inbred and lazy, but under the right circumstances, James's behavior suggests, they can be useful in furthering the elite's advantages.

McEvoy doesn't last long working for Gregg, and when he returns to Graniteville after a long absence, Dourif's performance reveals a young man who may be more used to his disability but is no less uncomfortable with himself or the world around him. He arrives in the back of a cart, and as he approaches town he uses a pocket knife to eat an apple. Instead of putting the knife aside, he unceremoniously sticks it into his wooden leg. There's no reaction shot of the boy who rides with him; McEvoy's action isn't a joke but an indication of his disdain for his prosthetic. He doesn't speak to the boy.

When he finally comes home, he pauses in the doorway of the dark house, staring at the mourning women who stare back at him. He loses his temper visibly, as he did with the gravediggers, and slams the door shut after he has kicked them all out. He moves through more thresholds as he seeks his father. The old Gregg greenhouse, too, is a changed place, once carefully tended by Patrick McEvoy but now a garden paradise in ruins; McEvoy stops in the doorway to take it in, looking almost as reluctant and surprised as when he stepped inside to see his mother's body. Captain Giles, now aged, finds him there, and the old timekeeper has himself had time to begin doubting the ways of industry. It's all about profit and efficiency at any cost, he implies, and mourns the loss of what was once a beautiful space: "Just because a thing ain't used," he says, "ain't no sign to rock it to death." McEvoy knocks on one more door that day, of the old barn where a group of local men pass the bottle. They welcome him into their circle but McEvoy sits awkwardly, as stiff and taciturn as the others are loose and drawling; Dourif's performance makes clear that this is no home for McEvoy either. He wakes alone the next morning and stumbles toward the mill, and to James Gregg.

In The Gardener's Son, *McEvoy trudges wearily through a doorway and into James Gregg's office, moments before the murder.*

In all of these scenes, Pearce shoots Dourif peering through doorways before moving slowly and reluctantly through them, a visual correlative for his discomfort with the changes that have overtaken his life, his family, and his town. He seems most reluctant to move into the mill's space, but he does—looking in a doorway before entering from outside, moving through the noisy, clattering machinery on his way to the office, and then appearing first as a shadow through the semi-opaque glass of the office window before slouching through the doorway and into the mill's heart, Gregg's office. One gets the sense that he doesn't want to breach these thresholds any more than he wanted to learn how to walk with a crutch—but he does, awkward and still alone, and the confrontation between him and Gregg has a sense of inevitability. When Gregg puts the money on his desk, McEvoy looks at the offering almost sadly, pulling his pistol after Gregg goes for his own. After the shootout ends outside in the street, children watch curiously from the windows of the mill, their spindles and gears temporarily forgotten.

What, then, happened in that office? Jerry Hardin plays Patrick McEvoy as a father who is visibly falling apart as he tries to understand, who laments to Whipper during the trial (in dialogue that is changed from the screenplay) that he "can't tell what they're thinking, them people on the jury. I can't see nothing in their faces." In the film, Whipper makes his own status as an outsider more clear: "The jury commissioner draws the jury from the voter list," he explains. "As you may know, I was called in on this case because of the high Negro population in this county. If you are asking me what I think it means to have 'them people' sit in judgement of your son, I have to tell you frankly that I don't know. But I doubt it's a consideration." Robert McEvoy, then, isn't the only one with sensitivities to how people are labeled, though as in the scene with Martha and Mrs. Gregg, this one is emblematic of a missed opportunity for commiseration. And Patrick McEvoy gets none of the explanations that he seeks.

Do we, as viewers, have any better ideas? Those who worked on the film have offered their own. Fred Murphy, the director of photography, notes that James's targeting of women, including Martha, is a "red herring," one that even the sister assumes is McEvoy's motivation, but he says that the real reason is "vaguely accidental." McEvoy didn't intend to commit murder, but it happened and "that's what the story's about: the forces that are driving Bobby are something that he doesn't have control over." Anne O'Sullivan, who played Martha, wishes that her character had been the reason: "I think it should have been more clear ... it would have upped the stakes a lot" (Josyph, *McCarthy's House* 175). Brad Dourif agrees, noting that the unclarified motivation was "very much intentional," but he ultimately doesn't think that it was "handled well." Upon watching the film after many years, however, he comments on what does come across:

> What struck me this time ... because I've played a lot of crazy people in my life, is how sane McEvoy is. He's arrogant, he's confrontational, but he is very sane in the way that he looks at people, and he really is unafraid to look at them as they are. You know, the South was built on the English system of class—it was people running away from Cromwell, that's how it was made—and McEvoy cannot stomach it. (177–178)

It's true that when the moment for McEvoy's death comes, he seems relatively at ease, certainly more so than he ever did while confronting the language and attitude of those like James Gregg. He walks to the hanging platform without a struggle and passes through his final doorway, the trapdoor that opens below him during his hanging, without making a statement—just the same silence that accompanied him through every other threshold. As Dr. Perceval waits to formally record his death, Pearce frames McEvoy's bound hands in the center of the shot—briefly violent, but now restrained and still. His inarticulate resistance to upper-class entitlement and the toll of industrialization on communities like his own is over, and his lifeless body is finally the only message that he sends. After his death, the film ends with shots of the sun still rising over the mill's tower, reflected in the water of the river, before everything fades to black.

Perhaps the closest McEvoy gets to articulating a reason for his anger and resistance is something he says to Martha in the street, on his way to execution. She reaches out to him but he backs away, speaking in anger and despair that she doesn't seem to comprehend. "You wake up sometimes of a morning," he tells her, "and you feel good for a minute and then you see where you are." The world has changed around him, and he despises the agents of that change. He urges his sister to go home and, with a little more tenderness, to "forget all this" and find a good man to marry. Then he walks away to face his final solitude and his last threshold.

MOVING THROUGH THE FUGITIVE PAST

Martha never does find a man to marry, though we don't find this out in the finished film. The published screenplay and the shooting script include two short scenes that were later cut; these scenes take place at the beginning and end of the story, bookending the major action, and function as a frame story set many years after the murder. A young man—eventually revealed to be William Chaffee, nephew of James Gregg—seeks information or insight about the long-ago murder of his uncle. In the first scene, an old timekeeper—the aged Captain Giles—leads Chaffee through James's old office, stacked with boxes and papers. As Chaffee sifts through the records, the timekeeper chides him: "They aint the thing," he says. "Old pitchers or papers. Once you copy something down you dont have it anymore. You just have the record. Times past are fugitive. They caint be kept in no box" (5). The truth of real experience is fleeting, he warns, and overreliance on mere artifacts can make it disappear entirely.

In the last scene of the screenplay as written, Chaffee goes to visit the state hospital and talks with Martha McEvoy, now an old woman. Her statements directly echo the timekeeper's: "I ort not even to of kept it," she tells him, speaking of a worn, yellowed photograph of Robert. "I think a person's memory serves better. Sometimes I can almost talk to him. I caint see him no more. In my mind. I just see this old pitcher" (93). Photos, records, artifacts—they make us think we know the truth. In accepting them passively, however, we may only blind ourselves further and strengthen our fetters in the cave, as Plato would put it. If Chaffee is daunted in his task to discover more about the murder, he doesn't say so, and McCarthy might add that what's needed are imagination and active engagement (something he states openly in the stage directions for *The Stonemason*). The "fugitive past" does come alive, after all, in the recreation that is *The Gardener's Son*, though the timekeeper's warning that reconstructed knowledge is always incomplete is reflected in the character of Robert McEvoy. Unlike the real-life person, the McEvoy of *The Gardener's Son* doesn't speak on his own behalf, doesn't make his motivations clear, and remains an ambiguous figure, stoking our interpretation and analysis.

Luce has noted the connections between Chaffee in these scenes and the boy Wes in "Wake for Susan," a short story McCarthy published in October 1959 in *The Phoenix*, a literary supplement to the University of Tennessee student newspaper; the character also resonates with that of John Wesley Rattner in *The Orchard Keeper*. In "Wake for Susan," Wes pauses by a gravestone and imaginatively reconstructs the life of a seventeen-year-old girl who died in 1834, an action that John Wesley echoes in *The Orchard Keeper* when he visits his mother's grave. John Wesley reaches out to touch the gravestone "as if perhaps to conjure up some image, evoke again some allegiance with a name, a place, hallucinated recollections in which faces merged inextricably, and yet true and fixed" (245). But instead of the vivid vision that Wes experiences, John Wesley finds the "carved stone less real than the smell of wood-smoke or the taste of an old man's wine" (245)—sensations, as Luce notes, that he associates with his mentors Marion Sylder and Arthur Ownby ("They aint the thing" 26). John Wesley's thought nonetheless "affirms the possibility of hallucinated recollection that mingles and even mangles images, yet somehow remains 'true and fixed,' suggesting at its very end that all of the narrative between the framing scenes in the cemetery has been John Wesley's partly remembered, partly imagined reconstruction of his past and his father's, Sylder's, and Ownby's" (26). Chaffee in *The Gardener's Son* could be understood as another "author-surrogate" like Wes and John Wesley, making the screenplay "Chaffee's attempt at a history of the inarticulate, as the screenplay itself is McCarthy's: history that requires sympathetic identification and creative imagination to fill the gaps and compensate for distortion in the artifacts and monuments" (31). *The Gardener's Son*, then, aligns not only with "Wake for Susan" and *The Orchard Keeper* in its engagement with history and memory as subject matter, but also with *Child of God*, *Blood Meridian*, and (to some extent) *The Stonemason* in its demonstration of McCarthy's own practice of the imaginative and self-conscious reconstruction of historical material. And of course these qualities as well as the complex narrative framing reveal the continuing influence of Faulkner, though by 1977 McCarthy was soon to leave the South and engage with a different regional and literary tradition.

Its ambiguity and the inarticulate nature of the protagonist make *The Gardener's Son* somewhat unusual as tragedy, at least in an Aristotelean sense. McEvoy is more aimless than ambitious (more like Meursault than Oedipus); seems largely unmoved by his peripeteia, or reversal of fortune; and certainly has no moment of anagnorisis in which he articulates his sudden understanding of the factors at play in his murder of James Gregg. But the murder and McEvoy's subsequent execution do prompt ample reflection on the part of other characters—about class, race, justice, God, and human nature.

In a draft of the screenplay that appears to be an earlier version of the published screenplay and the shooting script, McCarthy doesn't include the opening scene with Chaffee—the screenplay begins instead with McEvoy playing on top of a train, falling off, and suffering the injury that necessitates the amputation of his leg. McCarthy does feature Chaffee, however, in a long final segment that includes his calling on Martha as well as a visit to an elderly man named Oren Kneece and his wife, who live in the McEvoys' old house. Kneece remembers the Greggs and McEvoy and identifies the murder as the turning point for the community: "After that things—everthing started to go wrong here."[20] For Kneece, executing McEvoy for the murder was the wrong response, an unjust scapegoating. He describes the events similarly to the way that René Girard explains tragedy in *Violence and the Sacred*, as a ritual enacting of the attempted purgation of a community. When unchecked violence threatens to overwhelm the community, the people identify one who is deemed responsible for that violence and then banish or kill that person. Thus the community is united against the scapegoat and purged—temporarily, at least—until the cycle begins again. Kneece puts it this way:

> So there's a tragedy in a community and a young boy kills a man who is maybe the most prominent man in that community and the community is tore up. They think to mend it back by takin this young man and hangin him by his neck til he's dead, but then they cut him down and lower him into his box and they take the hood off his head and his eyes are pooched out like a frog's and they can see the light runnin out of them and it runs all the way back to Adam and before Adam and before man was and the soul is gone from this boy but it is also gone from the.... The spirit is gone from the community because they conspired together to let death in instead of standin together against him.[21]

Like Girard, Kneece sees this as less an enactment of justice than a mechanism for preserving peace and the community's sense of itself. In his eyes, McEvoy is more victim than villain, as he elaborates: "McEvoy, they made him to be this and to be that. A bad boy. What I believe he was was just a poor cripple boy never did have nobody to take up for him."[22]

As presented in this version of the screenplay, Kneece is something of a moral authority, a witness to the tragic events with the benefit of years of reflection. He greets Chaffee warmly, encourages him to join him and his wife for a meal, before which he prays that God "make us mindful of the needs of others."[23] The explanation he offers for McEvoy's actions and the town's response is a compelling one, though McCarthy cuts the Kneeces from his later versions of the screenplay. At thirty-one pages the scene is a lengthy one, and Kneece's description of McEvoy's scapegoating may hew too close to definitive explanation than McCarthy and Pearce had in mind—Pearce, after all, was initially drawn to McCarthy's work because of the artistic ambiguity he perceived in *Child of God*, what he called "'Negative Capability' of a very high order" (Foreword v). It distracts, too, from Martha's more unsettling final thoughts, which end each draft of the screenplay and the shooting script and are cut from the film.

In this final scene, Martha takes her observation about photos and other representations further, and wonders if names—the words that represent us—are purely a human invention, and an unnecessary one at that: "I wonder if God has names for people. He never give em none. People done that. I wonder if people are not all the same to him. Just souls up there and no names. Or if he cares what all they done. I dont know why Bobby done what he done. Once people are dead they're not good nor bad. They're just dead" (92). It's a radical idea, one that her brother articulated differently in his repeated insistence that "you dont know me": that the words we attach to things and people—their social value—might be not merely negligible, but meaningless. If so, then commerce—the transactions we make, whether aptly or not, based on those values—becomes a pointless or misguided endeavor and progress based on commerce is nothing but a perversion. But then justice, too, might just be another human transaction rather than a divine sanction; maybe God doesn't care "what all [people] done" (92). Whether this is indifference (as Whipper suggests) or grace is unclear.

Though it is lesser known than his novels, McCarthy's first screenplay is a key text. Luce calls it "his first historical work in the usual sense of the term" ("They aint the thing" 29), and in a basic sense McCarthy learned how to write historical fiction and how to write a screenplay, and he experienced the process through which that screenplay is transformed into a film. Further, in telling the story of Robert McEvoy, McCarthy engages themes that are prevalent across his career: the function of storytelling and, more broadly, representation; alienation and difference; violence and its causes and repercussions; fathers and sons; the changing landscape of the South in a period of industrialization; the frustrations of appealing to a silent God; and commerce and its relation to justice (a connection that, as Brad Bannon and others have pointed out, is later literalized in Judge Holden's, the dueña Alfonsa's, and Chigurh's statements about coins and fate).

McEvoy is the son in a loving family and a member of a close community, but he still sticks out because of some combination of temperament, disability, and unarticulated values. There are witnesses to his hanging, but he effectively dies alone. In the story as rendered by McCarthy and Pearce, there are no other rebels—no disgruntled millworkers or townspeople ready to take action, even though others express regret or frustration at the loss of the gardens and of readily available jobs. One wonders what might have happened if McEvoy had an ally instead of standing alone.

McCarthy himself understood that need, and his work with both Erskine and Pearce shows his willingness to collaborate in order to achieve the best expression of his vision. In the case of *The Gardener's Son*, the rewards were clear. Writing in the *Washington Post*, Alan Kriegsman said that it "may well be the finest 'Visions' installment thus far presented," and noted that the drama reflects "a writer's accurate ear for local vernacular, and a filmmaker's grasp of the revelatory power of imagery." The *New York Times* concurred, as John O'Connor called it a "haunting production" with "almost poetic vividness." The *Village Voice* was even more enthusiastic, saying that the film was "the most provocative unknown American movie of 1976 [sic]," and, in fact, "on a par with *The Battle of Algiers*." That publication also noted the balance between psychology and historicity that the film keeps in play, calling it "class-conscious filmmaking, a rarity in this country, that is squeezed for humanistic insights rather than doctrinaire propaganda" ("Film: *Gardener's Son*"). In 1977 the film was nominated for two Emmys, one for graphic design and title sequences and one for lighting direction. McCarthy and Pearce apparently tried to secure a theatrical release for the film as well, given its good reviews, but as McCarthy wrote Peter Greenleaf in 1981, to do that the film "needs to be cut a bit from its present 2 hours [and] it needs to be blown up from 16 to 35 mm." All of that, he notes, "takes money," which of course can be hard to come by.[24]

Those early offers from production companies may not have resulted in products or profit, but when McCarthy got his own hands into the making of a film, it paid off. The results were no doubt encouraging, and in the next decade he would enthusiastically tackle a number of film projects. Unfortunately, the success of this first screenplay didn't translate into subsequent accomplishments—at least not for many years.

CHAPTER TWO

The Unproduced Screenplays

"CITIES OF THE PLAIN," "WHALES AND MEN," AND "NO COUNTRY FOR OLD MEN"

*I*N 1984 SCREENWRITER BILL WITTLIFF WAS SERVING ON the selection committee of what is now called the Sundance Film Festival (then in its very early years and known as the United States Film and Video Festival) when he came across a screenplay by someone whose name he didn't recognize. It was called "Cities of the Plain," and it was by a writer named Cormac McCarthy. For Wittliff, it stood out right away. "I was just knocked out by it," he says. He loved what he read, especially "the brilliance of the dialogue." The rest of the committee, however, was unmoved. The long dialogue scenes that Wittliff liked so much were a sticking point with the others, and as he puts it, "it didn't go anywhere" (Wittliff).

Except, that is, with Wittliff himself. He was so struck by the power of the writing that its unusual qualities as a screenplay were unimportant, he felt. "It would not have been ordinary," he says, but it was precisely "the kind of thing that we ought to be looking at." And if the committee wasn't interested in finding out more, then he would. He tracked down McCarthy and began a correspondence as well as a longstanding friendship. Much later, in 2007, McCarthy's papers became a part of the Wittliff Collections at Texas State University, San Marcos, cementing the two writers' professional association—and surprising many who suspected that his archive might go to the Harry Ransom Center at the University of Texas at Austin up the road, home to collections of James Joyce, Norman Mailer, Ezra Pound, Doris Lessing, David Foster Wallace, and many others. But McCarthy's long friendship with Wittliff may well have been a deciding factor.

Wittliff knew McCarthy first, then, not as a novelist (as most of the rest of the world eventually would), but as a screenwriter—if an unproduced one. After McCarthy's encouraging experience working with Richard Pearce on

The Gardener's Son, in the late 1970s he delved into further screenwriting in earnest. By 1987 he had completed three projects: the story that Wittliff read, which was originally called "El Paso/Juarez" and later retitled "Cities of the Plain," about a young cowboy's love for a doomed prostitute; "Whales and Men," an ecologically minded story of an unlikely group of friends trying to save the whales; and a drugs-and-money thriller titled "No Country for Old Men." (The latter is an original screenplay that is quite different, as I'll explain, from both McCarthy's later novel and the Coen brothers' 2007 film adaptation of that novel.) With each screenplay, McCarthy worked intensely on extensive revisions and multiple drafts and shaped a complete, polished final version. None of them, however, were ever produced. Pearce did try to make something happen with "Cities of the Plain," and Sean Penn was reportedly interested, but—perhaps not surprisingly—producers shied away from the dark material (Woodward, "Venomous").

As I mentioned in chapter 1, McCarthy wrote to Howard Woolmer in 1985, lamenting the forthcoming end to his MacArthur Foundation money and noting his continuing but thus far fruitless efforts to get his film script produced. (Given the timing, he is likely referring to "Cities of the Plain" here.)[1] Despite his failure to find support in Hollywood, he does seem to have found the screenplay format an amenable one, and its influence on his writing style and the stories he would choose to tell is considerable. By October of the same year, he reported further work in this area to Woolmer: "I'm working on a couple of stories in filmscript form," he wrote. At this point McCarthy was the published author, most recently, of the 471-page novel *Suttree* and the 337-page *Blood Meridian*, and he apparently found the shift in format refreshing. "Very good form for conserving the word," he commented to Woolmer.[2]

Both stylistically and thematically, these screenplays constitute an important step in McCarthy's writing career. The three works evince McCarthy's evolving interests in tragedy, modernity, and ecology in ways that are particularly resonant with the Border Trilogy, the novel *No Country for Old Men*, and *The Counselor*, and his practice of "conserving the word" in his screenwriting is evident in his later, more minimalist novels *No Country for Old Men* and *The Road*.[3] Steven Frye has found McCarthy's engagement with the visual aesthetics of film to be an influence on his novels as well, specifically *Blood Meridian*, which McCarthy began researching in 1974 and was still writing when he began work on his first film treatment in 1978.[4] Frye notes the similarities, for instance, between the Yuma massacre scene in that novel and the final battle of Sam Peckinpah's *The Wild Bunch* (1969): "As in Peckinpah's scene, McCarthy's visual montage blends group movement and individual movement as the language pace is slowed by modifiers in the same manner as the film, in which slow motion is employed particularly when people are killed.... What marks this scene as cinematic is not the simple use of visual images, it is the precise combination of verbal pacing, interspersed wide-angle visuals, focused facial images, and the use of color and light" (113).

These screenplays, then, affect McCarthy's later aesthetic choices regarding style and theme, but most obviously they provide source material for other works. "Cities of the Plain" became the foundation for the Border Trilogy, and "No Country for Old Men" was extensively revised and published as a novel. "Whales and Men," though McCarthy didn't rewrite it in another form, is deeply resonant with *The Crossing* and, more generally, with his career-long interest in the natural world, language, and representation. McCarthy writes "Cities" in particular as a tragedy and describes the story in those terms in a synopsis. Those tragic elements are then amplified in the ensuing Border Trilogy by changes McCarthy makes to the major characters and the repetition of loss featured in the three novels. "Whales" is not structured as a tragedy, though it does emphasize the dual human/animal experiences of suffering and community as well as the role that language can play—sometimes advantageously and sometimes not—in working from the experience of violence to its communal amelioration. And finally, "No Country" was, surprisingly, originally written as an action-adventure screenplay complete with a happy ending for the good guys and is drastically different from the tragic novel and film adaptation that appeared two decades later.

INTRODUCING THE TRAGIC HERO:
"CITIES OF THE PLAIN"

Suttree, McCarthy's fourth novel set in the South, was published in 1979, though by then McCarthy's interests had already turned toward the West. He moved to Tucson, Arizona, in 1977, and at that time he was working on what he called his "western" in earnest.[5] Of the change in region, McCarthy told Richard Woodward simply that he had "always been interested in the Southwest" and that "[t]here isn't a place in the world you can go where they don't know about cowboys and Indians and the myth of the West." But his own Western would be more than a familiar cowboys-and-Indians yarn. This historical novel—eventually titled *Blood Meridian: Or the Evening Redness in the West*—is based in part on the real-life exploits of the Glanton gang, a group of men hired by the Mexican government in 1849 to scalp Native Americans. He compiled a great deal of research, much of which went into building the historical basis and regional setting for the novel, though the allure of genre storytelling and mythology that the region produced clearly wasn't lost on him.

Most scholars have agreed that *Blood Meridian* doesn't bear much similarity to classic Western novels or films. Robert Warshow has famously written about the appeal of the Western hero, who "comes into serious art only when his moral code, without ceasing to be compelling, is also seen to be imperfect. The Westerner at his best exhibits a moral ambiguity which darkens his image and saves him from absurdity; this ambiguity arises from the fact that, whatever his justifications, he is a killer of men" (708). *Shane* (1953), *The Searchers* (1956), *Pale Rider* (1985)—in these films the hero's skill with violence is his best and worst feature, and the films each end with him leaving the community he's helped save, headed back out into the wilderness. As Richard Slotkin has argued, that violence translates into victory for the community but personal loss, even tragic loss, for the hero, who is exiled from the community for the very qualities that make its continued existence possible.

Blood Meridian, of course, features conflict in the extreme, but it doesn't follow this narrative pattern, nor is its ambiguity restricted to the characteristics that Warshow discusses. Despite the cinematic qualities that Frye has pointed out, the novel's complex philosophical underpinnings and hyperbolic violence have proved to be particular challenges for those filmmakers who have sought to adapt it for the screen, as I'll explain in the conclusion. It's a novel that even a prodigious reader like Harold Bloom found "appalling" the first two times he tried—and failed—to get through it (though he tells that story as part of his celebration of the novel as a "canonical imaginative achievement") (255). Appalling though much of its violence may be, the novel is also consciously situated in the traditions of American historical romance that include authors like James Fenimore Cooper and Herman Melville (the latter, along with Faulkner and Dostoyevsky, one of McCarthy's favorite writers, he told Woodward). It also resonates with the American naturalism of Jack London and Ernest Hemingway and with the theological or philosophical writings of Nietzsche, Jakob Böhme, and the Gnostics. Simply put, it's a rich and unusual text. A number of critics, including Leo Daugherty, David Williams, Kate Montague, and Bloom himself have written about *Blood Meridian* as a tragedy, though this designation is neither an obvious nor Aristotelean one; Daugherty reads it as Gnostic tragedy, for example, and Montague as baroque tragedy through Walter Benjamin's understanding of the genre. These interpretations hint at the wide range of critical lenses one can productively bring to bear on the text.

"Cities of the Plain," however, the screenplay he began working on during the years leading up to *Blood Meridian*'s publication, is more recognizably palatable as a Western, a love story, and finally a tragedy. McCarthy describes it in precisely those terms in a synopsis of the screenplay. (The synopsis is undated, but it includes a short bio of McCarthy that mentions that his novel *Blood Meridian* "was nominated for this year's National Book Award."[6] That would indicate that McCarthy wrote the synopsis in 1985, when he told Howard Woolmer that he was actively trying to get the completed screenplay produced.) He begins by noting that the events of the plot "were related to the author by Jack Sanderson, a rancher of El Paso and Carlsbad New Mexico, who died five years ago," thus adding a bit of regional authenticity to the tale. McCarthy describes a story about "a young cowboy who fell in love with a prostitute in a Mexican bordello and became determined to marry her." She is murdered as a result, and the cowboy, John Grady Cole, can't be dissuaded by his friend Billy Parham from his "errand of vengeance." Revenge he achieves, though it also kills him. "Cities of the Plain," McCarthy explains, "is a story of doomed lovers and betrayal and the meaning and limits of friendship set in two cultures radically different and inextricably joined." Tragedy has certainly seen its share of doomed lovers, and McCarthy further indicates his conception of John Grady as a tragic hero in a document with descriptions of various characters in order of their appearance (also undated, but probably composed with the synopsis as supporting material for the screenplay). Although he doesn't include descriptions of Billy, John Grady, or Magdalena, he writes that Mac, an older rancher, "probably sees in John Grady the son he never had. John Grady is cut from the same bolt of cloth, but with the fatal romantic flaw."[7] In addition to the cultural conflict between the United States and Mexico, McCarthy emphasizes the tension between the cowboy codes of old and the new demands of modernity, a tension that contributes to John Grady's character and his eventual fate: "In the end," he writes in the same synopsis, "it is John Grady's romanticism and stubborn pride as emissary of the clearly defined values of the old west—values already well under siege—that bring him to a confrontation that can be neither avoided or survived." McCarthy summarizes the story in a way that evokes both Aristotelean hamartia and Vernant and Vidal-Naquet's understanding of tragedy as a conflict between older, heroic values and a modernizing society. John Grady Cole is the tragic hero here, and as a character he would be famous.

As it turned out, that fame didn't happen until 1992. That year he appeared as the protagonist of *All the Pretty Horses*, the novel that finally made McCarthy a bestselling author and was the first installment of his Border Trilogy. The second novel, *The Crossing*, follows a different character, Billy Parham, and John Grady reappears alongside Billy in the third, *Cities of the Plain*. The unpublished screenplay "Cities of the Plain," then, constitutes McCarthy's initial conception of both John Grady and Billy, and in each case that conception is quite different from the characters who are portrayed in the later Border Trilogy. Examining McCarthy's working and final drafts of the screenplay alongside the novels reveals how the characters, and thus the greater shape of this tragic narrative, evolved over time.

As in both *All the Pretty Horses* and *Cities of the Plain*, John Grady is the protagonist of the screenplay. With the assistance of his friend and fellow cowboy Billy Parham, John Grady tries to arrange his beloved's escape from her bordello and from her pimp, Eduardo. But John Grady's plan doesn't come together, and the girl is killed. John Grady manages to avenge her by killing Eduardo in a knife fight but sustains fatal injuries in the process. Billy finds him before he dies and cries out a curse on "goddamn fucking whores" as he holds his friend in his arms. (A lengthy epilogue, in which an aged Billy has a labyrinthian conversation with a stranger about a traveler who is both the subject of the stranger's dream and a dreamer himself, doesn't appear until McCarthy is drafting the novel.[8])

McCarthy sketched out the plot of "Cities" in a short treatment that is dated 1978 and titled "El Paso/Juarez." Here, he indicates setting with fragments like "Night in the barn" and includes Billy's cry of "Goddamn fucking whores" at the end but features little other dialogue.[9] Though his later drafts and fragments are undated, he completed the version that he sent to Sundance by 1984. In the draft versions of the full screenplay, McCarthy includes scene headings and capitalized names in dialogue headings, though he doesn't use formal screenplay format.[10] Instead, he sends the screenplay to a stenographer for the purposes of creating a shooting script. In a note to that stenographer, McCarthy writes that "[t]he primary purpose we have in typing a fresh draft of this script is to put it in the proper script format and to reduce the number of pages in the new format." He cautions that the punctuation is not "to be altered in any fashion" and that "[w]e would particularly like to get by with no *extra commas* inserted anywhere." Reformatting is a necessity, but McCarthy insists that his own well-established style remain in place in the process.[11]

McCarthy revises as he repeatedly redrafts the screenplay: he changes the title, alters the prostitute's name from Elvira to Magdalena, indicates that Magdalena has epilepsy, and gives Eduardo more lines, especially during the final knife fight. In the first complete typescript draft, all dialogue is in English, though he notes that conversations between John Grady and the girl will be in Spanish with English subtitles.[12] In a photocopy of that draft that McCarthy corrects heavily in pencil and into which he inserts additional, newly typed pages, he also inserts pages on which lines of dialogue are rendered in both Spanish and English; this is likely when McCarthy began to learn Spanish in earnest, which becomes such an integral part of his storytelling in the Border Trilogy.[13]

One scene in particular highlights the differences in John Grady's character as originally conceived and his portrayal in the Border Trilogy and shows how John Grady's stature as a tragic hero and the impact of his death are emphasized to a greater degree in the later novels. McCarthy writes what appears to be the earliest version of the scene by hand, on notebook paper.[14] In it, John Grady is attempting to ride an unbroken horse and is bucked off repeatedly, reinjuring a foot that was stepped on by a bull the week before, when John Grady competed in the Doña Ana County rodeo. The other cowboys stop him from trying again, but he returns to the barn that night, determined to saddle the horse. Billy arrives to stop him, and their confrontation turns intensely physical. John Grady takes a swing at Billy but fails to hit him, and then Billy punches John Grady in the face. John Grady falls down and then gets up again, "bleeding at the nose and he hits Billy in the side of the head and Billy knocks him down again." John Grady keeps rising and coming at Billy, "looking very grim and bloody," and Billy hits him fully four more times, including one "murderous swing at him which stretches him out in the chaff."[15] Here, John Grady is willing to endure a hellacious beating that causes one eye to swell shut just so that he can continue to be beaten up by the horse. In McCarthy's first complete draft of the screenplay, John Grady curses both the horse and Billy, insisting that "I can ride the son of a bitch" and telling Billy "Goddamn you" when Billy tries to prevent his further injury.[16]

By the time that the screenplay is reformatted as a shooting script, McCarthy has reduced the conflict slightly, though he still emphasizes the physical and emotional antagonism between John Grady, the horse, and Billy. John Grady demeans the horse by calling it "squirrelhead" and "that squirrel-headed son of a bitch" ("Cities" 12, 16). When he returns at night, the horse is clearly agitated and afraid, "Its eyes walled, wheezing" (17). "Will you leave that thing alone?" Billy implores him (17). John Grady's response is to take a swing at Billy, refusing to back down even as Billy says in amazement and frustration, "Will you quit? What the hell is wrong with you?" (18). Billy doesn't have to punch him six times, as he does in the handwritten version, but the violence of John Grady's encounter with the animal and the people around him is clear.

As originally conceived, John Grady's character was defined by stubbornness, grit, and an inability to take no for an answer. His approach to animals is literally rodeo-style, though that approach seems to fail both in the barn as well as in the actual rodeo in which he competes; his main talent seems to be his willingness to take a beating. The contrast with the John Grady of the Border Trilogy is striking. In the later novel version of *Cities*, the horse, rather than the young man, is the difficult one, described in the narration as "shrieking" and "crazed" (17). As Billy, Troy, and Joachín watch John Grady "work the colt" in the corral—rather than merely chase it around, as he does in the screenplay—Billy remarks that "I got a suspicion that whatever it is [John Grady] aims to do he'll most likely get it done" (14). Troy asks if John Grady "is supposed to be some sort of specialist in spoiled horses," and Billy refers the question to Joachín, asking him if the cowboy knows horses. Joachín just shakes his head. Billy clarifies to Troy, "Joachín thinks his methods is unorthodox" (15).

In the novel John Grady is not reckless or unskilled, but simply willing to take the necessary time to break the horse he considers his responsibility. Joachín's designation of "unorthodox" refers to the same considered and gentle horse-breaking method we see in great detail in *Pretty Horses*. In this version John Grady hasn't injured his foot while being rowdy and trying to ride a bull but while working with this same difficult horse. And finally, when Billy discovers John Grady in the barn late at night, continuing to work with the horse, he and the other cowboys convince him to cease and desist without the added persuasion of a heated conflict, much less a bloody fistfight. In the end John Grady's only comment to Billy about this is that it "wasnt any of your business" (19). He may be irked but is well in control of his emotions—a notable difference from the way the character was originally written. (Though the film adaptation of *All the Pretty Horses* doesn't portray John Grady as coarse or ineffective, it returns in some ways to the young man of the "Cities" screenplay, as I discuss more in chapter 4).

Though John Grady's more nurturing relationship with horses and other creatures—such as the litter of orphaned puppies he goes to great lengths to rescue (176)—is a significant element of *Cities of the Plain*, it is even more central to *All the Pretty Horses*, the first novel of the Border Trilogy. There, his gift for working with horses is almost preternatural, and he treats them with a respect and gentleness unfamiliar to his peers. But he can also endure physical hardship, romance the girl, and outfight an assassin. Though some reviewers found John Grady's many abilities unrealistic, especially given his youth,[17] critics have identified the character's place in a Bildungsroman or chivalric tradition. Gail Moore Morrison calls him "an unlikely knight errant, displaced and dispossessed, heroically tested and stubbornly faithful to a chivalric code whose power is severely circumscribed by the inevitable evil in a hostile world" (178). Charles Bailey has further argued that although John Grady in *All the Pretty Horses* may indeed be a knight errant, by *Cities of the Plain* he has become an antihero—not the "clumsy, often inept character of the picaresque novel that started the tradition, nor . . . the tortured, raging, mysterious, Satanic Byronic hero of Byron's own serious work. . . . Instead, I mean the character of highly developed sensitivities, the 'wandering outlaw' intent on self-realization and personal salvation, capable of great courageous moral action in the cause of human freedom, whose unconventional impulses rise from some inherent spiritual core" (294). Phillip Snyder locates both John Grady's and Billy's moral center as more specifically Western American, in that each character "still refuses to relinquish his essential cowboy self-identity—John Grady as the mythic cowboy in search of a lost homestead and Billy as the loyal saddle pard in search of a balance between the demands of idealism and pressures of reality" (200). These critics see in the Border Trilogy's John Grady both heroism and greatness, as well as anachronism—holding on to values that he "refuses to relinquish," even in the face of hostility and a changing world.

Chivalric knight or mythic cowboy—what either role requires is a horse, and there John Grady is indeed advantaged. McCarthy makes John Grady's character clear early on in *Pretty Horses*: "What he loved in horses was what he loved in men, the blood and the heat of the blood that ran them. All his reverence and all his fondness and all the leanings of his life were for the ardenthearted and they would always be so and never be otherwise" (6). John Grady finds his community in other passionate creatures, both human and animal, and as the story unfolds it becomes clear that his partnership with horses, based on that love and reverence, is unique. Another early passage in *Pretty Horses* dismisses even the idea that the young man and those animals would ever be separated:

> The boy ... sat a horse not only as if he'd been born to it which he was but as if were he begot by malice or mischance into some queer land where horses never were he would have found them anyway. Would have known that there was something missing for the world to be right or he right in it and would have set forth to wander wherever it was needed for as long as it took until he came upon one and he would have known that that was what he sought and it would have been. (23)

John Grady goes on to prove himself on a large Mexican hacienda by breaking sixteen horses in four days, a feat that draws a crowd as much for its audacity as for John Grady's method, which involves hobbling the horses, whispering to them, sacking them out (rubbing them with a gunnysack) using a sack that carries his scent, and gently familiarizing the horses with a blanket and saddle. When he climbs on the first horse and it responds to him, his friend Lacey Rawlins is both impressed and disappointed. "What the hell kind of bronc is that? You think that's what these people paid good money to see?" he comments good-naturedly (107). Despite Rawlins's joke here, the feat is still an impressive one, clearly establishing for both the people of the hacienda and the reader as well John Grady's credentials as a superlative horseman. (McCarthy describes John Grady's process in great detail, as I review in chapter 4. His accomplishment is unusual but still realistic; in a manuscript that McCarthy labeled his first draft of the novel, John Grady breaks nineteen horses in three days, a tally that he later chose to modulate.[18] John Grady is superlative, after all, but not superhuman.)

His partnership with horses is his way of life, but it's also a deep part of his psychology—something he can meditate on when things go wrong, or even horribly wrong. When he wakes up in a Mexican prison after being wounded, he can't think about his father or about the girl he loves, but "he thought about horses and they were always the right thing to think about" (204). In another prison, in the midst of dire circumstances, he dreams not of riding horses or controlling them but running with them, one of their number, a unity:

> … and in the dream he was running among the horses running and in the dream he himself could run with the horses and they coursed the young mares and fillies over the plain where their rich bay and their rich chestnut colors shone in the sun and the young colts ran with their dams and trampled down the flowers in a haze of pollen that hung in the sun like powdered gold and they ran he and the horses out along the high mesas where the ground resounded under their running hooves and they flowed and changed and ran and their manes and tails blew off of them like spume and there was nothing else at all in that high world and they moved all of them in a resonance that was like a music among them and they were none of them afraid horse nor colt nor mare and they ran in that resonance which is the world itself and which cannot be spoken but only praised. (161–162)

For John Grady in *All the Pretty Horses*, these animals are much more than how he makes a living and certainly more than an antagonist to be conquered. They are his community, and though he can't literally run with them the way he does in his dream, the "resonance" he imagines that is also "the world itself" is a mutual understanding that goes beyond language, one that "cannot be spoken." His human relationships don't end so well, but he does ride off into the sunset with his beloved horses at story's end, "their long shadows [passing] in tandem like the shadow of a single being," into "the world to come" (302). John Grady's relationship with his parents, his love affair with the hacendado's daughter, and his friendships with Rawlins and

Jimmy Blevins may drive the plot, but his character is most deeply defined by this transcendent resonance that he imagines and seeks. He is indeed ardent-hearted—and he's come a long way from the earliest drafts of the screenplay, where he appears to be just a hothead.

And so the screenplay reveals the humbler—though still tragic—origins of the character of John Grady and thus of the novels *All the Pretty Horses* and *Cities of the Plain*, but it also contains the seed of *The Crossing*. That novel follows Billy Parham's journeys into Mexico, the first of which he undertakes to return a pregnant she-wolf to the mountains. In the earliest complete draft of the screenplay of "Cities," John Grady asks Billy if he's ever seen a wolf, and Billy's answer indicates that there isn't much to say. "Nope," Billy responds. "Never did. They been trapped and poisoned out years ago. My daddy used to trap em up in the Organ Mountains and they wasnt plentiful then."[19] But when McCarthy makes extensive corrections to that draft and inserts additional pages, he changes Billy's story. Now, Billy has indeed seen a wolf, "in a trap one time." He says that his daddy used to trap them in Hidalgo County for the government, wolves that had likely come up from Mexico. He remembers the traps, "number fourteen Newhouse [that] looked big enough to hold a grizzly bear to me." Billy then describes the experience of seeing the trapped wolf in great detail. His father caught the wolf by burying the trap, building a fire over it, and letting it burn down—the same way Billy finally traps the she-wolf in *The Crossing*. "She was a real pale cream color, almost white," Billy says. "But that was the last one he ever caught and the first and last one I ever seen.... I carried that wolf home dead across the pommel of my saddle and I wasnt but seven years old but I felt bad about it. There was not no pleasure in it." He says his father may have also felt bad about killing the wolves, but that "I know that that was just another part of the west that was gone. There aint a whole lot of it left." He adds, "Hell, when I was a kid Apache indians used to come to the back door to ask for coffee and meal."[20]

Readers of *The Crossing* would recognize a good deal in this version of the screenplay from part one of that novel: the Indian who asks for food (and later kills Billy's parents in his absence); the she-wolf and the way Billy finally traps it; and his ambivalent feelings about doing so. But McCarthy apparently began to worry about the length of this passage and wondered if it might be better suited to a separate project. He cuts it down in a subsequent draft, and a page of notes referencing that draft includes the observation that this section is still "long." Maybe this is material, he thinks, for a "film about wolves?"[21] By the time the screenplay has been polished into a shooting script, McCarthy confines Billy to saying simply that he saw a wolf that his daddy had caught in a trap once and remarking on the size and type of the trap ("Cities" 10–11). *The Crossing*, then, begins as a story in "Cities of the Plain" that takes on a life of its own and that McCarthy initially thinks could make for another screenplay.

But instead of writing that "film about wolves," by 19 October 1987 McCarthy began a full draft of *The Crossing* in novel form.[22] Then in January 1988 he wrote to Peter Greenleaf and said that he had "finished a rough draft of a novel and put it away in a box and am about half way—make that ⅓ way—through another. More fun to start a new one than rewrite the old."[23] It's difficult to tell, but this may mean that he drafted *The Crossing* before *All the Pretty Horses*, because it isn't until 3 November 1988 that he began what he labels a "1st and early draft" of the novel *Cities of the Plain*.[24] He wrote again to Woolmer in April 1989 that he is "about half way through the 1st draft of the third novel in a series of three." It looks like "several years of rewriting," he reported.[25] Regardless of the precise order of composition—hard to determine because of his vagueness in letters like these, the many undated drafts of each novel, and the uncertainty that what McCarthy labels a "1st draft" for archival purposes is, in fact, a true first draft—the screenplay of "Cities of the Plain" is very much the foundation of the Border Trilogy, which McCarthy composed as a series rather than as three discrete projects.[26]

While I find the changes in John Grady's character the most notable when comparing the "Cities" screenplay to the Border Trilogy, Edwin Arnold sees the greatest differences in the depictions of Billy and considers it reasonable to wonder "if these two 'Billys' should indeed be considered the same character, for the young, melancholy Billy Parham of *The Crossing* initially seems worlds away from the garrulous, folksy cowboy we find here [in the screenplay]" ("Last of the Trilogy" 227). Arnold reads the screenplay version of Billy as "something of a comic misanthrope … who warns John Grady away from love and marriage," and whose final cry against "Goddamn fucking whores" reveals his feelings about women as well as his lack of understanding of John Grady's motivation. While Arnold does identify moments in the novel version of *Cities of the Plain* that depict Billy as a more boisterous, blustery character, and thus more like that in the screenplay—"I love this life," Billy jabbers to John Grady. "You love this life, son? I love this life. You do love this life dont you? Cause by god I love it. Just love it" (*Cities* 10)—he thinks ultimately that in the Border Trilogy generally and *Cities of the Plain* in particular McCarthy "found himself pulled closer to the older, wounded man than to the young, impulsive boy. And perhaps this explains why John Grady's story is so little changed from screenplay to novel, while the additions to Billy's are ultimately more profound and provide the novel its soul" (228). This Billy, Arnold writes in a different essay, "soon reveals his enduring capacity to love, even to risk once again losing the object of that love. John Grady Cole assumes Boyd's place in his still-damaged heart, and by the end of the book they are one in his memory" ("McCarthy and the Sacred" 234).[27]

In the screenplay Billy is a witness to John Grady's tragic death, but that witnessing is given greater weight in the Border Trilogy, compounded by Billy's own losses. Arnold celebrates Billy for his capacity to endure loss and still love, and the same could be said for John Grady, who, in addition to his love for and connection with horses, also loves and loses Alejandra and then Magdalena in the same way that Billy loves and loses Boyd and then John Grady. Aristotle believed that the tragic hero must be superior, which for him meant aristocratic—otherwise the reversal of fortune and tragic fall wouldn't be dramatic enough to impress the audience. John Grady's preternatural skills, his communion with horses, and his unironic ardentheartedness certainly make him "greater" in the Border Trilogy than in the screenplay, but the amplification of Billy's capacity to love and endure is also significant. Russell Hillier has noted the Border Trilogy's twelve-book structure—three volumes each divided into four sections—and its resonance with the twelve-book epic structure of the Virgil's *Aeneid* and Milton's *Paradise Lost*, as well as with the twenty-four books of Homer's *Iliad* and *Odyssey*. The Trilogy's protagonists, then, are "the Achillean John Grady, whose life, like Homer's fiery Myrmidon, is remarkable but short, and, second, the Odyssean Billy, who lives out his long years wandering the West and, despite himself, searching for a place he might call home" ("Like some supplicant" 7–8).

I've called Billy a witness, which might sound like the designation of a lesser character. Here, however, that status describes someone one who stands before—and indeed is enmeshed in—the violence of the world, and who then, denied the release of death, must somehow assimilate and shape it. Billy's struggle to make sense of the world may seem to him to be all for naught: after wending through the complex story told by a traveler in the epilogue of *Cities of the Plain*, the novel ends with him telling a woman named Betty that "I aint nothin. I dont know why you put up with me." But Betty, Billy's own witness, counters that: "Well, Mr Parham, I know who you are. And I do know why. You go to sleep now. I'll see you in the morning" (292). It's a validation and shift of focus from tragic hero to enduring witness that McCarthy will repeat in the novel version of *No Country for Old Men*.

In all of the iterations of this narrative, John Grady is defined by his determination and willpower, but only in the Border Trilogy does he seem truly connected to other beings, the horses that prove to be both his life's work and his soul mates—more so than either Alejandra or Magdalena, or even Billy, who struggles mightily to understand why his friend makes the choices he does. Hence his blaming "goddamn fucking whores" for John Grady's death rather than a host of other options—true love, a Western code of honor that calls for vengeance, the lethally exploitative economics of the sex trade, or simply John Grady's failure to wait for Billy to help him take on Eduardo. But as difficult as it may sometimes be, it's that sense of community with others that is sustaining in the face of suffering, and the Border Trilogy expands on the screenplay by imagining the possibility of community, or resonance, with nonhuman beings as well. That interest in a transcendent communion with creatures that are also fundamentally unknowable was likely influenced by another screenplay that McCarthy wrote in the 1980s.

MYSTERIES OF THE DEEP: "WHALES AND MEN"

In 1986 McCarthy traveled to Argentina with his friend Roger Payne, a whale biologist. Payne had become publically known in the 1970s when his recording *Songs of the Humpback Whale* was instrumental in bringing attention to the whale and to its complex vocalizations. When Payne published his book *Among Whales* in 1995, he dedicated it to his wife and to Cormac McCarthy, noting in the acknowledgements that McCarthy had read and commented on the manuscript as well as discussed it with him in depth. "In my experience," he went on, "there is no precedent for someone not a professional biologist being so well-read and so clearly informed about biology" (8–9). As Edwin Arnold has noted, parts of Payne's book and McCarthy's screenplay seem like sibling texts, especially as Payne urges creative people to build the beauty of whales into their art ("Whales and Men" 22).

In 1986 McCarthy and Payne spent about three weeks with the whales of Península Valdés on the eastern coast of Argentina.[28] Even before McCarthy left the States he was planning a new project; he wrote to Howard Woolmer in August that he was "working on a whale story."[29] In December McCarthy makes his fascination with the creatures clear in a letter to Albert Erskine: "You cant really see whales until you get under the water and look at them," he writes. "They are huge and in the middle of this great wall of living (presumably) material is an eye—not all that large, maybe the size of a tennis ball. And this eye is watching you."[30]

In McCarthy's archive there are four drafts of the screenplay he eventually titled "Whales and Men" as well as copious notes; it's clear that he worked on the project intensely, although it never came close to production and McCarthy never adapted the story for a different format the way he did with "Cities of the Plain" and "No Country for Old Men." A folder of notes on "Whales and Men" also includes a few pages of notes labeled "All the Pretty Little Horses," indicating that the two projects probably had at least some overlap.[31] Indeed, of all McCarthy's works these two narratives as well as *The*

Crossing have the most to say about the potential resonance between humans and animals. The screenplay's title invokes Melville, though the judge in *Blood Meridian* is closer kin to Moby-Dick that the gentle creatures here. In earlier drafts of the screenplay, the title is listed slightly differently as "Of Whales and Men," which suggests an additional debt to John Steinbeck's naturalist novel *Of Mice and Men* (1937).[32] Steinbeck, in fact, wrote that book as novel/play hybrid, what he called a "play/novelette" (an antecedent of sorts to McCarthy's *The Sunset Limited*, which bears the description "A Novel in Dramatic Form"), and also wrote its first stage adaptation. The obvious similarity of McCarthy's title to Steinbeck's may indicate a possible reason why McCarthy decided to approach the story cinematically rather than as a novel. In what follows, I'll refer to the final draft of the screenplay.

"Whales and Men" opens on the Florida coast, where Guy Schuler, a marine biologist, is moving among seventeen pilot whales beached on the shore. He is injecting them with panabarbitol, a tranquilizer that will kill them. A young woman follows him and asks tearfully why he would do such a thing; Guy explains that the dying whales are drawing other whales in to the beach and that if they don't act, the whales' numbers could increase to as many as three hundred. The girl wonders at the suicidal acts: "They're supposed to be so smart," she says ("Whales" 2). "No one knows anything about them," Guy responds. "They're like martians. What do you want me to tell you? Their love for one another overcomes all reason. They're not like other animals. They wont abandon one another. They wont allow any one of their kind to die alone. Not as long as he still has breath to call out" (3). The scene is a gloss on the story as a whole, which follows a group of people fascinated by this unity and appalled by the humans that would either ignore them or slaughter them for profit.

Guy soon meets the unlikely trio with whom he will travel: John Western, a wealthy former medical student and yachtsman; Kelly McAmon, John's girlfriend; and Peter Gregory, an Irish aristocrat. Sailing with John, the characters seek out and encounter whales, hearing their calls on one short trip and later, on a longer research voyage, swimming and kayaking among them. During the second trip, a whaling ship arrives and massacres all the whales but one baby, which Guy must kill with panabarbitol in order to save it from the agony of being eaten by sharks. The experience affects all of them: Kelly and John split up, and Kelly later marries and has children with Peter; John goes back to medical school and then begins work in a hospital in the developing world; and Peter takes a seat in the House of Parliament, giving his maiden speech about the plight of the whales.

As a screenplay, "Whales and Men" is much less conventional than *The Gardener's Son* or "Cities of the Plain," which themselves are hardly exercises in cinematic formula. "Cities" in particular evinces a visual imagination and a plot that moves quickly and with building tension. "Whales and Men" is different. Though the characters are memorable, and scenes like the whale hunt have strong cinematic potential, many scenes consist of long, unbroken speeches and philosophizing. The speeches, in fact, are much lengthier than the dialogue sequences of "Cities of the Plain" that apparently put off the Sundance committee, according to Bill Wittliff. (Not to mention the difficulties of shooting a film that takes place even partially on water, as the makers of *Jaws* have attested.) Despite the challenges a screenplay like this would face if it were actually produced and the fact that of the three screenplays discussed in this chapter this is the only one never to become public in a different form, "Whales and Men" is nevertheless a key work to consider—particularly for those interested in McCarthy's ecological imagination and his conceptualizing of language, both of which are framed in such a way as to emphasize their connection to suffering and to its potential abeyance.

The lengthy philosophical dialogues of "Whales and Men" and its concern for human-animal relationships make it resonate with all of the Border Trilogy. As Arnold has noted, the episode with the baby whale is a strong corollary to Billy Parham's experience with the pregnant she-wolf, which he ultimately kills in order to save her from being torn apart by dogs in a bloody wolf-baiting spectacle (Arnold, "Whales and Men" 25). Kelly's discussion of God reflects similar discussions in *The Crossing*, and when John Western describes seeing a bright light out at sea and wondering if it was "the sun misrisen at midnight . . . the skies given over to the access of sudden random moons, everything mindless and migratory," it presages Billy's witnessing of the Trinity Test, the "white light of a desert noon" seen at night, which gives way to "an alien dusk and now an alien dark" ("Whales" 126; *Crossing* 425). John Western even compares whales to wolves, which are cooperative because they are predators: "[Predators] have to understand each other. They share in the work of hunting and they share in the kill. Cooperative society among grazing animals scarcely exists.... If you're a hunter you have to learn to control your aggression. Wolves never kill each other" (87). "Cities of the Plain" was the genesis of the plot of the Border Trilogy, but "Whales and Men" may share the trilogy's soul in its deep appreciation for the communion of the animal world and the longing that people like John Grady and Guy Schuler have to be a part of that world.

Peter expresses his wonder at the whales' existence in a long disquisition about language and the nature of evil. In a conversation with Guy, he explains that he "distrust[s] language above all things," a distrust that was "brought on by the measles" (53). He was seventeen, he says, laid up in a dark room, thinking about how he had lost his father in a car racing accident and his brother to polio and about how the measles might leave him blind. It seemed like nothing so much as a punishment, and so he began to wonder about what evil is and where it comes from.

Seeing no evidence of evil in the rest of the world—because he couldn't see things like flood, famine, or shark attacks as the workings of malign intent—he concluded that the source of evil must be in humans. "What was there about us," he wonders, "that made us so suitable?" (55). The answer, he realized, is the thing that makes humans both unique and alien in the world—language. "What had begun as a system for identifying and organizing the phenomena of the world had become a system for replacing those phenomena. For replacing the world" (57). Peter's meditation on language and representation elaborates on the Platonic concerns voiced by the timekeeper in *The Gardener's Son* that "[o]nce you copy something down you dont have it anymore. You just have the record" (5). Peter goes further, however, when he compares language to the "evil aliens in the horror movie that take on the forms of things and gradually replace them altogether." Because, after all, any act of evil is characterized by "the refusal to acknowledge it. The eagerness [and ability, one might add] to call it something else" (58). If it's true that "[n]omenclature is the very soul of secondhandedness," as Peter puts it, then he wonders longingly if "there existed a dialogue among the lifeforms of this earth from which we had excluded ourselves so totally that we no longer even believed it to exist? Could it be that dialogue which we still sense in dreams?" (57). This, then, is the attraction of the whales, creatures that communicate purely, who are "transparent to each other," as John Western puts it later. There might be such a thing, then—a communion not based on symbols but on mutual being, like John Grady running with horses in his dream.

Guy, Peter, and John all despair at the state of the world and the possibility of humans ever achieving—or recovering—such a way of being, since they seem so hell-bent on actively destroying each other and their fellow creatures. (It's a despair that presages the brutal violence of the postapocalyptic world of *The Road*, though the characters' resumption of hope even in the face of suffering is also echoed at the end of that novel.) Kelly, however, seems to understand something about a communal existence from the beginning. "And I see that the similarities are so much greater than the differences and I know that there is a connection there that no separation in time or space can invalidate," she muses while visiting Peter's Irish estate. "I know that you are my brother"—a statement echoed by Black in *The Sunset Limited*—"and at another level which is harder to reach but just as real I know that you are me. Not figuratively. Not a metaphor. For real. In the flesh. It's an understanding that has nothing to do with problem-solving. It's an act of pure cognition.

It's an event. I guess what I would say is that yes I believe in God but I dont know who he is. I dont know what his name is. Why would he have a name? To distinguish him from what?" (45). Kelly's visceral understanding of one-as-another is made material by the end of the story, when she is pregnant with her and Peter's second child.

The male characters come to something like her understanding by the story's end as well. Guy continues to work with the whales, though he worries about the emotional toll it takes, the full realization of what their plight means to him. Fully empathizing with, and thus fighting for, the whales could lead him to a moral impasse: "I saw where the sort of commitment I contemplated could take me," he tells Kelly. "That there could come a point somewhere where I would have to choose. Between whales and men. That I could be called upon to take sides in some irrevocable way and that ultimately it could mean taking human life. And I knew that if I did that I was lost" (115). Guy isn't willing to lose himself, to violate his sense of communion with the whales by doing violence to another class of creature, even if it means protecting the ones he loves the most.

For his part, John returns to medical school and dedicates himself to helping others, writing to Kelly about his own new sense of unity: "They [the whales] changed us all. I know that one life can change all life. The smallest warp in the fabric can tilt all of creation to run anew. . . . Yet I cannot believe that whales and men are alien beings. . . . I know that we are lost but I no longer believe that we are doomed" (129–130). And Peter takes his seat in Parliament and speaks to the members about the need to protect "a nation that cannot speak for itself," whose "family and communal life is nothing if not exemplary," but which is being continually slaughtered. "Because it bore no arms against others it was put to the sword," he says. "Because it spoke an alien tongue it was given no hearing. Not in the world's courts and not in mens' hearts" (133). On the last page of the screenplay, the scene description says that the members are listening. It's a view of nature similar to what Arnold sees in *The Crossing*: a biocentric one that elevates the idea of a "rich matrix of creatures" (*Crossing* 127; Arnold, "McCarthy and the Sacred") that is both physical and spiritual, an interconnectedness that is observable and mysterious at the same time.

McCarthy's characters recognize the dark and bloody nature of the world around them, but in this case they also work to acknowledge and understand the interwoven relation of all creatures and to revere the love that overcomes all reason, as Guy puts it. If suffering is unavoidable, then community can serve as solace. Those relationships might be occasionally available as the transcendent and nonverbal awareness of the "rich matrix of creatures," but more often community must be established through language—this is a screenplay that itself consists mostly of dialogue, after all. And so "Whales" acknowledges the power of language to negotiate the chasm between suffering and union but also warns of the danger that it may be used as mere obfuscation—or even, in Peter's description, to perpetuate suffering as the mechanism for evil.

Despite that anxiety about language, "Whales and Men" is ultimately a fairly optimistic narrative, one that concludes with each of the major characters doing meaningful work in the world, aware and in support of the ties that bind humans and ecological systems together. The screenplay's emphasis on environmental concerns links it to the Border Trilogy and to *The Road*—the latter a novel that has proved to be of particular interest to ecocritics engaging with its presentation of ecology and community—though "Whales" takes a clearly activist stance that is an exception in McCarthy's work. As James Lilley notes, most of McCarthy's texts "engage issues of ecology and environmentalism in much more subtle ways" (118). The issues are common to McCarthy; their clear and unambiguous articulation is not. This could be why McCarthy never chose to revise "Whales and Men" for later publication as a novel—it may ultimately have functioned as a kind of exercise, a way to work through philosophical ideas that took on a more nuanced and complex hue in his later novels. Clearly optimistic endings seem to leave something to be desired for McCarthy as well, which is dramatically illustrated by the changes he makes to his original screenplay "No Country for Old Men" when he rewrites it as a novel.

"NO COUNTRY FOR OLD MEN": AND NOW FOR SOMETHING COMPLETELY DIFFERENT

The third screenplay McCarthy wrote during this prolific period is "No Country for Old Men," and it differs from the other two in its emphasis on fast-moving action rather than doomed romance or ponderous dialogue. Though the screenplay itself was no more successful than the others, the 2005 novel was a bestseller that the Coen brothers would then adapt for the screen in 2007, for which they won Oscars for Best Picture, Best Director, and Best Adapted Screenplay. Like "Whales and Men," this is a story that also demonstrates the value of alliance, though here that partnership takes the form of a buddy movie rather than a narrative about the interconnectedness of all beings. McCarthy appears to have worked on the screenplay most intensely in 1987, and on one page of an early draft he notes the date—20 July—his fifty-fourth birthday.[33]

Though John Grady's and Billy's characters undergo some notable changes when McCarthy adapts his "Cities of the Plain" screenplay into the third novel of the Border Trilogy, the story remains essentially the same. McCarthy makes dramatic changes to the plot, however, when he adapts "No Country" into the novel he publishes in 2005. While he maintains the main characters and the central narrative premise, the plot's development and conclusion, and the tone that conclusion strikes, are all remarkably different. As in the novel, the screenplay follows Llewelyn Moss as he stumbles across the money from a drug deal gone bad and Sheriff Ed Tom Bell as he investigates a series of crimes that he fears are beyond his power to understand. Both versions feature a formidable antagonist, though the enigmatically named Anton Chigurh appears only in the novel. In the screenplay the villain is Edward Ralston, a "tall man with a moustache, elegantly dressed" ("No Country" 1). He doesn't have Chigurh's penchant for coin tosses, nor does he insist on working alone. Ralston is less *a true and living prophet of destruction*" (as Bell calls Chigurh in the novel) than he is a bad guy quick to kill those who oppose him (*NCFOM* 4). He has a sidekick named Milo who drives him from place to place in a bulletproof Suburban. As the lives of the three main characters—Moss, Bell, and Ralston/Chigurh—begin to intersect, the differences between screenplay and novel become apparent. McCarthy revised a screenplay with a classically comic ending of union and fortune into a novel with the structure of tragedy.

The screenplay's opening does evoke a sense of tragic loss, though that tone will later change. Here, Sheriff Bell lives with his teenaged granddaughter Melinda, having lost both his wife and his daughter. The final version of the screenplay begins with a crime scene—a woman in her late thirties is being wheeled to an ambulance, but the police lieutenant at the scene doesn't have any hope for her survival. He speaks into a radio, and his words indicate that this isn't just a random victim. "I know she aint goin to make it," he says, and continues: "Charlie I dont care if it is his county. I dont care if its his house. You'll have to get somebody else to come up there. There's a pastor at the church that's a friend of the family. See if you can get a hold of him. I think it's Mullins" ("No Country" 1). Two scenes later Bell talks to Mullins, and it becomes clear that the woman was Bell's daughter. "You know I never expected to outlive my wife. Never even crossed my mind. But if somebody had told me I'd outlive my daughter. I dont know" (3). Bell wonders about his ability to cope with it all: "I wasnt cut out for it, Don," he goes on. "This talk about the Lord testin you and what not. He didnt need to test me, I can tell you that. I'd of owned up to whoever wanted to listen that without them women I just wasnt a whole lot of use to anybody" (3). Melinda cries at night for her mother and is engaged to a boy that Bell doesn't think much of. "Rides around on a goddamn motorcycle," as he puts it (88).

Bell is drifting, an unhappy man with a broken family. He tells Mullins that he's decided to retire. "I think the county could use a younger man," he says (2)—and the sentiment explains McCarthy's choice of title, a reference to the first line of Yeats's poem "Sailing to Byzantium." The poem initially seems to celebrate the sensual world of youth at the expense of the old man, "[a] tattered coat upon a stick" (197). Bell certainly feels reduced and irrelevant, and he laments how things have changed: "It seems like everything I see nowadays is designed to take the place of the real world," he says. "Drugs I guess just does it better. That's what I see. It's the ultimate future. It subverts everything else. It will subvert everything else including the law" (6). The young revel in drugs, in artifice, and avoid the real world, and that dangerous sensuality threatens to take over all systems of morality and order. Similar to the way that Peter in "Whales and Men" describes language's capacity to propagate evil through denial and obfuscation, Bell describes drugs as the worst kind of representation, a mask that also annihilates the real that it hides. (McCarthy makes the connection between drugs and dangerous representation explicit in a draft fragment of this same scene, on which he adds additional handwritten dialogue equating drugs with mindless television: "TV takes the place of human companionship. You cant live with real people, you live with artificial ones. Easier to get along with. After awhile people lose certain things about give & take. People spend more time alone."[34])

"Sailing to Byzantium," however, goes on to express longing for a different kind of artifice—"the artifice of eternity," the world of art and "[m]onuments of unageing intellect" (197). Only in "the holy city of Byzantium," a place associated in the poem with the Christian sacred and artistic purification, can one slough off the distractions or trials of the body and take a form "as Grecian goldsmiths make." Yeats ultimately celebrates being consumed by and gathered into a world of being that is not merely sensual but born of "holy fire" and eternal as artistic creation. Old age may be "paltry" and cut off from the revels of youth, but at least the old soul can "clap its hands and sing" and seek the permanence represented by Byzantium. Given this emphasis, the title and allusion "No Country for Old Men" is an appropriate one for McCarthy's later novel, but as I'll explain, it's rendered ironic by the plot of the screenplay.

In the screenplay Bell certainly feels his age and his losses acutely. But when a group of bodies is discovered in the desert, minus the drugs and the money that fueled the conflict, Bell is suddenly infused with purpose and determination, and the tone of the screenplay shifts. He becomes an active rather than passive character, a skillful lawman who is willing to break the rules if he needs to. At the crime scene he talks to a DEA agent and tells him plainly that if he finds the money, he doesn't intend to turn it over to federal agents. "If I find some money and there's no evidence linking it to this case," he says, "then I intend to see that the county gets that money. And since the money aint here, that's how I intend to find it. I dont think it's right. I thing [*sic*] the money ought to be burned along with the damned dope. But I'll take the lesser of the two evils, given the choice" (27). The comment reveals his pragmatism, honesty, and need to make the situation right any way he can.

Once he has a lead, Bell doesn't pause to doubt himself or to ruminate, as he does in the novel, about painful memories of abandoning his comrades during his service in World War II or to wonder about the ways that someone can "steal [his] own life" (*NCFOM* 278). Here, Bell is determined to catch Ralston and displays a level of control and efficiency that he lacks in that later version of the story. After he finds out about the missing money and about Llewelyn Moss, he catches up to Moss in Eagle Pass. Moss had been shot in an encounter with Ralston and Milo and went to Mexico to seek medical treatment; Bell finds him as he crosses the border to return to the States ("No Country" 79). It's a surprising moment for anyone familiar with the novel or the Coens' film, in which Bell doesn't catch up with Moss until he's already been killed.

The Sheriff Bell of McCarthy's screenplay is smart enough to figure out where Moss was going and where to find him when he made his next move. He convinces Moss to talk with him, and their conversation reveals that Bell has not only figured out what's already happened, he's also figured out what needs to happen next in order to outwit the bad guys. But he needs Moss's help to do it. Bell explains the situation to Moss, and he even understands how Ralston has been able to kill people without leaving any telltale bullet casings. "He kills people with a pneumatically operated cattlegun," he says, having deduced both Ralston's choice of weapon and its mode of operation (82). Ralston also knows, Bell emphasizes, who Margie Wallace is—Moss's wife (later renamed Carla Jean in the novel). Moss is suddenly worried, but Bell allays his fears. He's hired a private detective to watch over her, he says, and paid for it himself. It seems that Bell has thought of everything—he just needs a partner. "I appreciate what you're tellin me, sheriff," Moss responds. "But I dont think you understand the sincerity of my desire to be rich" (82). "I do appreciate the sincerity of your desire to be rich," Bell assures him. "You just dont appreciate the sincerity of mine to get Ralston" (83). So the two men come to a deal—if Moss will help Bell get the killer, then Bell will let Moss walk away with half the money (which, Moss is impressed to find out, Bell knows is $325,000) (84).

As Bell reveals in this scene, he doesn't just want Ralston because he's a criminal, or because of the drug-related destruction that he both causes and represents—he wants Ralston because Ralston is his daughter's killer. Moss senses that "There's somethin personal" about all this for Bell, and Bell assents: "Lets just say this man killed somebody that was pretty special to me" (84). Moss wants the money, but Bell is out for justice. When they join forces, the screenplay's debt to the "buddy movie" genre becomes clear.

Broadly speaking, the genre has a long history, as male duos were common in vaudeville and the early comedy films of Laurel and Hardy or Abbott and Costello. But as Molly Haskell has noted, "male camaraderie has cropped up with increasing self-consciousness and sentimentality" (24) in the 1960s and '70s in films like *Butch Cassidy and the Sundance Kid* (1969), a dynamic that Eve Kosofsky Sedgwick would later describe as "male homosocial desire," a continuum between homosocial and homosexual desire existing within a homophobic culture (2). Cynthia Fuchs writes specifically about how this dynamic works in interracial buddy cop movies, a subgenre that includes *48 Hrs.* (1982), *Lethal Weapon* (1987), and *Men in Black* (1997), and argues that in films like these the "initial axes of racial, generational, political, and ethnic difference [are contained] under a collective performance of extraordinary virility" (195). (And like Bell, one member of the partnership in each of these films is also working to overcome a personal loss — the murder of friends and fellow cops in *48 Hrs.* and the loss of a wife to death or estrangement in *Lethal Weapon* and *Men in Black*, respectively.) Moss and Bell are both white, but their partnership — an older, more conservative lawman paired with a younger wild card — is similar to the duos in those films, and the father/son relationship that develops between them reflects those that Susan Jeffords has identified in a number of 1980s films, including the Star Wars, Indiana Jones, Rambo, and Back to the Future trilogies. (Jeffords argues that the emphasis on patriarchal legacy "externalized the deep-seated anxieties for those in the conservative movement ... about the passage from Reagan to Bush" [66–67].) As Fuchs writes, the buddy movie ends in spectacularly violent victory: "Again and again, these movies conclude with the partners triumphantly detonating all villains and nearby vehicles. The profusion of these psychosexual displays (as expensive special effects and formulaic repetitions) demonstrates by unsubtle metaphor the incongruous nature of the buddy politic. Too much and never enough, the final catharsis remains untenable" (195).

And indeed the climax of "No Country" involves the spectacular detonation of villains and vehicles as well as the profession and demonstration of loyalty between the father/son buddy team of Bell and Moss. The two go to the desert to confront the bad guys; Moss approaches Ralston's vehicle while Bell stays hidden. "You dont aim to throw me in the creek do you?" Bell asks, worried that Moss might slip off into the night. "I'll be back, Sheriff," Moss assures him (94). But Moss is caught, cornered by Milo and Ralston. They want the money, and Ralston uses his cattle gun on Moss's elbow when he claims not to have it. "How did you get in a jackpot like this, Moss," Ralston asks, while coolly smoking a cigar (96). He's about to do away with Moss for good when Bell calls from out in the desert: "Leave the boy alone, Ralston. I got your money" (97). "There is a frozen moment," the screenplay reads, and then a firefight erupts—Bell starts shooting with an automatic. Everyone but Ralston is hit, and Milo is seriously wounded when a bullet pierces the compressed air tank next to him and the result is a fiery explosion. Displaying his trademark coldness, Ralston eliminates Milo by shooting him in the head, and then turns to Moss, lying on the ground. "He didnt come back for you," Ralston tells Moss (denying that Bell feels anything for Moss), "He came for me." Moss doesn't take the bait and simply responds, "It's the same thing." As Ralston moves to pull the trigger, Moss reveals a hidden pistol and shoots him in the face, killing him (98). He then finds Bell, assuring him that he won't leave him there. "I'll be back as quick as I can. I wont leave you, Sheriff," Moss says, cementing their partnership. "I know you wont, son. Go on. I'll be right here," the sheriff responds (99). The two men have not only outwitted a serial killer and nabbed a serious amount of cash, but in the experience have formed a familial bond. It's no coincidence that Bell calls Moss "son" in this moment—he is childless no more.

The story closes with two reunions and a payday. Melinda visits her grandfather in the hospital, telling him she loves him and that she's realized the no-account she was engaged to is "not good enough for me" (101). Bell's friend Doc White is depositing $320,000 into the bank, having enlisted thirty-two people to each make a deposit of $10,000 so that the banker doesn't have to report it. "And that's what this corporation is," the banker asks White to clarify. "To build a clinic." "That's it," replies White, and it seems that Bell has done exactly what he intended with his half of the money from the drug trade (101–102). Moss, meanwhile, has other plans. He returns home to Margie with a new truck and a promise to take her to Las Vegas. Go get ready, he tells her. "Well go on. I'll be right here," he says, echoing Bell in the desert, and the screenplay ends (104).

Bell may call himself an "old man," aged out of his job and beaten down by life, but he turns out to be just what the county—and the country—need. No "paltry thing" at all, he seizes the moment and shapes his story into a happy ending. Though Moss is the one who shoots Ralston, Bell is the one who saves Moss and finagles a substantial contribution to his community in the form of the clinic. This *is* country for old men, after all, and it's proved accommodating for enterprising young ones as well. The screenplay ends as a celebration of can-do masculinity and partnership, buffered by hardship but standing strong in the end.

When McCarthy rewrites *No Country* as a novel, he changes the plot drastically and thus the implications of the narrative and of the title's allusion to Yeats.[35] Rather than an action-oriented screenplay featuring a masculine partnership with a happy ending, the novel is a tragedy. Here, Bell never catches up to Moss. Instead, Moss is killed by members of the cartel; Chigurh kills Carla Jean and then walks off, injured but alive, to haunt other people's nightmares; and Bell retires in a gesture of defeat. Moss's decision to take the money is figured here not as canny opportunism but as a crossroads, an act of moral import that will have dire consequences. (As always with McCarthy, however, the calculus may not be quite that simple. Moss also decides to return to the scene of the drug deal to bring a dying man some water, and thus it's unclear whether the hamartia that brings the violent forces of the drug trade down upon him is greed or mercy.) Either way, as he tells a young hitchhiker that he picks up shortly before he's killed, your choices build your fate: "You dont start over. That's what it's about. Ever step you take is forever. You cant make it go away. . . . You think when you wake up in the morning yesterday dont count. But yesterday is all that does count. What else is there? Your life is made up of the days it's made out of. Nothing else" (*NCFOM* 227). (As I mentioned in the introduction, McCarthy explained his later screenplay *The Counselor*, which bears a number of resemblances to *No Country*, in a similar way: "The counselor is a classical figure in tragedy. He's a decent guy who gets up one morning and decides to do something wrong. And that's all it takes" ["The Counselor" commentary].) In this case Moss's choice to take the money puts him in the path of both the cartel and Chigurh, an antagonist who sees himself as the violent hand of fate itself: "Every moment in your life is a turning and every one a choosing," Chigurh tells Carla Jean before he kills her. "Somewhere you made a choice. All followed to this. The accounting is scrupulous. The shape is drawn. No line can be erased" (*NCFOM* 259).

Moss's choices drive the plot and situate him as a tragic hero, though Bell is the true focus of the narrative, the witness who must try and shape these violent events into some kind of understanding. The novel is interspersed with italicized monologues spoken by Bell, and in the final pages Bell recounts two dreams he had about his father, one of which finds them traveling together through the mountains, his father riding ahead and carrying fire in a horn "*the way people used to do.*" Bell knows in the dream that his father is going onward, "*fixin to make a fire somewhere out there in all that dark and all that cold and I knew that whenever I got there he would be there. And then I woke up*" (309). Alexander Barron has compared Bell to King Lear, both of whom "in the end, realize exactly what they are up against, and both ultimately acknowledge their defeat at the hands of a world they no longer understand" (17). Barron also interestingly notes that both narratives engage and then undo audience expectations—four versions of Lear appeared before Shakespeare's, all with happy endings, and Barron quotes Walter Kirn's notion that *No Country* defies the tendency for American crime fiction to emphasize "[f]reedom and space. The freedom (perhaps illusory) to make poor choices and the space (as real as the highways) to flee their consequences" (Kirn 2). McCarthy's novel, then, defies the expectations of the action/adventure genre as thoroughly as his previous screenplay fulfilled them, instead taking on the structure and tone of tragedy.

Barron finds that tragedy utterly devastating, writing that Bell's dream of his father provides only "scant relief" (17). But even McCarthy's most violent works are not without some glimmer of hope—quite literally rendered this time in the fire that Bell's father carries, an echo of the metaphoric fire, or goodness, that the father in *The Road* teaches his son to carry within him. Benjamin Mangrum agrees, writing that Bell's dream, as in Yeats's poem, "signals the hope 'Of what is past, or passing, or to come'" and that "[f]acing the world's chaos and violence requires justice—a distinctly human disposition to pursue the good in the face of its tragic absence.... Bell's vision thus suggests that the good life lies on a dark path through an inevitably tragic world" (129). And Steven Frye understands both the content and the style of the novel as an extension of Yeats's poem. He sees the novel as demonstrating a contrast between the style of the primary plot and that of Bell's monologues, the former noticeably more minimalist than McCarthy's earlier novels and the latter interiorized and folksily poetic:

> In this sense, in *No Country for Old Men* McCarthy juxtaposes two worlds: the external and objective world of sense, artless violence, disorder, and bloodshed, where passion vents itself in pain; and the interior world of Bell's consciousness, which is a realm infused with the same, but one that seeks and finds a stability and permanence in human love, spiritual transcendence, and a mild and mitigated acceptance. To convey the latter world McCarthy again resorts to an overt artifice, to image, to symbol, and to the language of indirection. ("Yeats's" 20)

South Texas in 1980 may be no country for this old, defeated sheriff, but as in Yeats's poem Bell has recourse to a different landscape, one represented in part by the stone water trough that Bell imagines could only have been made by someone with "*some sort of promise in his heart*" (NCFOM 308). Drugs may be the worst kind of artifice according to Bell, but the creation of the trough and McCarthy's rendering of it in heightened language are representations with the potential to reveal rather than conceal. The fire in the horn that Bell sees in his dream is akin to Yeats's holy fire, the house of the sages that can gather up the sick and dying into "the artifice of eternity" and provide solace for a dark and tragic world.

McCarthy originally conceived Llewelyn Moss and Ed Tom Bell as a can-do pair of tough guys, overcoming the odds and Bell's personal losses in their victorious quest to bring the villain to justice. But in the novel these two characters, like John Grady Cole and Billy Parham, become an Aristotelean tragic hero and the witness to that tragedy. Though Billy and the later version of Bell are certainly no strangers to suffering themselves, they nonetheless end these narratives struggling to make sense of the events around them. At the end of the novels *Cities of the Plain* and *No Country for Old Men*, Billy and Bell are enacting that struggle in conversation with others—the nameless stranger and Betty in the former, and Bell's wife Loretta as well as his unidentified interlocutor in the latter. That, then, is the hope these tragedies offer—a belief in community, even if it's ephemeral, just as the characters in "Whales and Men" believe in the fundamental resonance of those two species despite the vast differences between them. Each narrative offers that kind of promise in the heart even in the face of great reversal and great darkness.

CHAPTER THREE

Works for Theater

*F*OR ACTOR AUSTIN PENDLETON, WORKING WITH COR-mac McCarthy was a memorable experience. When Martha Lavey, the artistic director at the Steppenwolf Theatre Company in Chicago, called him to ask if he was interested in a part in *The Sunset Limited*, a play by McCarthy, he immediately said yes, he reports. Lavey responded, "Aren't you going to read it first?" But Pendleton, who was familiar with McCarthy's work, was eager to do anything that he had written. Lavey thought that Pendleton would be perfect for the role of White, an atheist, suicidal college professor, and told him that Mike Nichols was set to direct. That made Pendleton's eagerness flag a bit—he suspected that Nichols would prefer a famous actor for the part, "somebody with a bigger name" (Pendleton interview). But Nichols eventually stepped aside, and Pendleton was able to take the role after all.

McCarthy was present for two weeks of evening rehearsals, Pendleton says, which included himself, actor Freeman Coffey (who played the character Black), director Sheldon Patinkin, and a stage manager. McCarthy observed the rehearsals while sitting quietly at the back of the theater, "very friendly and respectful" but almost totally silent. McCarthy then had another commitment that took him away from Chicago, and he returned on the day of the "invited dress," a final rehearsal to which theater VIPs are also invited. The invited dress is a big deal, Pendleton explained, a "high-pressure night" which was also, in this case, the first time that this play would be performed for an audience.

On the afternoon before the invited dress, McCarthy observed a last run-through of the play. Afterward, the director gave the actors a few notes, and then McCarthy asked, "Can I say something to Austin?" "Of course," answered Patinkin, and McCarthy turned to Pendleton. "Austin, on pages 81 and 82, I think you really had a hold of the character," McCarthy said politely. "Uh, okay," thought Pendleton. He didn't have his script at hand and so wasn't even sure what scene McCarthy was referring to. Then he checked it and realized that he was, in fact, playing that particular scene differently. "Do I understand," he asked McCarthy, "that you want me to play the other 118 pages the way I'm playing those two?" "If you could," responded McCarthy, again politely.

Pendleton was floored. McCarthy wanted him to change all but two script pages' worth of his performance in a ninety-minute show, and to do it approximately two hours before the invited dress. Actors just don't work that way—doesn't he realize that? he wondered. But after taking a walk and thinking it over, Pendleton decided to take the chance. He told Patinkin and Coffey in order to prepare them for the change and began his performance. "Halfway through page 1, I realized he was right," Pendleton says emphatically. "It was an astonishing evening."

Pendleton had been playing White in a very agitated, volatile way. McCarthy identified the one scene that Pendleton had played more quietly and encouraged him to make his performance understated rather than emotionally dramatic—a decision that worked, Pendleton says, and worked remarkably well. (Pendleton doesn't remember which scene this was, though the McCarthy Papers include a script with McCarthy's annotations and reactions to the performance. The script is dated 30 March 2006, though it may have been annotated during this final run-through, as it has notes throughout and Pendleton remembers that McCarthy hadn't seen the full play performed until that point. In that script, pages 81 and 82 feature Black reading from a made-up news story about a man throwing himself in front of a train while asserting "I am right."[1] What Pendleton does remember about the scene is that it was a point at which "the conversation became a little less confrontational," and that it was a "relaxed, less abstract discussion," which is an apt description of that particular exchange.)

McCarthy also occasionally suggested during rehearsals that the two actors remain seated at the kitchen table for almost the entirety of the play, an idea that seemed laughable to those with extensive—indeed any—theater experience. But when the company took the show to New York a few months later, they decided once again to take McCarthy's suggestion, and they confined the two characters to the table. "We did it, and it worked," Pendleton reports. "He'd been right all along. McCarthy really knows what he's doing as a theater person, even though he has no real experience in theater." Both of these were unconventional interventions to say the least—Pendleton calls them "truly radical theatrically"—but they worked, and they demonstrate

McCarthy's understated but engaged involvement with the way that his play would be coming to life onstage.

Cormac McCarthy began as a novelist and then became a screenwriter—albeit one with a series of unproduced projects in the 1980s. Also in that decade, he moved into another new medium and began writing for the stage. To date McCarthy has logged one notable failure and one considerable success. His play *The Stonemason* has only been attempted three times, and the one production that actually reached the stage consisted of a much-abbreviated version of the play. *The Sunset Limited*, on the other hand, has seen a number of productions in the States and abroad as well as a small-scale but successful adaptation for HBO, which I discuss in chapter 5. Both plays concern characters struggling, and often failing, to understand one another, a struggle reflected in the production history of *The Stonemason* but overcome by *The Sunset Limited*. The importance of that struggle is emphasized in *The Stonemason*, which tells the story of Ben Telfair, a stonemason carrying on the physical and spiritual work of his grandfather while in conflict with the other generations of his family; the struggle appears again in the one-on-one metaphysical grappling that takes place between Black, an evangelical Christian, and White, a suicidal nihilist, in *The Sunset Limited*.

In its focus on a multigenerational family and its engagement with issues of class, race, labor, and justice, *The Stonemason* evokes Faulkner—as do many of McCarthy's works, of course—as well as the tradition of African American theater exemplified by playwrights like August Wilson and Lorraine Hansberry. *The Sunset Limited*'s psychological realism and pared-down staging aligns it most closely with plays like Marsha Norman's 1983 *'night, Mother*, an intimate conversation between two characters in which the threat of suicide is the primary conflict of the plot. Though focused solely on two characters in one room, *The Sunset Limited* is not properly called minimalist in the way that Luigi Pirandello's *Six Characters in Search of an Author* (1921) and Thornton Wilder's *Our Town* (1938) are, which both use a stripped presentation to augment their metatheatrical content. Nor is it akin to German Constructivism—the characters may be named Black and White, which is symbolically suggestive in several ways, but they behave as real people speaking from real experience.

Neither of McCarthy's plays evinces the Aristotelean tragic structure of the Border Trilogy or *No Country for Old Men*, though each features characters responding to suffering and attempting to navigate that response within a community. Ben in *The Stonemason* endures failure and loss but ends the play with a vision of hope. *The Sunset Limited* comes to a close more ambiguously, and different productions and interpretations have emphasized either a sense of stalwart faith or, in contrast, an atmosphere of shattering despair. As

William Quirk has argued, however, *The Sunset Limited* conforms to Nietzsche's ideas about what tragedy is and does, as the play pits the individualistic, Apollonian tragic hero against the Dionysian forces of unity and jubilation. *The Stonemason* fits that structure as well, though less obviously, as it also suggests that community and belief can ameliorate the inevitable suffering and pain of the world—that they should be, in fact, one's primary concern, even above the inherent justice of right labor and good work in the world.

TRYING TO BALANCE ACCOUNTS: *THE STONEMASON*

The Stonemason: A Play in Five Acts focuses on Ben Telfair, a thirty-two-year-old African American stonemason, and his relationships to other members of his family. McCarthy has said that he based the story on a family that he knew in Kentucky, and among the manuscript materials of *The Stonemason* in the McCarthy archive is an obituary clipping from the *Lexington Herald-Leader* for Frank E. Guy Sr., who died in 1987 at seventy-seven years of age. Guy's great-grandfather was a slave who taught himself stonework, and the family boasted six generations of stonemasons.[2] McCarthy was working on the project as early as February 1985.[3]

The play's setup is unusual and presents a number of challenges for a production company. The main character, Ben, is played by two actors, sometimes simultaneously—one who narrates portions of the play from a podium and another who plays out the scenes' action with the other characters. In an early draft of the play, McCarthy explains this briefly: "At far stage left is a podium or lectern at which Ben's double will speak his monologue. Ben's role is played by two actors who are to be as similar in appearance as is practical and who will be dressed identically. Only the principal actor will speak, and he will stand at the podium in those scenes where both appear."[4] As I'll discuss, McCarthy elaborates on these directions in the later published version of the play, explaining the purpose of Ben's dual presence. Here, however, they are presented as simply the method by which this story will be told.

This is an uncommon, though not insurmountable, setup for a theatrical production, and the conceit has both interested and put off companies who have considered the play. *The Stonemason* also necessitates numerous scene changes and settings, including, in one, a *"low partial wall of actual stone"* that the characters work on, as is noted in the published play (9). Peter Josyph has taken McCarthy to task for the play's apparent disregard for the practical restrictions of theater, writing that *The Stonemason* requires a number of different and detailed sets, a dog who can pick up cue lines, a kitchen stove with a working fire, a real stone wall, and "an actor who can pass for a hundred [who] has to be able—and willing—to do a nude scene" (*Adventures* 117).

Those challenges—or failings, depending on your perspective—have at least something to do with the play's production history (or lack thereof), though McCarthy didn't set out to write a peculiarly difficult piece for theater. He set out to write a screenplay, which isn't too surprising given that he conceived of the story in the 1980s, when he was writing "Cities of the Plain," "Whales and Men," and "No Country for Old Men." The earliest draft, titled "The Stonemason's Chronicle," is written in screenplay format, which lessens or entirely eliminates these production problems. A voice-over, for instance (as Ben's monologues are labeled), is a simple way for a character to both narrate and perform the story, with no look-alike pair of actors or podium necessary. Location changes are handled easily, a stone wall is easy to find and film, and dogs can be induced to "act" on command, though it may require a few takes to get it right. McCarthy worked through at least three complete drafts of *The Stonemason* as a screenplay, suggesting that his original vision for the narrative was thoroughly cinematic.[5]

It's not clear why McCarthy decided that *The Stonemason* was a story more appropriate for theater when all evidence suggests that it's not. By January of 1986 a draft of the story is in theatrical rather than screenplay format,[6] and McCarthy refers to it as a play in letters he writes to Albert Erskine, Howard Woolmer, and Peter Greenleaf in late February of that year.[7] Oddly enough, he mentions this to Woolmer in the context of moviemaking. "I'm just back from New Orleans where a friend of mine [Richard Pearce] has been filming a new movie with Richard Gere [*No Mercy* (1986)]. We went out one evening along Bourbon Street interviewing strippers in the clubs for parts in the film. I dont know why I mention this as it's an impossible adventure to describe, other than that I've been writing a play. Actually just finished it, but what I'll do with it, if anything, God knows." To Greenleaf he suggests that he just happened upon the theatrical form: "I've just finished writing a play. I dont think novelists in general do very well as playwrights but I didnt know what else to do with the story. What I'll do with it now I have no idea." McCarthy is still enmeshed in the world of film, in his other projects, and in accompanying his friend Pearce, and yet *The Stonemason*, by early 1986, was incontrovertibly a work for theater—simply because, as he puts it to Greenleaf, he wasn't sure what else to do with it.

But despite his uncertainty, initial interest in the play was strong. In June 1986 McCarthy wrote again to Woolmer about *The Stonemason*, saying that "agents and other interested parties" were enthusiastic about it. "A lady named Marcia [*sic*] Norman is very anxious to help get it produced," he adds, and asks Woolmer if he has heard of her play *'night, Mother*.[8] Woolmer sends him a copy of the two-person play, a dialogue between a daughter and her aging mother as the daughter prepares to commit suicide. McCarthy writes back after reading and enjoying it: "There is a sustained disbelief, against all evidence, as the drama unfolds, that this woman will actually kill herself. Which of course makes it very interesting and suspenseful (and which I may have some tendency to distrust.)"[9] A Norman-produced *Stonemason* never happened, but her influence likely planted an important seed; McCarthy's later play *The Sunset Limited* bears a close resemblance to *'night, Mother* in the small cast, the single setting, and the subject matter.

In 1988 McCarthy's friend Richard Pearce, another supporter of the play, directed a reading of *The Stonemason* at a small theater in Los Angeles (Arnold, "*Stonemason*" 143). McCarthy was present and enjoyed the experience. He wrote to Howard Woolmer that the reading was "[m]ostly for me to get to hear it and see how it tracks in the flesh, so to speak. We did it in a small theater with a small audience and people seemed to like it pretty well. The players I thought were excellent."[10] Though the group of Los Angeles actors liked the play, Pearce told Edwin Arnold that the reading "did not work out"—that is, didn't lead to a production—as the play was just "too ambitious for this theater to handle" (143), probably because of the aforementioned setup, the large cast, and the multiple locations. Pearce then put McCarthy in touch with director Lloyd Richards, then the dean of the Yale School of Drama and artistic director of the Yale Repertory Theater. Again, there was interest but no production.

In 1990, through the efforts of Wiley Hausam at International Creative Management (ICM), the play came to the attention of the Arena Stage in Washington, DC. As Arnold reports, *The Stonemason* was a compelling option for the Arena for a number of reasons. They liked the play itself, they appreciated the focus on an African American family working to preserve their heritage in a time of change, and they were eager for the chance to show the theater's awareness of cultural diversity. Despite their enthusiasm, they did worry about the play's format, which they found to be a kind of hybrid, "a mixture of narrative fiction, cinema, and stage" (Arnold, "*Stonemason*" 144). But everyone believed that those issues could be addressed during the production process. The Arena staff wasn't previously familiar with McCarthy, however, and given the play's subject matter, they assumed he was himself African American. "Based on the script, I assumed McCarthy was black. We all did," said Larry Maslon of Arena (qtd. in Arnold, "*Stonemason*" 144). They eventually discovered their error, but according to Wiley Hausam of ICM, it "was not a big deal. I don't think it occurred to anyone that it would be a problem" (qtd. in Arnold, "*Stonemason*" 145). Unfortunately, as plans for the production moved forward, the issue of race would indeed become a matter of contention.

In 1991 the play was chosen for funding by the Kennedy Center Fund for New American Plays, and in 1992 the Arena Theater began workshopping the play, with McCarthy in attendance. Those workshops again revealed the logistic problems of the doubled main character as well as the jarring contrast between the realistic interchanges among family members and the long, stylized monologues from the podium. McCarthy, Arnold reports, was willing to make changes but was uncomfortable with the speed with which he would have to do so as part of the workshop process. "Cormac didn't enjoy the workshop," said Maslon, "but he was always game. Still, he played his cards close to his vest, very Faulkneresque. It was fascinating for the first few days, and then it became frustrating" (qtd. in Arnold, "Stonemason" 148). There was friction, and the process wasn't working as smoothly as it might, but prospects were still promising. Doug Wager, one of the potential directors for the play, reported to Arnold that McCarthy was eager to "get into a real collaboration" with whoever was chosen to be the director (qtd. in Arnold, "Stonemason" 148). Though workshopping on a tight schedule was a new and difficult way for him to work, he looked forward to creative back-and-forth of the kind he shared with Pearce on The Gardener's Son.

But then problems arose, and the central issue wasn't logistics—it was race. As work on the play continued, several members of the Arena staff voiced objections to the play's depictions of African Americans, saying they felt that The Stonemason relied on racial stereotypes rather than more authentic portrayals. They pointed to the violent deaths of two of the play's four male characters as well as the lesser roles the women play in the story. Maslon recalls that McCarthy was polite about the objections but unmoved. "He was quite happy to work on it if there was a sense that it would be performed, but he would not make changes just to satisfy everyone" (qtd. in Arnold, "Stonemason" 149). The workshop ended, and radio silence ensued between the author and the theater. Finally, McCarthy's agent Amanda Urban called Arena to ask about it and was told that Arena had cancelled the play and, in an unprecedented move, returned the grant money. The decision seemed "unusually political," according to a Kennedy Center administrator (qtd. in Arnold, "Stonemason" 149). McCarthy's friend and correspondent Howard Woolmer was surprised by the development. In September 1992 he wrote McCarthy to ask about the production; he called Arena several times, he said, but they claimed they knew nothing about the play.[11] The following March Woolmer wrote McCarthy again to compliment him on the written version of the play, which he thought was excellent, and commented on how odd he found their apparent objection to a white author writing about African Americans. Isn't it the case, he asked rhetorically, that the opposite is possible as well—that an African American author could write well about white characters?[12]

The Stonemason did see the light of day in 1994, when McCarthy—by then a famous author—published the script with Ecco Press. In the stage notes to the published edition, McCarthy explains the "doubled Bens" in more detail. He says that they should be considered separate characters and that the purpose is to *"give distance to the events and place them in a completed past"* (5). He calls the monologue a *"chautauqua,"* indicating that it is a kind of didactic public performance, and cautions the audience: *"The speaker has an agenda which centers upon his own exoneration, his own salvation.... The audience may perhaps also be a jury. And now we can begin. As the mathematician Gauss said to his contemporaries: Go forward and faith will come to you"* (6). As text, of course, this works quite well and encourages the reader's skepticism of a character who may well be an unreliable narrator. Audience members would presumably not hear these stage directions before the show began, and so despite their best intentions and active engagement, that faith might not be as sustaining as it would for a reader.

For the reader, however, *The Stonemason* is a formidable work, one that demonstrates McCarthy's career-long interest in the grace of skilled physical labor, justice, God, violence, and community. It begins in Louisville, Kentucky, in 1971, as Ben speaks to the audience about his grandfather, Papaw. "I always wanted to be like him," he says in his first line, and he goes on to describe the depths of his commitment to the man and to the work they share in the world (6). This work is stonemasonry—not the kind that relies on Portland cement to hold everything together, but the kind that uses only gravity, "the warp of the world ... the stuff of creation itself. The keystone that locks the arch is pressed in place by the thumb of God" (9–10). (Note his use of the phrase "the stuff of creation," which also appears in what is likely *Blood Meridian*'s most important sentence.) In this labor of stonemasonry, which the two men call simply "the trade," one conforms to the divine patterns of the world, to that which is good and just. "The arc of the moral universe is indeed long but it does bend toward justice," Ben says, quoting Martin Luther King Jr., who was himself quoting minister and abolitionist Theodore Parker. "At the root of all this of course is the trade.... But it was not in any book. We kept it close to our hearts.... We knew that it was a thing that if we had it they could not take it from us and it would stand by us and not fail us" (32–33). McCarthy positions Ben's philosophy of labor and grace—a philosophy shared, if not always articulated, by many McCarthy characters—clearly in the intellectual and activist African American tradition.

Thus in *The Stonemason*, Ben says "we," not "I," since this shared work and legacy with Papaw is central to his conception of himself. In the concept of a day's good work is everything good: "rhythm and pace and wholeness. And truth and justice and peace of mind" (96). The trade is the physical link between God's justice and man's, and in Ben's telling, the proper handling of stone is access to the divine. Unlike in *The Gardener's Son*, justice here is freely accessible through cultivated skill and right action, even when the surrounding society remains unjust. A good day's work, then—as opposed to commodified labor—is independently performed, distinctly preindustrial, and uniquely rewarding. It's a similar emphasis to that in the Border Trilogy, where skills like horse breaking and wolf trapping are deeply respected, though the trilogy and "Whales and Men" suggest that labor is ultimately less important than the nonverbal partnership and empathy with animals that it affords. *The Stonemason* is perhaps more radical, offering an ecologically moral vision based on inanimate rock, consciously assembled. "[T]he laying of stone," Ben explains, "can teach you reverence of God and tolerance of your neighbor and love for your family" (65). Rather than relationships with and among animals, in *The Stonemason* the connections between stones are lessons about the connections of all things. For Ben, however, one relationship matters most of all. Papaw was already an old man when Ben was born, but even so Ben says he has "loved him all my life and love him now" (8). Even his wife, Maven, pregnant with their second child, is jealous of Papaw. Maven is right to feel that way, he admits, because "I know that he's going to die and I despise every hour not spent in his company" (26).

Stonemasonry leads Ben to goodness and closer to Papaw, whom he reveres, but it doesn't obviate suffering. His teenaged nephew, Soldier, falls in with a bad crowd and eventually disappears, much to the pain of his mother, Carlotta. Ben also has a distant relationship with his own father, Big Ben, a financially dubious businessman who owns their company but does no masonry himself. And good work may be justice itself, but it doesn't forestall racism or ill treatment by others. Papaw, at least, is sanguine about such troubles; when he tells Ben about stonework he did for which he was never compensated, his attitude is accepting rather than outraged. "They's lots of work in this world that aint never paid for. But the accounts get balanced anyway. In the long run.... They's a ledger kept that the pages dont never get old nor crumbly nor the ink dont never fade. If it dont balance then they aint no right in this world and if they aint then where did I hear of it at? Where did you?" (29). People's records may be inaccurate or even falsified, but the only thing that matters is the one true record—God's. There's no need, says Papaw, to rely on a mere document when the real thing never fades and always balances.

Ben's wife Maven quite reasonably questions him about his reverence for physical work: "Then why arent more workers wise?" Ben answers, "I guess for the same reason that more college professors arent wise. Thinking's rare among all classes. But a laborer who thinks, well, his thought seems more likely to be tempered with humanity. He's more inclined to tolerance. He knows that what is valuable in life is life." What matters, he suggests, is respect for one's fellow man, the valuing of others' lives—the community of all humans. The professor, he says, is "more apt to just be dangerous. Marx never worked a day in his life." When Maven responds that it all "sounds a little neat to me," Ben avers, "I think most people feel that books are dangerous and they're probably right" (38–39). For Ben, work, rather than book learning, can be the path to enlightenment, though his view is tempered somewhat by his later revelations to a reporter, who comes to write a story on Papaw when he turns 102. He tells the reporter that Papaw learned to read from his wife, who taught herself using the books owned by a family that she worked for as a live-in maid. She later became the first black registered nurse in Indiana and could recite all of Walter Scott's *The Lady of the Lake* (93). In this case, then, books are necessary tools for advancement and, apparently, pleasure. The danger, according to Ben, seems to be the utter dependence some people have for books as their basis for knowledge of the world, without the tempering influence of either intellectual or physical work, especially work that is shared with others. It's a suspicion of representation that echoes Papaw's comments about the superiority of God's records to humans'—and further echoes similar ideas in *The Gardener's Son*, "Whales and Men," and *The Sunset Limited*—though that suspicion is made even more ironic here than in those other works, all representations themselves, by its refraction through a character who is doubled. Ben, after all, appears as a character but also frames and offers the play as representation, standing as a witness to his own narrative. (And not only that, but McCarthy tells us directly that we should "have faith" in the complexities of its presentation.)

Ben is confident in his approach to life, supporting his loved ones and being supported by his work. However, despite that work, his belief in tradition, and his love for his family—his own quite substantial faith—Ben still suffers, and he can't make his way in the changing world he finds around him. He tries hard to find Soldier, cornering one of his friends and asking if Soldier's disappearance had something to do with street gangs. The friend's response is dismissive: "They aint no more Nighthawks. Aint no more clubs. They aint shit. Just a bunch of freelancers out roguin and doin drugs" (74). People don't form alliances anymore even for crime; they're just on their own, seeking some fleeting pleasure—a replacement of the real world, as Sheriff Bell describes drugs in the screenplay "No Country for Old Men." Big Ben asks him for six thousand dollars, in debt and in trouble, and Ben reluctantly finds him some cash, though likely not the full amount. Ben does celebrate Papaw's 102nd birthday and Maven's birth of a healthy baby, but those events are followed by Papaw's death and Big Ben's sudden suicide. Ben is haunted by both losses and burdened with guilt over his father. "If I'd ransomed everything and given it all to him," he wonders, "would it have saved him? No. Was I obligated to do so? Yes. Why did you not?" (105). He further confuses his obligations to Carlotta when he succeeds in finding Soldier but doesn't tell her about it, giving him money that he then uses to overdose on drugs. He hopes to avoid the pain of telling Carlotta about Soldier's death as well, but Maven challenges him again: "Dont you see what you're doing? You're getting to say, Ben. And it's not up to you. You cant know another person's torment. . . . You cant judge, Ben. You cant get to say" (125). The revelation of Ben's secrecy causes a falling out between Ben and Carlotta, and as the play ends Ben speaks at the podium about the need for charity and a strong, true love for others as well as the need for good work. He relates a dream he had, in which he waits "before the door of some ultimate justice" with his "jobbook" under his arm, all his hours and projects logged, only to find the writing faded and the book crumbling, just as Papaw predicted that human records would. Then God leans down to ask that solitary figure "perhaps not even unkindly—this single question: Where are the others?" (112–113).

Good work, then, is ultimately not quite enough, and the independence Ben prizes so much can also isolate him. However good the work, it remains incomplete until it includes the consideration and even the saving of others—what he called "justice" wasn't quite right, either. Though Ben intended to save Carlotta from harm, his dishonesty belied that intention; in his final speech to the audience, Ben says from the podium, "What I need most is to learn charity. That most of all" (131). Papaw is the ideal to which Ben will continue to look for guidance, though he is probably an impossible one to imitate successfully; perfect work and perfect righteousness may be worthy, if unrealistic, goals. As the world continues to change around him, he looks back for help, seeking that communion with Papaw as a source of the divine in the same way that the boy prays to his father at the end of *The Road*. He sees a vision of Papaw, "and as he began to fade I knelt in the grass and I prayed for the first time in my life. I prayed as men must have prayed ten thousand years ago to their dead kin for guidance and I knew that he would guide me all my days and that he would not fail me, not fail me, not ever fail me" (133). It's a communion like the one that John Grady experiences with horses in his dreams or like the characters in "Whales and Men" develop as they strive, painfully, to transcend their violent human world. Ben is a flawed seeker, more articulate than Robert McEvoy but with his own lessons to learn—and what he learns is that doing good work without authentic empathy and charity negates the righteousness of that labor, or at least reduces its value. That recognition of the ultimate significance of community as opposed to rigid isolationism is similar to Nietzsche's conception of what tragedy accomplishes:

> Not only does the bond between man and man come to be forged once more by the magic of the Dionysian rite, but nature itself, long alienated or subjugated, rises again to celebrate the reconciliation with her prodigal son, man … all the rigid, hostile walls which either necessity or despotism has erected between men are shattered. Now that the gospel of universal harmony is sounded, each individual becomes not only reconciled to his fellow but actually at one with him—as though the veil of Maya had been torn apart and there remained only shreds floating before the vision of mystical Oneness. (24)

Building stone walls can be true and right labor, but walls one builds around oneself must be shattered. This recognition, however, isn't achieved at the cost of Ben's life, as is the case with the Nietzschean tragic hero. For that reason and others, Nietzsche's concepts of tragic conflict and annihilation are more obviously applicable to McCarthy's second play, *The Sunset Limited*.

Ben's search is further reflected in Black, one of the two characters in *The Sunset Limited*. Mary Brewer notes that although Ben and Black can hardly be said to be immune to suffering, they "gain emotional sustenance and resilience from the acts of communication with the sacred—a position that is rarely granted to McCarthy's white characters" (49). Though this characteristic opens the plays to criticism that these African American characters are childishly devout and thus reflect a racist stereotype, Brewer argues that Ben's and Black's engagement with their faith is both complex and resistant to the dominant discourse. In particular, Brewer notes Ben's co-opting of the chautauqua format, the historical movement that was open to diverse Protestant voices but generally not to African Americans. Ben thus "disrupt[s] the historical racialization of this religious practice [and his] delivery of a Judeo-Christian message challenges that racism, especially the history of presenting black Christian practice infused with elements of folk culture as inferior to a presumed authentic white Christianity" (45). Ironically, given the controversy over *The Stonemason*'s production at Arena, this finally "reveal[s] the limits of white patriarchal discourse for potential individual and collective development" (51). That recognition and potential allows Ben in particular to avoid ending his story in the kind of devastation that we associate with tragedy, notwithstanding the painful losses of his nephew, father, and grandfather.

Ben may be flawed, but he has a sustaining faith. And in fact there was more faith to be had in the theatrical world where *The Stonemason* was concerned. In 1997 the McCarter Theatre in Princeton, New Jersey, began working on the play in earnest and conducted a reading in April and a workshop in June. In May, McCarthy corresponded with Janice Paran, the theater's literary manager and dramaturg. Paran writes that she and Emily Mann, the artistic director, were "very happy with the reading; it amply demonstrated the play's beauties and strengths, and no less importantly, its actor-friendliness." She thanks McCarthy for the chance to hear the play and "mess around a bit with it," and that the experience had "solidif[ied] our commitment to producing it at McCarter." Paran then continues with some questions and comments about the play's story and structure. In the reading they apparently "consolidated" the two Bens, which she considered a crucial step toward a successful production. It "gives the play greater structural integrity, fluidity, and dramatic interest without sacrificing the distance you want to inject whenever Ben adopts his 'narrator' pose." In this version, Ben would still directly address the audience, but only one actor would embody the character. She also asks about aspects of Soldier's story and includes another page of suggestions about places to cut. Based on McCarthy's own notes on the letter, he seems to have accepted most of them.[13]

The workshop took place on 20 June 1997; McCarthy attended and took notes. As Austin Pendleton said of his own interaction with the author, McCarthy appeared to prefer an understated delivery, especially from Ben, writing repeatedly that the actor should "tone it *down*."[14] In July, Mann followed up with McCarthy and wrote him a long letter requesting numerous changes and clarifications. "I think the play can be magnificent," she assures him, "but it needs to have more dramatic strength." A play is different from a novel or film, she says, and then provides detailed notes on how to clarify Ben's journey in act I and enrich the characters of Soldier and Big Ben in acts I and II. She closes with an observation:

> You said on the phone, Cormac, that it is a simple, classical story about a hero and his mentor, how the hero loses his way, and how he recovers it. I think we see the hero and his mentor. We, the audience, lose our way when the hero loses his. Why does the hero lose his way?[15]

Work continued, as did the conversations. In 1999 McCarthy sent along a revised script with notes responding to another set of suggestions. Some he took—"Yes, cut visible dog," he writes, perhaps agreeing that dogs *are* hard to stage train, as Josyph complained. Some he rejected, writing at one point about Ben's monologues that his "general comment" is that "if the character who plays Ben is not capable of holding an audience the play will not play, and nothing in the way of trimming these or getting more drama out of the dramatic sections will help. For a model I would hark back to the success of one such actor/monologue plays as Clarence Darrow, or Truman."[16] Paran responds in April, and in May the McCarter scheduled almost two weeks of rehearsals.[17] Both parties were fully engaged in the process, and McCarthy's responses to Paran are similar to those he wrote to Erskine prior to the publication of his first novel *The Orchard Keeper*. He considers all suggestions thoughtfully and responds to each, accepting some and holding the line on others that he feels are too important to let go—like Ben's long monologues.

By October, however, the play had been called off. *Playbill* reported on 14 October 1999 that the McCarter was replacing *The Stonemason* with Chekhov's *The Cherry Orchard* for its 1999–2000 season and that Emily Mann and McCarthy had agreed that the play "needed to be developed further and McCarthy could not find time in his busy schedule to do the necessary work" (Simonson). The collaboration was fruitful, and less fraught than that with the Arena, but ultimately not fruitful enough. Whether McCarthy was indeed "too busy" or just unwilling to make the changes Mann deemed necessary for a successful production is uncertain, though it's also true that the long monologues may have been too much for the company to manage. In 1999 McCarthy's career as a dramatist was not looking particularly strong.

Finally, however, in October 2001, the Arts Alliance Center in Clear Lake, Texas, put on a single performance of an abbreviated version of *The Stonemason* as a fundraising event. When the center's president contacted McCarthy about the idea, he reportedly responded, "That's very nice, Kay. But you might want to reconsider," fully cognizant, at that point, of the play's challenges (qtd. in Arnold, "*Stonemason*" 7). Peter Webster, the director, had the idea to cut the scale of the story down dramatically. A single actor, Manning Mpinduzi-Mott, delivered selected monologues from both Ben and Papaw's parts, and the readings were augmented by music from the Marian Anderson String Quartet, playing selections from Antonin Dvorak's "The American Quartet." Behind Mpinduzi-Mott, projected images of photographs reflected the subject matter of McCarthy's writing. The evening was considered a success, and McCarthy himself was unobtrusively in attendance. "Drama is the hardest to write," he told Arnold after the show, but he hugged Mpinduzi-Mott and complimented everyone on a job well done (11). When *The Stonemason* at last appeared as a production, it was as a multimedia experience of voice, music, and image rather than a multilayered linear narrative with many characters and settings. Sprawling theatrical productions are certainly not impossible, as various companies' interest in the play attests, but the relative ease of a more simplified approach was likely not lost

The program for the only public performance to date of The Stonemason, *held at the Arts Alliance Center in Clear Lake, Texas, on 12 October 2001.*

on McCarthy. Though his second play isn't stripped quite as bare as Beckett, for instance, it still demonstrates an appreciation for the advantages—both for staging and for storytelling—of a more modest style.

LIFE EVERLASTIN': *THE SUNSET LIMITED*

If McCarthy considered drama "the hardest to write" in 2001, it didn't stop him from taking up the task a few years later. In 2005 he began work on a very different play, *The Sunset Limited*, and just the next year the play was produced by the Steppenwolf Theatre Company of Chicago and then published by Vintage. With *Sunset*, McCarthy avoided the biggest problems of *The Stonemason*; the two-person play takes place in one spare room, with no doubled characters, real stone walls, or dogs necessary. The back-and-forth dialogue consists of some longer stories and speeches by each character, but no unbroken monologues.

In fact, McCarthy seems to have begun *The Sunset Limited* as a novel but, due perhaps to its essential theatricality, then rewrote it as a play. In his earliest draft materials, he titles the story "The Black"—after one of the play's two characters, who are known in the finished version simply as Black and White—and tries out versions that are written in the format of a novel very heavy on dialogue but with occasional sentences indicating action, such as "He shook his head from side to side, his eyes closed." He even experiments with telling the story in the first person from the professor's perspective, evident in sentences like "He held the pad away from him and squinted at me."[18] But these draft fragments are tough reading—in them, McCarthy follows his usual conventions of eliminating quotation marks and rarely including indications of who's speaking (such as "said the professor.") The dialogue is clearly front and center, to the extent that a descriptive sentence might not occur for several pages. Despite all the production difficulties that became evident with *The Stonemason*, McCarthy likely realized that this new story had to be a play—because a play, after all, would allow him to put the focus on the dialogue without the confusion that the novel format would inevitably cause.

Nonetheless, the published version of *The Sunset Limited* appears with an unusual qualifier. When the play was being prepared for publication, someone crossed out the subtitle "A Play in One Act" on the title page of the copyedited manuscript. Written in is the odd equivocation "A Novel in Dramatic Form," which appears on the published version.[19] The note is not in McCarthy's handwriting, and my assumption is that this change came from the publisher rather than McCarthy. In addition, McCarthy makes a few corrections to a description of *The Sunset Limited* to be used on a "sell sheet" for Vintage, and adds: "Please note that in the list of previous works cited at the bottom of the sheet, *The Stonemason* should be called: *His play* and not his *previous* play, as the present work is *not* being presented as a play."[20] McCarthy's use of the passive voice here could also indicate that this was not, in fact, his own decision — rather, he seems to have been thinking about the story theatrically from very early in the work's composition. On one of the folders that held an early draft of the play, McCarthy scrawled the names "Samuel L Jackson" and "John Malkovitch [*sic*]" — notable not only because McCarthy was thinking of Jackson well before he starred in the HBO adaptation but also because he was, in fact, thinking of actors rather than considering his characters to be purely literary creations.[21] It's also possible, however, that McCarthy is indeed considering the play as a kind of hybrid. As the title of his unproduced screenplay "Whales and Men" attests, McCarthy is writing in awareness of his literary predecessor John Steinbeck — and in fact the screenplay's original title, "Of Whales and Men," is even more allusive. Steinbeck wrote three works that he called "play-novelettes": *Of Mice and Men, The Moon Is Down,* and *Burning Bright.* Steinbeck hoped, he said, that this would increase the work's potential audience, as the combination "gives a play a wide chance of being read and a piece of fiction a chance of being played without the usual revision" (qtd. in Morsberger 271), though Steinbeck did rewrite *Of Mice and Men* when it was to be performed for theater. McCarthy, then — or at the very least, his publisher — may have also been thinking about how *The Sunset Limited*'s form could help it reach the widest possible audience. (Nonetheless, in what follows I'll refer to it as a play.)

As he did with both the Arena and McCarter productions of *The Stonemason,* McCarthy got involved with Steppenwolf as the company worked on the play. He took extensive notes on the draft of *The Sunset Limited* that is dated 30 March 2006, which may correspond to the "invited dress" that Pendleton describes. Similar to the way his notes urged the actor playing Ben in the McCarter *Stonemason* to "tone it down," his notes here express frustration that the actors, particularly Freeman Coffey as Black, are reading their lines jovially or while laughing when they should be serious. McCarthy writes that particular lines are "NOT FUNNY" and that the actors should "STOP the fucking yucking." Pendleton as White he urges to "STOP," presumably so that he will take more time with his lines.[22] As Pendleton confirms, McCarthy values an understated performance, though in Pendleton's telling he vented none of this apparent irritation in his dealings with the actors and director, instead comporting himself entirely "like a gentleman" (Pendleton interview).

And in fact the process seems to have been a productive one for everyone. Director Sheldon Patinkin said that McCarthy was a "delight to work with," and commented specifically on his collaborative skills: "At first he was resistant to rewrites but then he realised he had less experience of theatre than we did and he did some major rewrites before rehearsals began. He was very open and interested in the whole process" (McBride). Patinkin has also said that McCarthy's script initially called for an intermission, but that he convinced McCarthy to eliminate it in order to maintain the story's momentum (Luce, "*Sunset*" 18–19). McCarthy, then, was willing to make major changes based on his collaborators' input.

The play ran at Steppenwolf from 18 May through 25 June 2006 and was generally well received, though many reviewers noted, for better or for worse, the play's lack of physical action.[23] Chris Jones of the *Chicago Tribune* titled his review "Brilliant, but Hardly a Play," and says that some of McCarthy's prose is "so good—so astonishingly effecting [*sic*], so powerful, so stimulating—it actually makes the rest of this completely static play worth it." If too much was going on in *The Stonemason*, many worried that too little was going on here, despite the clear life-and-death focus of the story. But the company embraced that feature and took it even further when the play moved to the 59E59 Theaters in Manhattan for a run with the same director, cast, and crew from 24 October through 19 November. As I noted earlier, in this second production they followed McCarthy's previous suggestion that the two actors perform the entire play while seated at the kitchen table, without building in any movement or "business" around the apartment. The risk paid off; the *New York Times* review by Jason Zinoman doesn't even mention the restriction and introduces the play as "one of Cormac McCarthy's unfortunately rare forays into theater." Pendleton agreed, and he loved the decision to keep the play physically quiet: "Even apart from the thrill of doing this play again, with this group of people, there is a thrill of finding something about the power of stillness that I hope won't ever fully leave my awareness" (Pendleton, "Austin").

The unusual qualities of the play generally proved to be an attraction rather than a hindrance for other companies. *The Sunset Limited* was published by Vintage in October 2006, and in the summer of 2007 it was produced at the Galway Arts Festival in Ireland. Since then it has been performed in Atlanta, Charlotte, San Francisco, Los Angeles, Birmingham, and Kirribilli, Australia, among other venues. HBO premiered a film version in 2011 directed by Tommy Lee Jones, who co-starred with Samuel L. Jackson (thus fulfilling McCarthy's earlier imagining of the role of Black), a production that I discuss in chapter 5.

The Triad Stage, a regional theater in Greensboro, North Carolina, produced the play as part of its 2010–2011 season. Artistic director Preston Lane said that although he is deeply skeptical of plays written by novelists, this one works — and it works especially well in a place like Greensboro. Lane remembered a conversation he had with an African American member of the theater's board, who was "bemoaning the fact that there aren't a lot of plays that actually have white people and black people in conversation together about things beyond race." When Lane read *The Sunset Limited*, he realized that this was that play. "It enables the audience to see black and white people talking together … and the issue isn't about oppression or empowerment — McCarthy strips away all of that. The issue is much bigger" (Lane interview).

Speaking about the HBO film, McCarthy said in an interview that "I think the issue some people have with it is it would be confining, you know, two people in a room, what is that? But as it turns out it's not that at all. That stage, that room, is the world. Besides," he added, "literature is about tragedy" (Carr). McCarthy is speaking more about spare dramatic form than the content of tragedy, though *The Sunset Limited* makes that interpretation available in a more substantial way than *The Stonemason*.

In the play, Black, an unorthodox evangelical Christian, rhetorically grapples with White, an atheist professor whom Black has just prevented from committing suicide by throwing himself in front of a train, the aptly named Sunset Limited. The two are in Black's apartment, where they have come from the train station, and White has been prevented from leaving by a collection of elaborate locks on the apartment's door, which can only be opened by Black. The two argue, tell stories, and engage in a complex dialogue about the existence of God, the natures of the world and of humanity, and the proper response to pain and suffering.

White is precisely the kind of professor that Ben Telfair voices his suspicions of in *The Stonemason*. "dangerous." White has proved to be exactly that, if only to himself. Though he doesn't believe in God, White did once believe in culture, in the books, music, and art that brought beauty to the world and happiness to him and others. But those representations have now lost their meaning, he says, especially in the wake of horrors like the Holocaust. Without religion, loved ones, or the refuge of art, White is ready, even eager, to end his life. "The things I believed in dont exist anymore," he explains. "It's foolish to pretend that they do. Western Civilization finally went up in smoke in the chimneys at Dachau but I was too infatuated to see it. I see it now" (27). Though White bristles a bit at the idea that books themselves are dangerous, he does make reference to the story of the Garden of Eden — "Knowledge as destructive to the spirit. Destructive to goodness" — and further elaborates that the purpose of such a story might be to warn people that knowledge is vanity, that it gives people "the unhealthy illusion that they can outwit the devil" (111). And illusion is something that White insists must be given up — the world must be seen truly, with all its "bloodshed and greed and folly the import of which is impossible to ignore" (112). Any representations that pretend otherwise are simply fragile, misleading veils over an ugly reality.

Black, on the other hand, has lived a hard life, but since discovering the truth of God's grace he is happy to live in a spartan apartment and to try to help the drug addicts and criminals surrounding him. He was once on the wrong path, he explains, and was even imprisoned for murder. Then during a jailhouse fight, he severely injured another prisoner and almost died himself. Black tells White that while he was lying in recovery, in incredible pain, he heard the voice of God: "If it was not for the grace of God you would not be here" (49). That moment of revelation changed his life, and he devoted himself to God's work from then on. Black's jailhouse conversion may seem like the conventional trope of a prison story, but as the conversation goes on, he reveals his faith to be decidedly unorthodox.

White questions the logic both of this religious conversion—which he characterizes as the story of "how a fellow prisoner became a crippled one-eyed halfwit so that you could find God"—and of Black's current endeavors (49). "Why not go someplace where you might be able to do some good?" White challenges him. "As opposed to someplace where good was needed," Black responds. White can't believe that God would be "interested in coming here to this cesspool and salvaging what everybody knows is unsalvageable. Why would he do that? You said he didnt have a lot of free time. Why would he come here? What would be the difference to him between a building that was morally and spiritually vacant and one that was just plain empty?" (77). Black's response emphasizes his belief not just in God, but in the necessity of loving one's fellow man:

> He said you could have *life* everlastin. Life. Have it today. Hold it in your hand. That you could see it. It gives off a light. It's got a little weight to it. Not much. Warm to the touch. Just a little. And it's forever. And you can have it. Now. Today. But you dont want it. You dont want it cause to get it you got to let your brother off the hook. You got to actually take him and hold him in your arms and it dont make no difference what color he is or what he smells like or even if he dont want to *be* held. And the *reason* you wont do it is because he dont deserve it. And about that there aint no argument. He *dont* deserve it. (*He leans forward, slow and deliberate.*) You wont do it because it aint just. Aint that so? (78–79)

Black senses that White's notions of fairness, or justice, keep him from loving or even appreciating other people, and insists that one must release the notion of love as a transaction, something to be deserved. In some ways his vision reflects Martha McEvoy's at the end of *The Gardener's Son*, of a God who releases people from their names as well as their past actions. Ironically, however, for Black letting go of that idea of human justice is in fact the proper currency for the ultimate transaction, the only one that matters: the realization of God's love and life everlasting, of justice that is divine. (Black and Papaw of *The Stonemason* have quite a bit in common, too, as Mary Brewer details.) And for Black, that realization can happen without reading the Bible, believing in original sin, or understanding Jesus in the traditional sense of a savior (67, 95). These may be heresies of sorts that make him "an outlaw," but he also avers that a man "should be … a questioner," even "a man with a powerful belief" (66, 67).

The truth that Black sees, and the work that must be done, is simple: "[Y]ou must love your brother or die," as he puts it (121). "That's another world from anything I know," White responds. Rather, his own world is one where any kind of labor is painful, pointless, and leads only to death:

> It's that the world is basically a forced labor camp from which the workers—perfectly innocent—are led forth by lottery, a few each day, to be executed. I dont think this is just the way I see it. I think it's the way it is. Are there alternate views? Of course. Will any of them stand close scrutiny? No. (122)

As the play ends, none of Black's jokes, elaborate stories, homespun theology, or even his excellent cooking can change White's dark view of the world, which he finally reveals in full. All human lives are battered by "[t]orment, betrayal, loss, suffering, pain, age, indignity, and hideous lingering illness. All with a single conclusion" (138). But what about the others? Black insists. After all, there must be other "fellow commuters" who have suffered like White, who might find communion in their shared vision. White finally admits that he does see himself in other people—but, he adds, it sickens him, because he wants neither communion nor salvation. "You tell me that my brother is my salvation? My salvation? Well then damn him. Damn him in every shape and form and guise" (138). The revelation of White's extreme isolation, alienation, and despair silences Black, who finally relents and opens his door, only to shout after White that he will be there at the train station again in the morning.

As White rushes out to greet Death and the hope of nothingness and solitude, Black mourns his inability to convince White to stay. He talks to God: "I dont understand it," he objects. "If you wanted me to help him how come you didnt give me the words? You give em to him. What about me?" But just as quickly he stops bartering, his transaction already complete: "That's all right. That's all right. If you never speak again you know I'll keep your word. You know I will. You know I'm good for it" (142). Still, he craves some small reassurance that his work is right, and his repeated query ends the play: "Is that okay? Is that okay?" (143).

Black, like Ben Telfair, believes fervently in the order of the world and in God's justice and power, but even a man who's been privy to a moment of revelation can have his doubts. Also like Ben, he understands the imperative to help others, but the proper way to do that is often elusive. Soldier and Big Ben die, and White presumably will as well, but Black and Ben each end their stories by reaffirming their need to keep trying, to keep seeking. White, on the other hand, is an educated, articulate version of Robert McEvoy, raging against the forced labor camp that is the world they know and striking back with a gesture of annihilating violence. Though White speaks in erudite refrains and McEvoy says almost nothing, they both disdain representations that veil the ugly truth about the world, where justice is a sham, just a name co-opted by the powerful—a view also articulated at length by Peter in "Whales and Men." *The Sunset Limited*, then, takes McCarthy's earlier thematic concerns and dramatizes them in a rhetorical showdown that is more complex, and less Manichean, than its characters' names would suggest. Black's religious conversion, after all, is inseparable from the violence that engenders it, and the "heresies" he enumerates for White reveal a radically unorthodox understanding of Christ, the Bible, and faith. Likewise, though White rejects his fellow man, he also feels the pain of the world so acutely that it—rather than just his own pain—drives him to suicide. Neither of these characters is easily reducible to a simple, partisan stance. That McCarthy's more recent dramatic work is also the more widely produced reflects his adjustment to the form, I think, as well as his simultaneous distillation and complication of ideas and character types from the earlier screenplay and play.

It's a work that emphasizes real engagement and requires it from the performers and the audience. Most actors will comment on the difficulty of getting off-book (that is, thoroughly memorizing the lines), as the play not only has a great number of lines to memorize but also lacks a traditional act-and-scene structure. "It's like a boxing match without rounds," commented Kevin Kelley, the actor who played White in the Triad Stage production (Kelley interview). And *The Sunset Limited* leads up to an ending that can be interpreted and performed variously: as a true tie between the two characters' exertions of rhetoric and will; as a clear victory for White, who succeeds in escaping back into the darkness; or as a clear victory for Black, who seems as determined as ever to continue his work for God. When 3M Productions in Charlotte put on the play in 2010, Jacobi Howard, playing Black, yelled his last lines, "*Is that okay?*" in a display of frustration and anger at a silent God, which had the effect of calling his determination and steadfastness into question. In reviewing the original Steppenwolf production, Chris Jones saw all of it as a "deconstruction of the secular, middle-aged, liberal elite." He calls it a deconstruction, but claims that White is clearly the main character and that Black functions "mainly as an interlocutor." Other productions, like HBO's filmed version, indicate that Black may instead inhabit the privileged position here; Tommy Lee Jones said that he thinks it is a "pretty happy ending [for Black] as far as I'm concerned" (Carr).

Preston Lane, in directing Triad Stage's production, was careful to preserve a balance in the ending. "We don't know who won," he says, although our impulse as an audience is always to embrace plays that clearly indicate "which way our feelings are supposed to run." That's a hard impulse to thwart, but *The Sunset Limited*, he says, "should leave it up to us to continue that conversation and dialogue." Lane had unique cause to think through the content of *The Sunset Limited* when he suffered a stroke while the play was in previews. He recovered, but the experience was jarring and refocused his thinking about this struggle between light and darkness. "I often find myself torn between these two viewpoints, and I do have a dark side. . . . If I believed in fate, I would say that there's a reason I had a stroke in the middle of this play," he commented. "As you make decisions about how to stay alive, you realize . . . The reality is that I think life wins. That as much as I can think like White does, I do the whole thing because ultimately I love directing, reading, theater, and there's a lot more I want to do. That became so true to me during this process. I have a sense of coming back to theater. A sense that I have stuff to do, and that I agree with Black" (Lane interview). As Lane's own experience with the play indicates, a staging that maintains a sense of balance or ambiguity in its closure provides the richest interpretive possibilities for the audience, allowing them to bring their own backgrounds to bear on a sense of what has finally happened between these two characters.

As a result of different decisions about line readings, characters' movements, and lighting, productions of *The Sunset Limited* have ended with varying degrees of devastation or hope. William Quirk has called the play a "minimalist tragedy" following Nietzsche's ideas in *The Birth of Tragedy*—a struggle between the Apollonian White, suffering from an excess of knowledge and from isolation, and the Dionysian Black, who loves Coltrane, good food, and calls for the unity of all people. (Quirk uses the term "minimalist" here as a general indicator of style rather than to signal a connection to the more specific minimalist theatrical tradition.) "When in the course of the drama it becomes clear that individuation is a source of suffering," Quirk explains, "the tragic hero [in this case White] is destroyed. The destruction is joyous, however, because it means the 'Apollonian' individual returns to the original unity of all being ('das Ur-Eine'), which is the Dionysian state and its intoxicated musical jubilation" (40). White can't stand other people but experiences his solitude painfully as well. "In some sense, then, if White desires release from the suffering of his extreme case of Apollonian individuation, he and Black offer remedies corresponding to two facets of Dionysianism. White wants the release in the destruction of individuation as death, and Black proposes a reunion with the 'unity of being' by finding some sort of community with which White might feel at home" (42). Though White ultimately walks away from Black's conversation and the communal significance of their shared meal, Quirk points to the play's subtle suggestions of cyclic temporality and Black's description of "life everlastin" to show how "Black and White's story unfolds as an unlikely drama of Apollonian and Dionysian tendencies, one that ultimately declares, despite White's seemingly victorious nihilism, a kind of Dionysian affirmation of life" (34). Quirk's reading of the play as tragedy describes another iteration of the community that McCarthy so often represents as a response to violence and suffering—a community that, however briefly, White assents to in his conversation with Black.

If tragedy teaches anything, it's that justice, whether human or divine, can be tremendously hard to reckon, as Ben and Black both discover, even if individuals have their hands on the keystone of the world or are spoken to directly by God. With the exception of Papaw, who can seem more like an ideal than a real person, McCarthy's characters struggle with the demands of working in the world and with determining how to properly navigate the sea of records, names, books, and other representations that may not be "the thing itself," but must still be engaged and dealt with—a navigation that sometimes leads to communion and sometimes to more suffering. We are, after all, creatures of language and are therefore defined by these kinds of transactions, a commerce that the stage and screen traffic in particularly well. The dialogue ends, the curtain falls, but even when the show's over, we keep talking.

CHAPTER FOUR

Keeping the Faith

ALL THE PRETTY HORSES AND THE ROAD

W HEN DIRECTOR BILLY BOB THORNTON WAS SHOOTING the final scene of his film adaptation of *All the Pretty Horses*, he was hoping to get in one last shot—a good one—before the day's light faded. In that scene John Grady Cole and Lacey Rawlins say their final words to each other. Lacey asks John Grady if he'll stick around San Angelo, maybe get a job at the oil rigs, but John Grady is intent on moving on. "It ain't my country," he says, and adds, "I don't know what happens to country." It's a moving moment and an appropriate culmination of this story about a young man who has suffered great losses, including the region and landscape that used to define him. John Grady turns away from his friend and rides off, into what McCarthy called "the darkening land, the world to come" (302).

On set, Matt Damon, playing John Grady Cole, turned his horse and rode away. The camera kept rolling as he kept riding, letting the impact of the moment fully take hold. Henry Thomas, playing Rawlins, loved it. "The whole shot is played out in one take. It's about six minutes long, I guess—maybe longer," he says. "But it's brilliant. Because you're stuck there. And you don't mind it! I get so tired of seeing everything cut up. It gives you a license to be a lazy audience member, spoon-fed these scenes without ever feeling them.... That's one of my favorite moments in the film, because I think it captures the whole essence of what we're all trying to say" (*Acting McCarthy*). That long take allows the audience to inhabit the open landscape and feel the slow pace of traveling through it on a horse, and is the opposite, Thomas suggests, of the quick, rapid cuts used in many contemporary films.

But in the midst of getting that lengthy shot, Thornton's heart suddenly sank. He heard an airplane overhead, spoiling the ambient sound, which was supposed to reflect a 1949 West Texas landscape. "Well, it ain't a 'period' jet either, you know?" he explains. "And so a jet comes over, for the whole important stuff in this last scene. Fairly loud jet—it ain't gonna get out of there, you know what I mean? I don't want to loop this scene. So guess what, I watched it for the first time, in dailies, and I'm like, damn, that's all we had, then we lost the light ..." He started to resign himself to the need to shoot the scene again, but was hit by a realization. "And it's like, oh my God, of course we'll leave the airplane in. A jet that's not 'period,' that's the future? I mean, you know, are you kidding me? Against America, with him riding off into this? Boy"—he grins widely—"sometimes fortune smiles on you, so that's in the movie" (*Acting McCarthy*). It was lucky, and at another time Thornton called it "the most beautiful scene he ever shot" (qtd. in Josyph 146n6). In a film about a boy who leaves a steadily modernizing United States for what he sees as a more authentic life in Mexico—a way of being that he briefly experiences and then loses, dramatically and painfully—the roar of a jet engine could be considered an apt background indeed.

Beautiful as the shot may have been, it's not, as Thornton says, actually "in the movie"—at least, not the movie that was released in theaters on Christmas Day 2000. That scene, along with many others, was cut so that the film would have a running time of under two hours, a reduction that was required by Miramax, the film's distributor. The resulting film was both a critical and a popular flop, and the conflict with the studio over the film's content, length, and marketing was devastating enough to Thornton that he didn't direct another film for twelve years. Thornton's adaptation of *All the Pretty Horses* and John Hillcoat's of *The Road* (2009) both benefited from McCarthy's increasing fame, positive prerelease press coverage, and even Oscar speculation. Despite all that, however, neither was a hit. The worldwide gross for *Pretty Horses* was slightly over $18 million for a movie with an estimated production budget (excluding marketing) of $57 million. *The Road* did better, though it was hardly a sensation, with a worldwide gross of $27.6 million over a production budget of about $25 million (*Box Office Mojo*).

THE PRACTICE OF ADAPTATION

Film is, of course, a collaborative art. Even in the case of directors who could be considered auteurs, many pairs of hands contribute to the final product. As such, the stories behind such efforts, like this adaptation of *All the Pretty Horses*, often spur considerations of mastery, ownership, artistry, and skill similar to those McCarthy has written about in that novel and many others. The directors, cast, and crew of *Pretty Horses* as well as those for the adaptation of *The Road* were open about their reverence for McCarthy's novels and their desire to do justice to their films' source material. "I remem-

ber being terrified because the book was so important to me," commented
Matt Damon in an interview. "Just feeling like, you know, I can only blow
it" (*Acting McCarthy*). Adapting a beloved novel for film, of course, can indeed be a bit of a minefield. As Robert Stam and other critics have noted, the
language that has been used to describe failed adaptations is often moralistic,
and more specifically invokes the specter of sexual wrongdoing. Adaptations
that don't meet the audience's expectations are said to be "unfaithful," to "betray" their source text, and in particularly egregious instances, to be outright
"violations" or even "perversions." The notion of fidelity is an unhelpful one
for scholars, as Stam observes, and reveals a deeply rooted prejudice for literature over film—notable in early adaptation studies like George Bluestone's
1957 *Novels into Film*, or even further back, in Gotthold Ephraim Lessing's
1766 *Laocoön: An Essay on the Limits of Painting and Poetry*, in which he argues that textual and visual arts should be clearly demarcated and not permitted to "take unbecoming liberties in the heart of the other's domain" (91).
Using the idea of fidelity to evaluate adaptations "is essentialist in relation to
both media," Stam writes. "[I]t assumes that a novel 'contains' an extractable
'essence,' a kind of 'heart of the artichoke' hidden 'underneath' the surface
details of style.... But in fact there is no such transferable core: a single novel-
istic text comprises a series of verbal signals that can generate a plethora of
possible readings, including even readings of the narrative itself.... The question of fidelity ignores the wider question: Fidelity to what?" (15). It's also a
less applicable concept in an age in which adaptations can draw on literature
but also from other films, television, graphic novels, theme-park rides, and
video games. How would a film "stay faithful" to a theme-park ride? "Adaptation has run amok," writes Linda Hutcheon, and she means it as anything
but a condemnation (xiii).

If not fidelity, what then is a better framing concept for the analysis of
adaptations? Stam notes the many tropes that have been suggested in the
years since Bluestone: "adaptation as reading, rewriting, critique, translation,
transmutation, metamorphosis, recreation, transvocalization, resuscitation,
transfiguration, actualization, transmodalization, signifying, performance,
dialogization, cannibalization, reenvisioning, incarnation, or reaccentuation"
(25). The angle one chooses, of course, also depends on which facet of adaptation one wishes to examine. Hutcheon discusses film adaptations as formal
entities, as processes of creation, and as processes of reception; she finds the
Darwinian metaphor of evolution a generative one, in which stories "adapt to
those new environments *by virtue of* mutation" (8–9, 32). Thomas Leitch has
sought to dethrone the source text and the method of comparative evaluation
by emphasizing that every text is an intertext "that incorporates, refracts, re-
futes, and alludes to many other texts, whether literary, cinematic, or more

broadly cultural" and that "source texts must be rewritten; we cannot help rewriting them" (17, 16). As for Stam, he draws on Gérard Genette's idea of transtextuality, all the ways that one text can refer to other texts (a concept that itself draws on Bakhtin's understanding of dialogism and Kristeva's of intertextuality). Adaptations, he concludes, "redistribute energies and intensities, provoke flows and displacements; the linguistic energy of literary writing turns into the audio-visual-kinetic-performative energy of the adaptation" in what he calls—in a nice counter to the moralistic condemnation of "unfaithful" films—"an amorous exchange of textual fluids" (46).

Fidelity may be outré as an organizing principle in adaptation studies, but it can still be a problem "variously conceived and defined by the filmmakers at hand," as Thomas Leitch notes (20). Certainly those who have adapted McCarthy's work for the screen have openly acknowledged the author as a source, though as I'll explain in the next few chapters, they do so with differing degrees of deference. In the case of *All the Pretty Horses*, the deference was considerable, even to the point of considering the book a kind of sacred text. "I had that book with me all the time," said Julio Menchoso, who played the captain in Billy Bob Thornton's film. "It was my bible, you know. All the time." Henry Thomas echoed that sentiment: "It was pretty easy to embody these characters because I had a bible that was the book, that I could look at and see more than what the script was telling me." Thornton's own comments were more equivocal. Echoing Thomas's preference for an appropriate pace over a zippy spectacle with rapid editing, he vowed not to "cut it down into nothing just so we could have an exciting movie or whatever, a commercial movie." He expressed a strong sense of ownership of the project, though he also imagined telling McCarthy, "I apologize in advance about screwing up your book up because it ain't going to be your book. It's going to be as close as I can get to getting the spirit of it across" (*Acting McCarthy*). Thornton acknowledges the inherent difference of text and film and the fact that a translation of one to the other is impossible—but also apologizes for that difference and positions the film as inherently lesser, something that can only "get close" to the spirit of the book. (That said, it's also worth noting that in this same set of interviews, a number of actors remark on Thornton's famously folksy humility, which they say masks a sure-footedness and self-confidence evident in his working practices. Many of the actors gush over McCarthy, but Thornton may not be quite as deferential as he sounds.)

Those involved in adapting *The Road* also found McCarthy's novel inspiring and expressed a desire to tell the story appropriately and well. In one interview Viggo Mortensen, who plays the father, holds a worn copy of the novel that is fairly bursting with Post-it Notes—but Mortensen also seems to understand that the film will be telling its own story. He talks about speaking with McCarthy on the phone and trading conversation about his son and McCarthy's son, "and after I hung up I realized I really hadn't asked him any of the questions about the book." He laughs and adds, "And I thought, well, you know, I don't ... maybe I don't need to" ("Making of *The Road*"). The screenwriter Joe Penhall speaks glowingly of McCarthy: "There's only ever a writer like that once every few decades," he says. "Hemingway, Carver, Faulkner ... and he's in the pantheon of those great American writers." Of their own project, he says that "we were on a mission, from God, to tell this unvarnished, you know, unadorned." It sounds like extreme devotion, though he tempers it with a chuckle that perhaps acknowledges his allusion to *The Blues Brothers* here, and frames their "mission" not as a precise translation from page to screen but rather a desire to avoid altering the story for the purpose of making it less challenging or more palatable for an audience.

Overall, however, Thornton's *All the Pretty Horses* and to a large degree John Hillcoat's *The Road* take what Leitch calls a curatorial approach, one that "impute[s] to their literary sources powers beyond their own" and seeks to "preserve their original texts as faithfully as possible" (96). Leitch cites Kenneth Branagh's 1996 *Hamlet* as an example, "whose four-hour length bespeaks its determination to avoid the usual cuts in the play." As we'll see, length would also be an issue in the production of *Pretty Horses*. Thornton's film hews close to those that Leitch singles out for their "exceptional fidelity": David O. Selznick's *Gone with the Wind* (1939) and Peter Jackson's *Lord of the Rings* trilogy (2001, 2002, 2003). As with *Pretty Horses*, Leitch quotes those involved with the films referring to the source texts as the bible, and notes that the pious attitude developed in each case results from a combination of financial motivation (that is, the desire to draw in as much of the books' popular audiences as possible) and deep respect for the texts (133).

Despite the largely curatorial approaches of the adaptations of *All the Pretty Horses* and *The Road*, both of the finished films do make small but significant changes to the narrative—in one case, as I've noted, against the director's will. Those changes have the effect of avoiding the potential for tragedy in each film. As novels, neither *All the Pretty Horses* nor *The Road* is obviously tragic in an Aristotelean sense, as are other works like *No Country for Old Men* and *The Counselor*, though *Pretty Horses* does serve as the first part of the ultimately tragic arc of the Border Trilogy, and some have called *The Road* an ecological tragedy, a warning about humankind's hubristic refusal to care adequately for our environment. (This reading of *The Road* depends, however, on how one interprets the cataclysm that devastates the landscape that the man and boy move through.) Both works emphasize that suffering is not easily ameliorated and that you can't go home again, emphases that the two film adaptations elide in favor of more positive senses of closure. Both Joe Penhall and Thornton spoke about their desire to avoid making their films "commercial," to keep them "unvarnished," but in fact the finished films do soften the impact of what could otherwise be more tragic endings.

All the Pretty Horses was the first film for which "Cormac McCarthy" was a major selling point. The author's career has seen a number of changes: his move from the South to the West; his switches between maximalist and minimalist prose style and among novels, screenplays, and dramas; and his forays among the Southern Gothic, revisionist Western, and postapocalyptic genres, among others. But 1992 saw perhaps the biggest change of all. His novel *All the Pretty Horses* was an instant success when it hit the shelves, garnering critical acclaim and selling 180,000 copies in hardcover and 300,000 in paperback by June 1994 (M. Jones 54). As I mentioned in chapter 1, McCarthy granted a substantial interview to Richard Woodward of the *New York Times*, something he wouldn't do again until speaking with Woodward for *Vanity Fair* in 2005. *Pretty Horses* won both the National Book Award and the National Book Critics Circle Award. After six novels and twenty-seven years as a published author, McCarthy was famous.

The early '90s marked another kind of transition for McCarthy as well. After continuing to work closely with Albert Erskine on all of his Southern novels as well as on *Blood Meridian*, Erskine provided only a few suggestions for an early draft of *Pretty Horses*. The problem wasn't lack of interest but rather Erskine's age and failing health. He had already been semiretired when McCarthy was working on *Blood Meridian*, and after that novel's publication he began treatment for cancer. McCarthy moved from Random House to Knopf (which is an imprint of Random House but can still be considered a different press) and began working with editor Gary Fisketjon. Erskine died in 1993 (Luce, "McCarthy and Erskine" 329).

Thus his life as a writer changed rather dramatically in two ways. What was perhaps the most intense working relationship of his life came to an end, and he had become something of a literary celebrity, even if he avoided the fruits of that particular kind of achievement. The success of *All the Pretty Horses* also meant that after McCarthy's many frustrations with unproduced screenplays in the 1980s, filmmakers were now knocking on *his* door, eager to bring his work to the screen.

THE FIRST ADAPTATION: PUTTING A
BEST-SELLER ONSCREEN

As I noted in chapter 2, John Grady Cole was originally conceived as a cinematic character in McCarthy's screenplay "El Paso/Juarez," though his depiction changed considerably as McCarthy revised the screenplay and then as he wrote the Border Trilogy. But because that earlier screenplay was almost completely unknown in 1992, any interested filmmakers would be dealing solely with the novel; they also wouldn't have any hints about how John Grady's story would eventually end in *Cities of the Plain*. And it wouldn't be up to McCarthy to tutor them in how to understand the character. Unlike *The Gardener's Son*, which McCarthy wrote as a screenplay and stayed involved with during production, *All the Pretty Horses* would be the first McCarthy novel to be adapted for the screen by others.

And others were indeed immediately interested in taking on that challenge. "My agent told me that at one point, more than twenty directors had said they wanted to do this movie," noted Ted Tally, the film's screenwriter (*Acting McCarthy*). *Variety* called the bidding war over rights to the novel a "heated battle," and Columbia emerged the victor, with legendary director Mike Nichols at the helm (Fleming, "Thornton Holds Reins"). Enthusiasm was so high, in fact, that Nichols planned to direct two sequels to the film, presumably the other volumes of the Border Trilogy that hadn't even been published yet (Weinraub). Ted Tally finished a first draft of the screenplay in September 1993.

After that initial burst of interest, however, the project lagged. In 1993 *Variety* reported that Columbia had "flinched," worrying that the film would be "high on budget, [but] low on star power, since the stars are kids"—that is, since the book's protagonists are teenagers (Fleming, "Calley's Coup"). United Artists then acquired *Pretty Horses*, with Nichols still on board to direct, but the film was pushed back behind other Nichols projects in development like *A Simple Plan* (which was eventually directed by Sam Raimi in 1998) and *Primary Colors* (1998). Interest kicked up again in 1995, largely because Brad Pitt wanted to get involved. Pitt, who would eventually record audiobooks for all three Border Trilogy novels, had been a fan of *All the Pretty Horses* since its publication—though in 1992 he was much less well known than he would be by the mid-'90s, when roles in *A River Runs Through It* (1992), *Interview with the Vampire* (1994), and *Legends of the Fall* (1994) had made him a significantly bankable actor. This reengaged Columbia, which considered partnering with United Artists if Pitt signed on or if the film's budget grew to above $18 million (Peers). Pitt, who was thirty-two in 1995, would have been exactly twice John Grady's age in the novel, a fact that industry bigwigs were likely willing to ignore in favor of his star power.

But that lineup didn't work out either, and the film went back to Columbia. Given Nichols's involvement with his other projects, he withdrew as director (just as he did later with Steppenwolf's *The Sunset Limited*). Billy Bob Thornton, who starred in Nichols's *Primary Colors* and had a deep interest in the project, took the reins instead in 1997. Because Thornton owed Miramax another film after his first, the sleeper hit *Sling Blade* (1996), that studio became an equal financial partner on the film. Harvey Weinstein, producer and cofounder of Miramax, pushed hard to bring in Leonardo DiCaprio for the role of John Grady; DiCaprio was a hot property after the record-breaking success of *Titanic* (1997) and knew Weinstein from the Miramax film *Marvin's Room* (1996) (Fleming, "Sony, Miramax"). But DiCaprio didn't jump at the opportunity, and so Columbia and Miramax went to Matt Damon, who is said to have committed to the deal within twenty-five minutes (Petrikin, "Damon"). The studios wanted Tobey Maguire to play the role of Lacey Rawlins, but like DiCaprio, Maguire couldn't strike a deal, and so the role went instead to Henry Thomas, still known to most as the child star of Steven Spielberg's *E.T.* (1982) ("E.T. Boy"). Penélope Cruz, a big star in Spain, was cast as Alejandra, and so the slate of main characters was complete (Hopewell). As the production finally picked up steam, Columbia negotiated a seven-figure deal for rights to the other two Border Trilogy novels, *The Crossing* and *Cities of the Plain*, in April 1998 (Petrikin and Cox). Hopes were high for *All the Pretty Horses*, both as a film unto itself and as the first of a series.

Shooting took place in New Mexico and Texas in 1999. According to Bruce Dern, who plays a small role as a judge and appears near the end of the film, when Sam Shepard found out that Thornton was working on *All the Pretty Horses*, he called up Thornton and said, "I don't care what there is in the movie, just tell me to show up, what day—I want to be in the movie." Thornton explained that almost all the roles were already spoken for, except for the very small part of the family lawyer. It was enough—Shepard showed up and filmed two short scenes in two days. "Just because, he says, I loved the book" (*Acting McCarthy*). Like Shepard, many of the actors were already familiar with McCarthy's work generally and *All the Pretty Horses* in particular, and that fueled their enthusiasm for the project.

Soon, however, obstacles arose. Ted Tally's screenplay made few changes in plot, character, or dialogue from McCarthy's novel, and partly as a result of hewing so closely to the source material, the finished version was 158 pages long. That's long—about 30 pages longer than what would already be considered a long screenplay. Thornton's writing partner Tom Epperson worked on the story as well, but his version wasn't any shorter. "Billy didn't ask me to shorten it," he said. "It seemed to not be an issue that it was a long script … [But] that was the whole downfall of the movie" (qtd. in Biskind 420).

Epperson simplifies a complicated situation, but the film's length did indeed become a major sticking point. Late in 1999 Thornton screened a cut of the film that was three hours and forty minutes long to executives at Columbia. Reactions were apparently mixed, and studio president Amy Pascal began pressuring Thornton to reduce the film's length (Biskind 420); for his part, Thornton complained to the press about that pressure, wondering to *Premiere* magazine why "a major studio [would] buy this book if all they're going to want in the end is a damn hour-and-a-half chase movie?" (qtd. in Brodesser). Compression, Thornton implies, would affect the pace, the rhythm, and thus the tone and even the genre of the film. Then in August 2000, Columbia handed over domestic distribution and marketing to Miramax while continuing to share production costs; that way, they reasoned, the film wouldn't have to be crowded in with Columbia's many other winter releases. The deal stipulated that *All the Pretty Horses* would be cut to a running time of two hours and fifteen minutes or less and that sexual content would be handled carefully in order to ensure a PG-13 rating and the bigger audiences that entails. The film, in turn, would benefit from Miramax's expert advertising, which had proven particularly adept at trolling for Oscars (Brodesser).

That was the idea, anyway. As the release date approached, news stories began to appear about the continuing conflict over the film's length, which in the final version was 116 minutes, just a hair under two hours. In an article titled "Cutting 'Horses,'" Chris Hewitt wrote about the stars' and director's reluctance to address the issue: "So many people at the press junket for *All the Pretty Horses* have so many things they don't want to talk about," he notes, "that you can't help wondering why some of them are there." In that piece, clearly doing some damage control, Thornton says that the long cut he screened for Columbia was "just an assembly of footage, not a finished print. … So the myth of the four-hour cut came from that screening." Matt Damon chimed in with the team, too: "The cut we have now is the cut everybody feels good about," he insists. "There's nothing missing. Nothing got cut out." Still, more articles appeared, with titles like "Billy Bob Thornton's Rough Ride: Thornton Battles Rumor Mill on 'Pretty Horses'" (McGee) and "After Choppy Seas, a Film Nears Port" (Lyman). The story that developed featured the blunt-spoken director facing off against studio execs, and in particular Harvey "Scissorhands" Weinstein, known for cutting down films in ways that were extreme and only sometimes effective (Biskind 90). Billy Bob wanted a four-hour cut; Harvey wanted ninety minutes; and the idea of a showdown between the idiosyncratic Arkansan and the curse-spewing New Yorker was too good for the press to pass up, regardless of everyone's attempts to quell the rumors. The finished film debuted in theaters on Christmas Day 2000.

In the film Matt Damon plays John Grady Cole as a young man with confidence, physical ability, and a strong idea of what kind of world he wants to live in, but who finds himself—quite literally—up against a wall, the world stubbornly beyond his control. The film opens with a slow-motion shot of horses running off into the night, which then cuts to John Grady and Rawlins looking up at the night sky and talking about similarly unknown destinations. "You ever think about dying?" John Grady asks, and they wonder about the existence of heaven and hell. "You think you can believe there's a heaven if you don't believe there's a hell?" Rawlins asks, and John Grady responds, "I guess you can believe what you want to." It's homespun philosophizing that emphasizes their youth and comfortable friendship, though it also foreshadows the trials to come and hints at Rawlins's nervousness about the endeavor. John Grady advocates a freedom of belief, a freedom that is later explicitly countered by the dueña Alfonsa, who tells him that "in the end we all come to be cured of our sentiments. Those whom life does not cure, death will." The two boys want to go to Mexico to escape their unsupportive families and to live like the "old time waddies" — "real cowboys" — in a way that they can't do in the States. A slow-motion shot during the opening credits emphasizes that disjunct, as a horse and rider race alongside a pickup truck. Both will take you places, but in different ways and on different roads. John Grady and Rawlins's road to Mexico intersects with Jimmy Blevins, whose loss of his horse during a thunderstorm, subsequent reclaiming of horse and gun, and killing of three men in the process condemns John Grady and Rawlins by association and leads to their imprisonment and Blevins's execution.

The plot and the dialogue follow the novel closely, although Thornton notably departs from that source narrative in the way he chooses to dramatize the horse-breaking scenes at La Purísima, the enormous ranch in Mexico where John Grady and Rawlins stumble on work after separating from Blevins. At this moment in the story, La Purísima's vaqueros have brought sixteen wild colts down from the mountains, and the two boys decide to try and break them themselves in four days. Just as the evolution of John Grady's character can be seen in how the horse-breaking sequence from the original screenplay of "Cities of the Plain" changes when McCarthy writes drafts of that screenplay and then the later novel, the horse-breaking scene in *All the Pretty Horses* as rendered in the novel and then in the film reveals key differences in how McCarthy and Billy Bob Thornton present this protagonist, despite the largely curatorial approach taken by the adaptation project as a whole.

Making Them Believe: John Grady on the Page

McCarthy was meticulous in his research for this sequence, which is John Grady's chance to demonstrate his knowledge of and skill with horses to Don Héctor, the ranch's patriarch, as well as to the reader. Don Héctor, it seems, has some four hundred horses up on a nearby mountain and is breeding *media sangres*. Rawlins has to ask what that means, and John Grady explains, "Quarterhorses, what we'd call em" (101). "That roan yonder," he goes on, "is a flat-out Billy horse if he does have bad feet." John Grady knows his horses, and pegs this one as an offspring of the Steel Dust line. According to the American Quarter Horse Association, the "legendary Steel Dust came to Texas around 1844, and five years later the great horse Shiloh also arrived. Shiloh's son Billy, out of a daughter of Steel Dust, became the fountainhead of Texas Quarter Horses" (Hedgpeth ix). John Grady further adds that the horse is part of the breeding line of "José Chiquito," or Little Joe, a horse from the early twentieth century. Rawlins has heard of Little Joe, but John Grady goes on, imparting even more information:

> Both of them horses were sold in Mexico, said John Grady. One and Two. What he's got up yonder is a big yeguada of mares out of the old Traveler-Ronda line of horses of Sheeran's.
> What else? said Rawlins. (101)

John Grady has a detailed understanding of horses' history and breeding and is also well acquainted with the appropriate terminology both in English and Spanish. Gail Moore Morrison has aptly noted that "in an ironic double entendre on his estate's name," Don Héctor has "conceived a breeding strategy to produce a superior cutting horse by crossing his quarter horse mares with a thoroughbred stallion" (180). Morrison observes that this echoes John Grady's memory of a painting that hung in his family's home:

> They had the long Andalusian nose and the bones of their faces showed Barb blood. You could see the hindquarters of the foremost few, good hindquarters and heavy enough to make a cuttinghorse. As if maybe they had Steeldust in their blood. But nothing else matched and no such horse ever was that he had seen and he'd once asked his grandfather what kind of horses they were and his grandfather looked up from his plate at the painting as if he'd never seen it before and he said those are picturebook horses and went on eating. (16)

These "picturebook horses" could indeed be cutting horses, the result of breeding Billy horses—horses from the Steel Dust line—with a thoroughbred. And so the union of the horses John Grady and Rawlins intend to ride with Don Héctor's prize stallion would produce a horse such as one has never seen, and John Grady is given a "miraculous opportunity" to do just that (Morrison 180). But first he has to break those horses.

McCarthy details the equipment they will use: forty-foot maguey catch ropes, saddle blankets, a *bolsalea* or riding hackamore with a metal noseband, sixteen rope hackamores, and coils of all kinds of rope, and John Grady has a pair of gunnysacks that he has slept in and a Hamley saddle. Rawlins asks if John Grady is "dead set of sackin these varmints out," or rubbing them with the gunnysacks to familiarize the horses with the smell and feel of a blanket and also of people (103). This is a common procedure, but John Grady adds his own touch when he uses sacks that smell of him in particular. He takes great care with the action, absorbed in the task at hand and dedicated to what he believes to be necessary attention to detail. Rawlins advocates a more straight-ahead method: "My old daddy always said that the purpose of breakin a horse was to ride it and if you got one to break you just as well to saddle up and climb aboard and get on with it" (103). John Grady grins and asks if his daddy was "a certified peeler," and Rawlins answers that although he never claimed to be, he had sure seen him "hang and rattle a time or two." Rawlins appreciates the show put on by a good bronc peeler, or bronc buster, who simply gets on a horse (often with the help of other cowboys) and attempts to stay on until the horse is exhausted, in a contest of will between man and horse. John Grady has different ideas—he declares that there is "no such thing as a mean colt" and that he will "make them believe."

Then he gets started. First he ropes the forefeet of one of the horses, drops it to the ground, and talks to it while holding its head in his lap. He allows it to rise and he and Rawlins begin fitting several of the horses with hackamores and tying up one of each horse's hind legs. This hobbling, or "sidelining," makes it impossible for the horses to kick or move about freely. When the boys have three horses arranged in such a way, the other vaqueros of La Purísima take notice, and a few wander over to watch. It's unclear if they are unfamiliar with the approach—which, though different from bronc busting, is still a common method of horse breaking—or if John Grady's facility with it is simply a sight to see. On the evening of that first day, "the vaqueros seemed to treat them with a certain deference but whether it was the deference accorded the accomplished or that accorded to mental defectives they were unsure" (105).

After each of the sixteen horses has been arranged in such a way and all of the vaqueros have come to watch, John Grady begins the sacking out, rubbing the sack that he has slept in all over the horse's body while talking to it. "What good do you think it does to waller all over a horse that way?" Rawlins asks skeptically. "I dont know," John Grady answers, "I aint a horse" (106). Finally John Grady places a blanket and saddle on the horse, which doesn't move, replaces the hackamore with the *bolsalea*, unhobbles the horse, and climbs up in the saddle. The horse briefly starts, and then responds, following his lead with the reins. Rawlins "spat in disgust" and complains, "What the hell kind of bronc is that? . . . You think that's what these people paid good money to see?" (107). Rawlins wants a rodeo, and he's gotten nothing of the sort. By dark John Grady has ridden all of the horses, and the crowd has grown to "something like a hundred people" who are picnicking and watching the show (107). In the following days he rides them all again, and then Rawlins does as well.

More than any other sequence in the novel, these scenes demonstrate John Grady's deep affiliation with horses as well as his practical skills with them. Though he and Rawlins "dont have no leaders" and are just buddies, as he tells Don Héctor, it is very clear that John Grady is the primary horse breaker and Rawlins does little more than assist him. Something about John Grady's method and talent is enough to draw a substantial crowd, though most of what happens here is relatively standard horse breaking: restraining the horse, getting it used to the touch and smell of people, sacking it out, saddling it, and eventually beginning to ride it.

Phillip Snyder has noted that John Grady's attitude, if not his method, is similar to "horse whispering," or natural horsemanship, as popularized by Monty Roberts and represented in Nicholas Evans's novel *The Horse Whisperer* (1995), as well as in the 1998 film adaptation of the same name. In his book *The Man Who Listens to Horses* (1996), Roberts explains his own technique of horse breaking, in which the breaker learns to mimic the body language of a dominant mare in a herd and thus creates a partnership with the horse. When this happens, the horse will move voluntarily toward the breaker rather than away (234). Other than the enclosed area of the pen, no restrictions are placed on the horse—and the pen itself may not be necessary, Roberts notes (233). Roberts emphasizes cooperation and earning the trust of the horse, so much so that he calls his method "starting" rather than "breaking" horses, and a similarly nonviolent approach has become relatively standard in contemporary approaches to horsemanship; other advocates include trainers like Tom and Bill Dorrance and Pat Parelli.

John Grady uses more traditional horse-breaking methods than someone like Monty Roberts—he does restrain the horses, for instance, and approaches them on his terms rather than theirs—though he does so in a way that largely divests these processes of the brutality that Roberts claims they often entail. He doesn't use the noncontact body language Roberts describes, but he does communicate with the horses, talking to them softly and at length. He doesn't "bust" these broncs, and no one—person or horse—has to hang and rattle.

John Grady dominates these horses with skill and care and does not enforce his domination with violence. And yet his relationship with them is still characterized by the imposition of control that is quite different from the partnership that Roberts and others would advocate. The horses, after all, are restricted from free movement and subjected to the application of force—if not physically violent or abusive force—that operates as a kind of mental colonization: "They looked like animals trussed up by children for fun and they stood waiting for they knew not what with the voice of the breaker still running in their brains like the voice of some god come to inhabit them" (105). John Grady clearly loves horses, but here that love is expressed as a desire to master them. Gentle and compassionate as he is, he still exerts his efforts *on* the horses rather than *with* them, and he doesn't doubt his ability to bring these objects of his affection under his complete control. Neither does he doubt the appropriateness of doing so.

This love and mastery is seen most notably a few pages later in the book when he rides Don Héctor's prize stallion and speaks to him in Spanish. The passage is remarkable for its use of language as well as for what John Grady actually says to the horse:

> He'd ride sometimes clear to the upper end of the laguna before the horse would even stop trembling and he spoke constantly to it in spanish in phrases almost biblical repeating again and again the strictures of a yet untabled law. Soy comandante de las yeguas, he would say, yo y yo sólo. Sin la caridad de estas manos no tengas nada. Ni comida ni agua ni hijos. Soy yo que traigo las yeguas de las montañas, las yeguas jóvenes, las yeguas salvajes y ardientes. While inside the vaulting of the ribs between his knees the darkly meated heart pumped of who's will and the blood pulsed and the bowels shifted in their massive blue convulsions of who's will and the stout thighbones and knee and cannon and the tendons like flaxen hawsers that drew and flexed and drew and flexed at their articulations and of who's will all sheathed and muffled in the flesh and the hooves that stove wells in the morning groundmist and the head turning side to side and the great slavering keyboard of his teeth and the hot globes of his eyes where the world burned. (128)

The Spanish sentences John Grady speaks indicate an assumption of complete control, mastery, even enslavement: I am the commander of the mares, he says, I and I alone. Without the charity of these hands you don't have anything. Not food or water or children. It is I who bring the mares from the mountains, the young mares, the wild and passionate mares. John Grady claims control over the stallion's sustenance and his breeding, all the aspects of his survival. And if the "world burns" in the stallion's eyes, then John Grady likewise claims mastery over the world itself. At this point in the story, that mastery seems plausible—John Grady, after all, has successfully ridden from the United States into Mexico, demonstrated his skill with horses to great acclaim, and risen to prominent employment for a wealthy landowner. And he has met and danced with Alejandra, that landowner's spirited and beautiful daughter, with whom he will soon begin an intense and intimate relationship. That relationship, of course, begins and develops around the horses each appreciates and rides so well. "What he loved in horses," McCarthy writes of John Grady, "was what he loved in men, the blood and the heat of the blood that ran them. All his reverence and all his fondness and all the leanings of his life were for the ardenthearted and they would always be so and never be otherwise" (6). Alejandra, impulsive and passionate, certainly qualifies. In consummating his love for her, it seems—at least initially—that John Grady has mastered yet another remarkable challenge.

Georg Guillemin has argued that, whispering aside, John Grady's relationship with horses in these earlier scenes is indeed characterized by dominance, or "the master-subject relationship of traditional animal husbandry" (133). Later in the book, however, this changes. After John Grady is arrested and jailed for his previous involvement with Blevins—now known as an assassin for killing three men—his expectations of mastery begin to falter. While in jail he dreams of running with horses over a high plain, and the fact that he runs *with* them rather than rides or commands them signals a shift. As Guillemin notes, the "dream image makes for a parable of an ecopastoral, rather than just pastoral, utopia because John Grady runs among the horses as their equal and not their master" (137–138). Certainly we do see evidence of more equality between boy and horse in the dream:

> ... and they flowed and changed and ran and their manes and tails
> blew off of them like spume and there was nothing else at all in that
> high world and they moved all of them in a resonance that was like
> a music among them and they were none of them afraid nor colt nor
> mare and they ran in that resonance which is the world itself and
> which cannot be spoken but only praised. (161–162)

Here, their partnership is a resonance, like music, and none are afraid—there is no creeping plague of fear or mental colonization by the voice of "some god," and no creature withholds anything from any other. Their partnership *is* the world, which is not controlled, or even spoken of, but rather praised. It's a communion that the characters in "Whales and Men" would envy, the "dialogue among the lifeforms of the earth" that humans might "still sense in dreams," as John Grady does here (57).

Much later, after John Grady has been released from prison and unsuccessfully attempted to reclaim Alejandra, he seeks revenge on the Encantada captain who arranged to have Blevins executed and who conveyed Rawlins and John Grady to the prison in Saltillo. Immediately before "men of the country" appear to take the captain from John Grady and, presumably, punish him appropriately, John Grady dreams of horses again. McCarthy writes that "what he saw in his dream was that the order in the horse's heart was more durable for it was written in a place where no rain could erase it" (280). Men's ordering of the world, John Grady realizes, pales in comparison to the durable and eternal order in a horse's heart. It is, by now, a familiar sentiment, echoing the timekeeper in *The Gardener's Son*, Peter and Guy of "Whales and Men," and Papaw of *The Stonemason*—that men's records and reckonings are fragile, especially in comparison to that which comprises the bedrock of the world. John Grady sees it in horses, while Guy sees it in whales and in nature generally, and Papaw in God.

The order that John Grady previously sought to impose with his voice and physical control of the horses has been trumped, and his love for horses thus matures into a corresponding respect. The novel ends with the image of John Grady riding off from Rawlins's home and into the sunset, appearing to be literally at one with the horses who travel with him: "and horse and rider and horse passed on and their long shadows passed in tandem like the shadow of a single being. Passed and paled into the darkening land, the world to come" (302). The John Grady of *All the Pretty Horses* is a character whose skills with and relationship to horses undergoes a subtle shift, deepening into true partnership, though his facility with these animals is remarkable both before and after this change. Unfortunately his relationships with other people haven't fared as well. He loses his grandfather, father, and Blevins to death, and his mother, girlfriend Mary Catherine, and Alejandra to what might generally be called a failure to communicate. Even Rawlins now seems to live in a different world than he does. But he and the horses end the novel together, poised on the cusp of "the world to come," whatever that may bring.

Hang and Rattle: John Grady on Screen

The film handles this sequence very differently, and in so doing harkens back, interestingly enough, to John Grady's earliest incarnation in McCarthy's screenplay of "Cities of the Plain." If the Rawlins in McCarthy's novel thinks a horse breaker should "hang and rattle a time or two," then the Rawlins of the film gets that wish and more. After John Grady and Rawlins have been signed on as cowhands at La Purísima, they linger outside the bunkhouse, smoking and watching the sixteen wild horses in the pen. As they watch, the camera cuts briefly and repeatedly to close-up shots of the horses'

flanks, punctuated by the sound of their agitated whinnies. John Grady proposes breaking them all, and Rawlins reluctantly agrees. As they carry equipment toward the pen, Rawlins emphasizes the importance of succeeding at
their task, and thus establishes the horse breaking as a high-stakes effort
rather than a lark: "We mess this up, bud, it's going to be a long ride back
to Texas."

The horse-breaking sequence, which is presented in montage, begins with
a slow-motion shot of a lasso swinging against the sky. A quick cut puts the
viewer right in the middle of the action, as John Grady ropes one of the
horses and loops the rope around a pole. The horse resists, bucking and moving away, and when John Grady approaches with a saddle he is forced to drop
it in the dirt. A slow-motion shot of a saddle swinging through the air toward
a horse's back is repeated three times during the montage, and we see wide
shots of John Grady being bucked off the horse followed by other shots of
him staying on successfully. Another repeated shot reveals John Grady ap-
proaching a horse with a saddle, intoning "whoa, whoa."

A crowd gathers, first the vaqueros and then others—families, a band—
who cheer and applaud as the boys attempt to ride the bucking horses. Both
John Grady and Rawlins are shown flying through the air in slow motion and
taking hard falls. At one point Rawlins nods after rising to acknowledge the
approval of the crowd. Finally night falls, and the audience watches, rapt, as
the boys ride around the pen. Their task completed, the two boys exit the
pen and walk toward the bunkhouse, accepting sips of tequila from one observer and their forgotten jackets from a small child who chases after them.

Though the film sequence features a great number of slow-motion shots
that linger on the lasso and saddle, it reveals few details about the variety
of equipment used or the entirety of the process. Here, no real philosophy
or special technique is explicated or demonstrated—both John Grady and
Rawlins just get on until they can stay on, and more often than not they are
shown hitting the dirt. This is a sign, as Roberts might note, that the two are
working for dominance rather than partnership—and it's a dominance born
of intense conflict.

Also in the film, the crowd that gathers comes more for the entertainment
of a rodeo and the spectacle of two young Americans getting the stuffing
beaten out of them rather than to witness a form of horse breaking so new
or otherwise impressive that fathers would hold up babies to see it, as they
do in the novel. As we see in the film, children laugh at the beat-up pair, and
adults offer tequila to dull their aches and pains. John Grady does speak to
the horses but only very briefly; he says "whoa" and intones that he's "gonna
put a saddle on you right now," but hardly maintains the ongoing and lengthy
communication that he does in the novel. Finally, when their work is done,

John Grady Cole (Matt Damon) bustin' broncs in Billy Bob Thornton's film adaptation of All the Pretty Horses *(Columbia Pictures, 2000).*

John Grady and Rawlins sit and eat a meal. As he does in the novel, Rawlins asks, "You tired?" The response is still definitely affirmative, but in the film it entails not only a hard day's work and mental exhaustion but a good bit of hanging and rattling as well.

The changes in the horse-breaking sequence elide John Grady's relationship with horses in favor of his friendship and partnership with Rawlins. The sequence is narratively significant for different reasons than in the novel, and it is shot and edited beautifully, its striking composition second only to the scene leading up to Blevins' execution. In one of the rare positive pieces about the film, Jim Kitses calls the horse-breaking sequence one of "three brilliant passages that effectively translate McCarthy's themes into film, relating the characters' inner life to history and myth." He goes on to note the ways the sequence succeeds:

> In what is at once a private experience and a spectacle, the boys assert their identity and establish their skill, commune with and master the animals, and contribute to their community. The effect is also one of timeless ritual—the play of light, the horses' defiance, the repeated falls and remounts.
>
> Such a scene goes beyond thematic statement and achieves an extraordinary power by successfully marrying realist action to dreamlike, stylised effects. (15)

As Kitses implies, the film makes Rawlins more of a key player. This is less John Grady's chance to show his mystical communion with horses than for *both* young men, as Kitses says, to show their grit, determination, and masculinity. The two boys are figured as partners rather than as master and assistant, or hero and witness.

If Rawlins is elevated in the film, then John Grady is also, in some sense, lowered. He never says, "Soy el comandante de las yeguas ... yo y yo sólo. Sin la caridad de estas manos no tengas nada. Ni comida ni agua ni hijos," or anything like it. He says "whoa." This film sequence demystifies John Grady as a character, and thus the story as well. It becomes tougher, less metaphysical. The John Grady of film is more like a real boy—he makes bad decisions, loses a friend, is left by a girl, and is gravely injured, but he manages to keep his best friend and recover their horses. And if he wants to break a horse, he gets on the thing until it kicks him off.

Interestingly, Ted Tally's screenplay for the film tries to play it both ways. It includes John Grady sidelining the horses, sacking them out, and eventually riding one without any protest from the horse. Rawlins spits in mock disgust, as he does in the novel, and laments the lack of a good show (57–61). The following scene, however, is a montage of John Grady and Rawlins getting thrown and thrown again, "[hitting] the dirt with an awful thump" as the crowd applauds and whistles (61–62). In the last scene of the sequence, "John Grady is riding a final mustang, which rears and twists and kicks. Somehow he hangs on, the crowd cheering him like a rodeo performer, until finally the horse stops bucking and stands still, trembling" (62). Tally tries to capture both John Grady's preternatural connection with horses as well as his grit, though featuring one method right after the other makes for a strange (and confusing) combination. It's possible that Thornton may have shot both horse-breaking methods before cutting the first, whether in service of logic, aesthetics, or length.

Regardless of the particular way that John Grady and Rawlins accomplish this feat—which does indeed impress Don Héctor and land John Grady a promotion—it's all for naught when he and Rawlins are ejected from that paradise once their connection with Blevins is verified. After reuniting with him as prisoners, they sit against a wall in an isolated outcrop of buildings as Blevins is hauled across a dry riverbed to be killed. The camera pans over their faces and those of the young men guarding them as they hear the shots; they flinch at the noise, and there's nowhere to go except to the Saltillo prison. There, they are up against the wall again, this time wearing the striped uniforms of a more official incarceration, and one with greater dangers. "I never dreamed that there was such a place as this," Rawlins says. John Grady responds that "I guess there's probably every kind of place you can think of." Their comments reveal how much the world has changed for them since Blevins's death.

While in the Saltillo prison, Lacey Rawlins and John Grady Cole (Henry Thomas and Matt Damon, center at rear) are up against the wall with other prisoners during a dream sequence in All the Pretty Horses.

After Rawlins is stabbed in the prison yard, John Grady buys a knife, which he needs soon enough during an attack in the mess hall. Whereas McCarthy describes an elaborate dance between John Grady and the *cuchillero* that lasts for four pages and includes swings with trays and knives, feinting and slashing, and blood spilled on both sides, Thornton shoots the fight as a quick and brutal confrontation. John Grady is hurt badly, but as soon as he gets the edge, he pushes the man up against a post and stabs him repeatedly — sixteen times, by my count, an unsettling parallel with the earlier feat of breaking sixteen horses. His injuries lead to unconsciousness, which leads to reverie. He sits with Blevins, asking what it's like to be dead, and then stands with Rawlins and a group of prisoners, one of whom sings "The Red River Valley" in both English and Spanish. "From this valley they say you are going," he sings, as everyone, this time, is up against the wall.

Salvation comes from dueña Alfonsa, who buys the boys out of prison in exchange for Alejandra's word that she will give up her relationship with John Grady. The boy attempts to persuade both women otherwise, but to no avail, and he must content himself with rescuing the three horses — his own, Rawlins's, and Blevins's — that were taken from them. He does so under great duress, getting shot in the process, and then goes back to Texas. The film as released in theaters ends with the moment of reunion between John Grady and Rawlins. "I thought you might want your old horse back," John Grady says, and Lacey's response is the last line of the film: "Damn, bud."

Without the conversation that ensues in the novel and that was cut from Thornton's film — about John Grady's feeling that this is no longer "his country" — and then his iconic ride off into the sunset, this ending emphasizes recovery and reunion rather than loss. (The adaptation of *The Road* does something similar, as I'll explain.) The film's John Grady may have had to give up the girl, but he's got the horses and his good friend, and he's back on his native ground. The Border Trilogy suggests instead that John Grady's friendship with Lacey may be effectively over, a result of their dramatically different experiences in Mexico and their respective reactions to those experiences—Lacey isn't present in the later *Cities of the Plain*, after all—and indicates that John Grady will have ongoing difficulties finding a place to belong. John Grady's decision to help Blevins steal his horse back and then to conceal that association from Don Héctor can be read as his Aristotelean hamartia. In Hegelian fashion, his insistence that he is a worthy suitor for Alejandra pits his American, masculine values irreconcilably against those of the dueña, her own life the product of very different assumptions about gender, family, culture, and history. The result, in the novel, is suffering and alienation. John Grady still has his connection with horses—and that matters deeply and does sustain him—but he also realizes that "the world's heart beat at some terrible cost and that the world's pain and its beauty moved in a relationship of diverging equity and that in this headlong deficit the blood of multitudes might ultimately be exacted for the vision of a single flower" (282). This, it seems, reflects something of the tone that the filmmakers wished to strike with the longer version of their film.

For those who worked on Thornton's *All the Pretty Horses*, the curtailed ending was an egregious example of editing choices that affected the pacing and storytelling of the entire film, creating a happy ending that largely eliminated John Grady's sense of loss and doubt as experienced in a modernizing America. Once Matt Damon had escaped the necessity of defending the film at press events, he described his take on the theatrical release in these terms: "[Y]ou bake a soufflé and somebody wants you to make it half the size, and you just chop the thing in half and try to mold it and make it look like that was how you made it to begin with. It can't work" (qtd. in Biskind 422).

The director and cast were disappointed with what happened, and reviews of the film were disappointments as well, often noting the project's attempts at fidelity but judging it a failure nonetheless. In one of the earliest, Todd McCarthy, writing for *Variety*, called the film "a half-broken adaptation of Cormac McCarthy's great modern Western novel," and says that the "faithful script by Ted Tally ... is underserved by director Billy Bob Thornton's lack of a coherent visual style and inability to catch a proper rhythm." Mike Clark titled his USA *Today* review "Slow 'Horses' Saddled with Flaws," and Bob Longino blames the studio's imposed editing: "It's a shame. Thornton reportedly brought in 'All the Pretty Horses' at nearly four hours. It's been hacked to two. It feels like three—easy." Rick Groen identified the film's missing element as an "ardentheartedness" that is in many ways the subject of the novel and called his review "Playing It a Bit Too Cool: Careful in Its Plotting and Easy to Watch, *All the Pretty Horses* Lacks the Passion that Fuelled the Book." Writing in the *New York Times*, A. O. Scott used similar language to describe the film's failure: "But the movie, for all its prettiness, manages to be shallow and portentous at the same time. The material to which Mr. Thornton and Mr. Tally have been so ardently faithful has betrayed them" ("Lost Souls"). For Scott, Thornton and his collaborators didn't betray the source text—rather, the slippery, troublesome source text betrayed them instead. There was hardly a review that didn't mention McCarthy's canonical status as an author or use the concept of fidelity as a way to criticize the film.

Much later, more of the story of the film's making—or unmaking, depending on how you see it—came out, at least from the side of those who worked on the film. In his 2012 memoir *The Billy Bob Tapes*, Thornton includes a conversation with Daniel Lanois, the Grammy-winning producer, musician, and composer who worked with him on the score for *Sling Blade* and who also wrote an original score for *All the Pretty Horses*. Weinstein replaced that score, however, with the one by Marty Stuart. It was huge blow, not least because Lanois's score, said Thornton, "was *the* best and the most haunting musical score for a movie I've ever heard in my lifetime. Ever" (195). He goes on to deny that he ever argued for a four-hour cut of the film, claiming rather that his final cut was two hours and forty minutes—"the exact length," he notes, "of *The English Patient*, made by one of the studios that made *All the Pretty Horses*" (196). The studio's insistence that the film be cut to under two hours was "just an arbitrary cut ... because they get more showings in theaters" (196). Finally, he blasts the way the film was marketed as a love story. "The movie was about the end of the west as we know it," he says. "It wasn't a love story between a guy and a girl, but at the time *Titanic* was popular and I begged the studio, 'Please don't make the poster where Matt and Penélope are all airbrushed and staring at each other like the *Titanic* poster,' and sure enough, that's what they put out" (196). Matt Damon made similar comments speaking with Peter Biskind in 2001:

> In the end, there was a lot of animosity and anger directed at Harvey, because he ran the marketing of the movie, and he pulled the trigger on how it was released and what cut was released. He tried to make it look like a love story, so that teenagers would go see it. He made a trailer with me and Penélope Cruz swimming around in the water, skinny-dipping, with Bono singing, and Billy's going, "Look, I love U2, but it's just not appropriate." And on the poster, they put, "Some passions can never be tamed," which is exactly what the movie's not about. (qtd. in Biskind 422)

In Lanois's conversation with Thornton, he asks the director if his own version of the film still exists in any form. "I have it in the house," he says. "I've got the complete movie with the score" (197). He remembers that the studio had given him the chance to put that version on the DVD but that "I turned it down because this was back when we were still feeling pretty raw from it. We were feeling a little beat-up and you weren't real keen on giving them your score to put on the DVD when they didn't put it in the fucking movie on the big screen. I agreed with you, and said no, I stand with my pal Dan" (197). Someday, then, it might be possible to see the film that Thornton made and intended to be released, but one wonders if Thornton will ever feel up to making it public. "[I]t's heartbreaking to watch the beauty of what we did at that time," he says. "The movie came out, it was a good movie, but it wasn't what we made. That ranks as my biggest disappointment" (198). While reviewers used the tropes of fidelity and betrayal to evaluate the adaptation as it was released, Thornton is very clear about where he thinks the betrayal happened. While this story is hardly tragedy—Thornton calls it a "disappointment" rather than a devastation—both the film and its making reflect the pursuit of an ideal that eventually slips painfully out of reach.

THE ROAD FROM PULITZER TO OPRAH TO FILM

If, as I noted at the beginning of this chapter, 1992 was a significant year for McCarthy, 2006 was similarly eventful. His books from *All the Pretty Horses* onward continued to be best-sellers: all three novels of the Border Trilogy as well as *No Country for Old Men*. That most recent novel featured the most contemporary setting of all of McCarthy's work to date (excluding the epilogue of *Cities of the Plain*, which is set in 2002), a cat-and-mouse chase plot, and a lean, relatively spare prose style. The news that Joel and Ethan Coen had agreed to adapt the novel for film and that, by May 2006, they were shooting in New Mexico and Texas certainly increased the popular interest in the author. But for McCarthy's career, the biggest event of 2006 was the publication of *The Road*.

That postapocalyptic tale of an unnamed father and son navigating a gray, ash-covered landscape is similar to *No Country* in its more minimalist prose and its engagement with, as well as revision of, popular genres. Writing in the *New York Times*, Janet Maslin called it "pure poetic brimstone" that is "simple yet mysterious, simultaneously cryptic and crystal clear." Michael Chabon offered high praise in the *New York Review of Books*, and *Entertainment Weekly* named it as the best book of the last twenty-five years ("New Classics"). In 2007 *The Road* won the Pulitzer Prize for Fiction and Oprah

Winfrey chose the book as the next selection for her book club, guaranteeing that the novel would find an even wider audience than it already had. Critical interest surged as well, and articles began to appear that took a number of different approaches to *The Road*, though discussions of the novel's theological and ecological concerns have been the most prevalent. (*The Road* has already garnered as much critical attention as *Blood Meridian*; a recent MLA Bibliography search turned up 173 entries on each of the two texts.)

That interest was compounded by the runaway success of the Coen's *No Country for Old Men* when it was released in 2007 as well as the public's appetite for apocalypse stories generally. The genre, which dates back to the flood stories of Gilgamesh, Genesis, the Quran, and the Hindu Dharmasastra as well as the book of Revelation, came to life on film fairly early, as in August Blom's Danish film *Verdens Undergang* (*The End of the World*, 1916), though it's been most popular onscreen in the years since World War II. In Blom's film a comet passes close to Earth and wreaks havoc, a scenario revisited in later films like *Deep Impact* and *Armageddon*, both from 1998. But the culprits of disaster in this multifaceted genre are various: they can be environmental, as in the Mad Max films (1979, 1981, 1985, 2015) and *The Day after Tomorrow* (2004); the result of artificial intelligence run amok, as in the Terminator films (1984, 1991, 2003, 2009, 2015) and the Matrix trilogy (1999, 2003, 2003); zombies, as in *Night of the Living Dead* (1968), *28 Days Later* (2002), *I Am Legend* (2007), and the popular television series *The Walking Dead* (2010–); or war, as in *Things to Come* (1936), *La Jetée* (1962), *Planet of the Apes* (1968), and *The Day After* (1983); as well as monsters created by nuclear radiation like *Godzilla* (1954), *Them!* (1954), and *Mothra* (1961). "Apocalypse" or "post-apocalypse" are the common terms used to refer to this genre, indicating simply that the narratives involve widespread and catastrophic destruction. Religious studies scholars, however, would be quick to point out that apocalypse means something much more precise in their discipline. Apocalypticism, writes Lorenzo DiTommaso, can be found in ancient sacred texts as well as contemporary narratives, and can be defined as

> *a distinctive combination of axioms or propositions about space, time and human existence.* It presumes the existence of a transcendent reality, which defines the cosmos and everything in it, but remains almost entirely concealed from observation and beyond the grasp of human intellection. It contends that the present reality is constitutionally structured by two antagonistic and irreducible forces, which are typically identified with good and evil. It maintains that a final resolution of the conflict between these forces is both necessary and imminent, and that it is also redemptive, in the sense of a deliverance from the

present reality. The apocalyptic worldview further assumes that the revelation of these mysteries orients existence, and gives life meaning and purpose. (474)

The *Left Behind* films (2000, 2002, 2005), which imagine events of the Rapture and the Tribulation occurring contemporarily, obviously fit that definition, as do, in DiTommaso's reading, the Matrix films, though not most zombie films.[1] In much the same way that calling *Blood Meridian* a Western doesn't provide adequate explanation of its content, *The Road* sits uneasily within the apocalypse genre. If one defines the genre broadly to include the films I listed above, *The Road* stands out for its paucity of large-scale spectacle and refusal to reveal the specifics of the disaster itself. If one considers a definition like DiTommaso's, on the other hand, the narrative hardly lays out a definitive understanding of the world and a "transcendent reality," and it certainly doesn't offer an imminent final resolution of the conflict between good and evil. But as I'll discuss, both the book and the film do depict a father in search of or grappling with the possibility of an apocalyptic understanding of the world in the way that DiTommaso defines it. And although the film is largely a curatorial adaptation, its conclusion takes a notably different approach to the final "revelation of mysteries" than does the novel, emphasizing deliverance instead of loss.

The Road was clearly not going to be *Mad Max* or *The Terminator*, but producer Nick Wechsler pursued and optioned the novel even before it had been published. He liked what he read and beat out other offers to option it—because, he said, his competition was "afraid of the material, obviously. It's very dark stuff" (qtd. in Chiarella). Wechsler enlisted John Hillcoat to direct, whose only other feature film was *The Proposition* (2005), a darkly beautiful and quite McCarthyesque Australian Western. Hillcoat then hired Nick Cave, with whom he had worked on *The Proposition*, to compose the score and the Australian playwright Joe Penhall to write the screenplay; as Penhall and Hillcoat worked on the script, the novel gained traction and fans, and they were suddenly aware of the "incredible pressure" to make the film a worthy adaptation (Chiarella).

The production company was 2929 Entertainment, with Dimension Films (run by Harvey and Bob Weinstein after they left Miramax in 2005) handling domestic distribution. Viggo Mortensen as the father was the first role cast, and in early 2008 Charlize Theron had signed on to play the mother—a small role for a big star, but one she was enthusiastic about because "she's a big fan of the book" and because she enjoyed working with Wechsler on *The Yards* (2000) (Siegel, "Road"). Australians Kodi Smit-McPhee and Guy Pearce (who had starred in Hillcoat's *The Proposition*) joined the cast shortly thereafter as the boy and "the veteran." Filming began in February, with the finished product slated for release in late 2008 (Vancheri).

The shoot received positive press coverage, which often focused on the devotion that Mortensen and the eleven-year-old Smit-McPhee were bringing to their roles, as the two actors appear in nearly every scene in the film. No one was surprised by Mortensen's dedication, which had already been noted in coverage of the *Lord of the Rings* trilogy (2001–2003), *A History of Violence* (2005), and *Eastern Promises* (2007). Child actors, however, have generally been cause for more anxiety. But although he was a relative unknown at the time, people were also praising Smit-McPhee. In a long piece about the film's production, Charles McGrath reported for the *New York Times* that "[s]ome of the crew privately referred to [Smit-McPhee] as the Alien because of the uncanny, almost freakish way that on a moment's notice he switched accents and turned himself from a child into a movie star. Days after the filming of a climactic, emotional scene, people on the set were still marveling at Kodi's performance." Anticipation was high, and there was even some talk about Academy Award nominations.

In October 2008, however, Dimension moved the film's release from November of that year to 2009, citing the need for "more post-production time and a less crowded theatrical calendar" (Zeitchik). As with any delay, this caused concern that this meant the film was somehow foundering or would be the subject of the same kind of conflict that plagued *Pretty Horses*. In fact, instead of cutting out material, the filmmakers used the extended postproduction time to add about fifteen minutes to the running time as well as some voice-over narration by Mortensen that directly echoes McCarthy's prose (Strauss). And as I've noted, McCarthy's prose was indeed the inspiration and guiding light of the production.

The novel that the filmmakers thought so highly of reveals its setting and focus in the opening sentences:

> When he woke in the woods in the dark and the cold of the night he'd reach out to touch the child sleeping beside him. Nights dark beyond darkness and the days more gray each one than what had gone before. Like the onset of some cold glaucoma dimming away the world. His hand rose and fell softly with each precious breath. (3)

The world is cold, dark, and gray, but the nameless man and his son survive together—the child's every breath is precious to him. For the father, the world is shaped by the loss of nearly everything that was familiar: family homes, communities, warmth, animals, crops or any readily available food, social structure, safety, and even language, as the "names of things [are] slowly following those things into oblivion. Colors. The names of birds. Things to eat. Finally the names of things one believed to be true" (88). The boy's mother chose to commit suicide rather than wait to suffer what she thought was inevitable: their capture, rape, murder, and consumption by the wandering bands of cannibals desperate for any kind of food. The man endures in order to protect his son, whom he loves completely and sees as a kind of divine light in an otherwise dark world: "He sat beside him and stroked his pale and tangled hair. Golden chalice, good to house a god" (75). McCarthy titled an early draft of the book "The Grail,"[2] likely referring, as that and other passages suggest, to the son. But though the son is unquestionably a source of goodness and light for the father, the father's belief in an externally divine source of guidance is vexed at best: "He raised his face to the paling day. Are you there? he whispered. Will I see you at the last? Have you a neck by which to throttle you? Have you a heart? Damn you eternally have you a soul? Oh God, he whispered. Oh God" (11–12). The father's love for his son makes their existence in this endarkened world all the more unbearable.

The cause of all this darkness and suffering is left ambiguous. McCarthy only writes that the clocks stopped at 1:17 a.m. when there was suddenly "a long shear of light and then a series of low concussions," followed by "a dull rose glow in the windowglass" of the family's home (52). The result is ash that clouds the skies and seas and kills all plant and animal life, making it necessary for humans to live on canned food—or on each other. Many postapocalyptic narratives dwell on the apocalypse itself, but *The Road* simply doesn't offer enough information to draw a conclusion. The earth and humanity have been devastated, but what's to blame? As a cause, nuclear war could provoke discussions about humanity's scientific hubris and propensity to violence, a tragic flaw that leads to massive devastation; on the other hand, a meteor could lead to reflections on fate or the purpose of a God who would allow such a thing to happen. David Kushner reported that at the Santa Fe Institute, McCarthy had asked questions of his colleague Doug Erwin about the meteor strike that caused the dinosaurs' extinction sixty-five million years ago and what the ensuing environmental effects would be. Though the details of the environmental devastation rendered in McCarthy's novel are somewhat different from what Erwin describes as the aftermath of a meteor—Erwin notes that skies would be blue rather than gray and that there would be "a lot more ferns"—he read *The Road* and decided that "this is what McCarthy was up to." Even so, Kushner writes that while "McCarthy suggests that the ash-covered world in the novel is the result of a meteor hit, [McCarthy's] money is on humans destroying each other before an environmental catastrophe sets in. 'We're going to do ourselves in first,' he says."

The characters themselves never speak about what caused the cataclysm—

perhaps because it no longer matters or perhaps because they don't actually know what the cause was. For his part, the father blames both God and his fellow man for their suffering and for the pain of loving a son in such circumstances. He damns God, wishes to throttle Him—perhaps God orchestrated such a downfall, or at least did nothing to stop it. Yet other humans are also at fault. When one of the cannibals grabs the boy and holds a knife to his throat, the father must shoot him, grab his son, and run to escape the others. "This was the first human being other than the boy that he'd spoken to in more than a year," he thinks later. "My brother at last. The reptilian calculations in those cold and shifting eyes. The gray and rotting teeth. Claggy with human flesh. Who has made of the world a lie every word" (75). How people like this "brother" have responded to calamity, bomb or meteor, denies what makes them human and thus makes the world—which is a world of narrative and meaning-making as much as it is a physical place—a lie.

Lest we think that such a thing is only possible in speculative fiction, McCarthy reminds us that humanity has a long history of treating others like mere objects. When their search for food grows particularly desperate, the father and son approach a once-grand house. They cross a porch where "[c]hattel slaves had once trod those boards bearing food and drink on silver trays" (106). McCarthy's use of the term "chattel" emphasizes that the slaves who served this plantation house were the personal property of the master, thereby making the slaves' children property as well. It makes sense, then, that this house built on the backs of slaves is also the site of the father and son's most horrific discovery. As they explore it, they find a locked cellar, which the father hopes contains a storehouse of food. It does, in a sense. When the father forces the door open, they look in and see "naked people, all trying to hide, shielding their faces with their hands. On the mattress lay a man with his legs gone to the hip and the stumps of them blackened and burnt. The smell was hideous" (110). To the cannibals living in the plantation, these people are merely a food source to be used as needed. The image of them suffering naked in a confined space also evokes the gas chambers of the Holocaust, a point that McCarthy drives home when he writes a few pages later that the boy, starved, exhausted, and traumatized, looks like "something out of a deathcamp" (117). Jay Ellis argues about this sequence that "cannibalism in *The Road* cannot be considered outside our historical memory of slavery, but also our awareness of the fragility of human interactions around commerce" (61). This is no far-fetched sci-fi tale, in other words—humans, as the father knows all too well, are entirely capable of treating one another as objects and are at times seemingly eager to do so. It's a landscape in which people can become commoditized, and one's willingness to commoditize others renders one a kind of soulless zombie. In that sense, *The Road* isn't as different from an apocalyptic zombie movie as it might seem, as iterations like George Romero's *Dawn of the Dead* (1978) make a fairly obvious connection between American consumerism and the consumption of human flesh. In the father and son's understanding, the cannibalistic consumers here have indeed lost their souls — become bad guys, or zombies — although arguably that loss is possible whenever people are seen and treated as objects, or commodities.

It's a bleak world — "[b]arren, silent, godless," as a sentence in the novel's second paragraph succinctly puts it (4). Reason enough, perhaps, to justify the mother's suicide, which she saw as the only option in the face of those dangers. Even the father, who begged her not to do it, sees the logic behind her decision and tries to prepare himself for the moment when he might have to kill his son in order to save him from the same fate as the people in the cellar: "[H]e knew that if he were a good father still it might well be as she had said" (29).

In all this darkness, however, the father's love for his son is an illuminating force. He may shake his fist at an absent God, but the father does see a divine goodness in his son, calling him "the word of God" and "God's own firedrake," and sees him "glowing in that waste like a tabernacle" (5, 31, 273). That goodness often conflicts with the father's survivalist instincts, as the boy wants to help the other people they see regardless of the potential danger of doing so. That conflict arises most obviously when a thief steals their food and supplies; they track him down and the father forces the thief to give everything back, and further, to strip naked. "I'm going to leave you the way you left us," he explains, eye-for-an-eye style, but the boy sobs (257). Later the father relents and goes back to the spot where they left the thief, returning the clothes, but the man is gone. "You're not the one who has to worry about everything," the father reminds the boy. "Yes I am," the boy corrects him. "I am the one" (259). The father worries about their survival, but the boy worries about their morality, their goodness. "I am the one," he says, a Christlike statement appropriate considering his advocacy of mercy and forgiveness. (Critics have been somewhat divided on the theological implications of passages like these. Allen Josephs has argued, for instance, that one can make "a textual case for God, or more specifically, a Christ-like figure in the boy" [137], while Erik Wielenberg claims instead that the book presents a "morality [that] does not depend upon God for its existence or justification" [1].)

Whatever the source of the boy's goodness, it wins over the father in the end. Weakened by illness, injury, and starvation, the father dies, but not before he tempers his pragmatism with a statement of faith, an apocalyptic understanding of the world. After reminding him to keep going south, keep the gun with him, and not to take any chances, he also says, "You need to find the good guys"—and they are out there, he now believes. "You have to carry the fire," the father insists, and he assures the son that the fire is real and that it's "inside you. It was always there." Finally, he tells the boy that after he dies, the boy can talk to him and will hear him respond. "You can talk to me and I'll talk to you. You'll see" (278–279). The fire is real—a transcendent reality that defines their existence and gives their lives meaning. And because of that transcendence, the love between the two of them will exist even after the father dies. He doesn't talk about a final conflict between the good and the bad guys, though he does still invoke that Manichean duality and believes that his son will go forth and find some kind of deliverance.

And indeed he does. The boy mourns his father and then ventures out to the road, where he encounters a man who takes him into his own family and affirms that he is carrying the fire despite his unfamiliarity with that phrase (283). It's an ending for the boy that "reconciles barbarous destruction with eloquent hope," as Ashley Kunsa has written (69), and Lydia Cooper has similarly described how the novel "expresses a deep pessimism regarding humanity's self-destructiveness, but it concurrently proffers an affirmation of the individual's ability to experience a transcendent, and perhaps ultimately redemptive, empathic connection with others" ("Grail Narrative" 234). The boy's apocalypse story ends with a validation of his faith in the existence of good in the world and the ability to find that good in other people.

The ending of the boy's story, however, is not the end of the novel, which closes with a much-remarked-upon passage:

> Once there were brook trout in the streams in the mountains. You could see them standing in the amber current where the white edges of their fins wimpled softly in the flow. They smelled of moss in your hand. Polished and muscular and torsional. On their backs were vermiculate patterns that were maps of the world in its becoming. Maps and mazes. Of a thing which could not be put back. Not be made right again. In the deep glens where they lived all things were older than man and they hummed of mystery. (286–287)

The passage echoes some of the father's vivid memories of life before the disaster, descriptions that contrast the inescapable, haunting grayness of the postapocalyptic world. In one memory that is redolent of the sublime, he remembers watching "a falcon fall down the long blue wall of the mountain and break with the keel of its breastbone the midmost from a flight of cranes and take it to the river below all gangly and wrecked and trailing its loose and blowsy plumage in the still autumn air" (20). In other passages the father recalls "the perfect day of his childhood," spent towing an old stump behind a rowboat with his uncle, the shore "lined with birchtrees that stood bone pale against the dark of the evergreens beyond," the edge of the lake "a riprap of twisted stumps, gray and weathered, the windfall trees of a hurricane years past" (13). A few pages later he remembers watching trout "swaying in the current, tracking their perfect shadows on the stones beneath" (30). Those trout reappear in the final passage, in a world that existed "once," so long gone it seems like a fairy tale. Following as it does the son's meeting with and welcoming into his new family, this passage offsets the hope of that new beginning, though it does so with undeniably beautiful imagery. The trout are simultaneously touchstones of a beginning, "the world in its becoming," and heralds of its end, "a thing which could not be put back" or "made right again." The patterns in their skin are both maps and mazes—twisted trails, some that show you where you're going and some that deliberately obscure your destination. After the close attention to the father and son that is sustained throughout the entire novel, and the focus on the deep significance of their human choices, this final passage performs a very cinematic cut to an extreme wide shot. Here, all things are older than man—that is, they are unanthropocentric, not focused on the human. The final word of the novel, "mystery," emphasizes that though the boy's story has concluded with an affirmation of principles and a validated understanding of the world, the world's own story is much more ambiguous. This is not a "revelation of apocalyptic mysteries," to use DiTommaso's phrase, but rather their continued obscurity.

In their interpretations, however, critics have found ways of understanding the significance of that final passage, even in revelatory apocalyptic terms. Michael Chabon has argued that the book is a kind of ecological tragedy, in which the loss of the world is felt most keenly through this father-son relationship:

> What emerges most powerfully as one reads *The Road* is not a prognosticatory or satirical warning about the future, or a timeless parable of a father's devotion to his son, or yet another McCarthyesque examination of the violent underpinnings of all social intercourse and the indifference of the cosmic jaw to the bloody morsel of humanity. *The Road* is not a record of fatherly fidelity; it is a testament to the abyss of a parent's greatest fears. The fear of leaving your child alone, of dying before your child has reached adulthood and learned to work the mechanisms and face the dangers of the world, or found a new partner to face them with. The fear of one day being obliged for your child's own good, for his peace and comfort, to do violence to him or even end his life. And, above all, the fear of knowing—as every par-

ent fears—that you have left your children a world more damaged, more poisoned, more base and violent and cheerless and toxic, more doomed, than the one you inherited. It is in the audacity and single-mindedness with which *The Road* extends the metaphor of a father's guilt and heartbreak over abandoning his son to shift for himself in a ruined, friendless world that *The Road* finds its great power to move and horrify the reader.

Like Chabon, those who consider the novel from an ecocritical angle note that the book's serious reflection on the realities of living in this altered environment raises issues relating to global warming, mass extinction, nuclear war, and environmental politics. Regardless of what caused the tragic loss of the world in the novel, reading it should spur us to think about the consequences of our actions on both the personal and political level—reading it should be an environmental revelation. McCarthy's novel, then, can be understood as an eco-tragedy, though the causes of the earth's peripeteia are left unclear. The aftermath, however, is quite clear, and despite the significance of the father and son's choice to remain "good guys" and "carry the fire" of humanity and morality, on a larger scale McCarthy reminds the reader that some things really can't be made right again.[3] Though the film adaptation depicts the bleak environment and the depth and moral significance of the father-son relationship, it backs off somewhat from the novel's eco-tragic elements, suggesting in the end that broader recovery may indeed be possible.

The opening of the film emphasizes the harsh transition from the pre- to postlapsarian world. A montage of bright, sunlit images of trees, flowers, a comfortable house, and a happy husband (Viggo Mortensen) and wife (Charlize Theron) gives way to a scene of father and son (Kodi Smit-McPhee) waking to the sound of "just another earthquake" in a dark and dirty camp in the midst of a gray landscape. "Cold, gray days, no animals, crops long gone," the father explains in one of his occasional voice-overs. "As the world slowly dies." As the man and boy move through the desolation, he further describes the roaming gangs of cannibals and the constant concerns about food, the cold, and their shoes.

"Sometimes I tell the boy old stories of courage and justice, difficult as they are to remember," the father explains. "All I know is that the child is my ward, and if he is not the word of God, God never spoke." The voice-over accompanies an image of the man reading to the boy by firelight, turning the pages of a worn book. "If you flicked your tongue like a chameleon, you could lick the food off your plate without using your hands," he reads. "What would your mother say? ... If you had eagle eyes you could spot a running rabbit." The book—which is not included in McCarthy's novel—is *If You Hopped Like a Frog*, by David Schwartz, and is designed to teach children about proportions and also about the abilities of animals. The snippet of text that we hear is rendered deeply ironic in the context of the film—animals are now gone, food is hardly plentiful enough to be toyed with, and there are much worse hunters in the world than eagles. Finally, the question "What would your mother say?" has a much bleaker resonance than simply as a comment about table manners. Like the animals, the mother is also gone, an absence that the film underscores with frequent flashbacks to the father's life with her both before and after the disaster. The father's prelapsarian memories of her are sensual and wordless, and their lush coloration is all the more striking for its contrast with the unremitting grayness of every other scene.

While many films focusing on large-scale disasters and/or their aftermath rely heavily on computer-generated imagery or other special effects to create the setting, Hillcoat filmed in real places. A number of locations in Pennsylvania were used because of state tax breaks for film companies as well as the availability of seemingly postapocalyptic scenery: abandoned stretches of freeway, deserted coalfields, a burned-down amusement park (McGrath). But the filmmakers also "deliberately used America's real apocalyptic zones," said Hillcoat (Chiarella). They shot in a ruined shopping mall in post-Katrina New Orleans, and a brief vista that shows two ships sitting beached on a freeway isn't a visual effect—it's real film shot in the aftermath of Katrina. "We had to doctor the image, grunge it up, make it more toxic, set it into our world," said Hillcoat, "but these places were not hard to find. There's a fair amount of devastation already in the American landscape." The area around Mount St. Helens also features in part of the film. While McCarthy reminds readers of humans' atrocities toward other humans with references to slavery and the Holocaust, Hillcoat uses visual evidence of disasters like Katrina and Mount St. Helens to underscore nature's ravaging power (though in the background of another scene, Hillcoat inserted footage of smoke from the Twin Towers' destruction on 9/11, an allusion to a man-made ashen landscape [Chiarella]).

Much of the novel's theological content derives from the father's statements or, more often, his thoughts. The film represents some of these considerations visually. In the opening sequence the man and boy walk by a billboard spray-painted with the message "Behold the valley of slaughter / Jeremiah 19:6." In the Old Testament the prophetical book of Jeremiah addresses Israel's infidelity to God and calls for repentance. Verse 19:6 reads: "Therefore, behold, the days come, saith the LORD, that this place shall no more be called Tophet, nor The valley of the son of Hinnom, but The valley of slaughter." This refers to Gehenna, a place outside ancient Jerusalem where people worshipped false gods and sacrificed their children, "[filling] this place with the blood of innocents" (19:4). Thus, among other punishments, "I will cause them to eat the flesh of their sons and the flesh of their daughters, and they shall eat every one of the flesh of his friend in the siege and straitness, wherewith their enemies, and they that seek their lives, shall straiten them" (19:9). Someone, then, sees the disaster and the practice of cannibalism as God's punishment for wrongdoing, an apocalypse with a discernible cause and effect, similar to that prophesized in Jeremiah.

The film also depicts the warmth, light, and bounty of an underground bomb shelter that the father and son discover, and the boy's untutored offering of thanks to "the people" who are no longer there but whose stockpile made their continuing survival possible, at least for a while. He doesn't "say grace" in the traditional sense, but his sincerity gives the moment the resonance of prayer. Later, as the father's consumptive cough grows worse and the boy worries he'll die, they take shelter in a ruined church. The two embrace in close-up after the boy begs the father to stop coughing, and then the scene cuts to a wide shot that includes the dim daylight coming in through a cross-shaped window in the church's wall. They are illuminated here by the cross, a visual corollary for the metaphorical fire they urge each other to continue carrying and a reminder, the film suggests, of the transcendent reality of love itself.

These moments of religious imagery are small but significant and indicate that a Judeo-Christian understanding of the story is possible if not overtly evident. In fact, the filmmakers attempted to market the film to a specifically Christian audience, working with A. Larry Ross Communications to make faith-based communities aware of the film. Phil Hotsenpiller, teaching pastor at Friends Church in Yorba Linda, California, "developed a discussion guide and sermon series for the movie around such topics as life and death, good and evil, love, and the environment, and [traveled] to cities throughout the country hosting screenings for pastors and other faith-based leaders" (Kwon). *Christianity Today* gave the film four out of four stars and called it "a triumph of beauty, tragedy, prophecy and redemption" (McCracken).

What some critics have lamented about the film, however, is the portrayal of the mother, a less-seen but significant character. As Charlize Theron plays her, the decision to leave the man and boy by committing suicide is an abandonment. The film flashes back to the father and mother's conversation across a kitchen table, two bullets on the surface between them. "I should have done it when we had more bullets," she says. "I don't know why I listened to you." Her tone is harsh and accusatory. "I should just go ahead and empty every goddamn bullet into my brain and leave you with nothing," she adds. "I would take him with me if it weren't for you." "Listen to yourself," the man pleads. "You sound . . . crazy." "Other families are doing it," she responds.

Theron says these lines with cold hostility, which may be true to the character but undermines the philosophical strength of her argument. Suicide could be considered a rational choice in the face of their probable capture by blood cults who, as she puts it, will "rape me and then they're going to rape your son and then they're going to kill us and eat us." And despite his words in this scene, the father comes to agree with her. Later in the story, when he and the boy are about to be overtaken by a group of particularly ruthless cannibals, he gives the boy the gun. "Don't be afraid," he says. "You're going to have to do it just like everybody else." Seeing the boy's incomprehension, he then takes the gun and points it at his son's forehead. "What are you doing?" the boy asks. "Will I see you again? When will I see you?" The father is ready but not quite able to do what he earlier condemned his wife for contemplating—but as his will is tested, the cannibals are briefly distracted and the two instead make a harrowing escape.

And so the mother's argument for suicide has a force that is belied by the writing of her character and by Theron's performance. In the novel McCarthy gives this argument fuller articulation, an articulation that he expands further in *The Sunset Limited*; there, suicide as a response to both personal and collective human suffering is the central narrative and thematic issue of the play. (McCarthy wrote *The Road* and *The Sunset Limited* in 2005–2006, so this overlap makes sense.) In McCarthy's *The Road*, the father remembers the "hundred nights they'd sat up debating the pros and cons of self destruction with the earnestness of philosophers chained to a madhouse wall," and the mother's eloquent, if bleak, statements that a "person who had no one would be well advised to cobble together some passable ghost" (58, 57). She says, echoing White in *The Sunset Limited*, that her "only hope is for eternal nothingness and I hope for it with all my heart" (57). The father, for his part, thinks at times that his and his son's survival is a failing rather than a triumph: "You will not face the truth," he tells himself when there's only a single round left in the revolver. "You will not" (68). In drafting the novel, McCarthy himself clearly considers the mother's character and actions significant and labels many pages of an early draft concerning her decision to commit suicide "The Mother."[4] How and why she makes her choice are as important as its effects.

In the film her decision is stripped of the bulk of that reasoning and rather appears as an inability to properly care for or about her family. Though the man cries when he remembers her after her death, he also struggles to release her memory, throwing away her picture and pushing his wedding ring off the edge of a high overpass with reluctant finality. "She was gone," he says

The mother (Charlize Theron) represents all the beauty of the lost world in John Hillcoat's The Road *(Dimension Films, 2009).*

in voice-over after a flashback to her final departure, "and the coldness of it was her final gift. But she died somewhere in the dark and there's no other tale to tell."

Though the justification for her actions is reduced, the mother remains a significant presence in the film. Casting a star like Charlize Theron clearly necessitated expanding her screen time—though this was never going to be a leading role—and the result is that the loss of the wife is the primary loss, the absence that creates the coldness of the new world. In the novel, given the setting and circumstances, many things are mourned—lost youth, other family and friends, language itself, and of course the flashing brook trout in the novel's final passage. But in the film the mother represents the totality of this lost community and beauty. Susan Hawkins has written that the flashbacks of the mother contextualize her absence at the expense of those other emphases, and thus the film "substitutes the loss of the mother for McCarthy's realistic insistence on what the extinction of the natural world would not only look like but what it would feel like to live each day in a disappearing world" (56). Dianne Luce has written similarly that "[t]he film's exclusive representation of memories of the wife and rejection of all the man's other memories suggest far more than the novel that the loss of her overshadows for him all other losses." While this is "largely true to the spirit of McCarthy's depiction of their marriage," these omissions also "work together with other small changes to diminish the novel's profound depiction of ecological loss" (Luce, "Hillcoat's *The Road*" 2). The film's addition of small hints of the possibility of renewal, like a beetle wondered over by the father and son, leaven the film with a level of hope that, for Luce, "undermines the devastating impact" that the story should have (4).[5]

McCarthy has said that his young son John, born in 1998 and eight years old when *The Road* was published, was very much his inspiration for the story and the character of the boy. "[A] lot of the lines that are in there are verbatim conversations my son John and I had," he told John Jurgensen of the *Wall Street Journal*. "I mean just that when I say that he's the co-author of the book." But as much as the relationship between father and son powers the novel and is its undeniable heart, the father still cares very much about the lost world as well. His memories, particularly those of natural scenes like streams, trout, or falcons, have real weight and imbue the final passage's tone of both celebration and elegy with an ambiguous power. The film, by using the mother as the primary site of loss, makes recovery more possible as well. Hillcoat's adaptation ends with the boy being taken in by the new family, with another little boy and a girl, and it gives the mother (Molly Parker) a new line, an assurance that "we don't have to worry about a thing." It also reveals that the family is accompanied by a healthy-looking dog, a visual indication that the family can look forward to something more than brute survival. The novel emphasizes the boy's deliverance from imminent torture and death, though the film offers the possibility that the world itself may avoid tragedy as well with the addition of the dog, the beetle, and the absence of a final statement that things cannot be put back or made right again. Here, perhaps they can, even on a larger scale.

Loss, the action of the film suggests, can be ameliorated. Over the credits the filmmakers include the distant sounds of families at leisure on summer lawns—children playing, a sprinkler, a lawnmower, a barking dog, birds, and a call to supper. Those sounds fade out into a low, minor tone, and this ambiguous combination of hope and lament is the only gesture the film makes toward a less than positive conclusion; it's left uncertain if this final soundscape is intended to indicate the possibility of recovery or serve as an elegy for the lost world and a reminder of the simple beauty we may take for granted.

The boy finds a new, loving mother (Molly Parker) at the end of The Road.

(Alfonso Cuarón's film *Children of Men*, released in 2006, also uses the sound of children at play over the end credits to similarly ambiguous effect, after following the story of a woman who gives birth to a child after two decades of human infertility have devastated society.)

Like the ambiguity of the novel's ending, taken as a whole the reviews of *The Road* were neither decidedly positive nor negative. *The Road* was put into wide release on 25 November 2009, though the earliest reviews were in response to screenings at film festivals in Venice, Telluride, and Toronto. Many were measured but positive—Geoffrey MacNab captured the tone of most in the title of his review for the *Independent*: "Bleak but Moving Tale of the Apocalypse." (Terrence McSweeney has aptly noted that "bleak" is "a word that almost every review of the novel and film seems contractually obligated to contain" [42–43].) However, two essays in particular were the most striking precisely because they weren't measured. Tom Chiarella, writing for *Esquire* in June 2009, explained in a lengthy piece why "*The Road* Is the Most Important Movie of the Year." In contrast, in one of the first reviews after the film's premiere in Venice, Todd McCarthy wrote for *Variety* that "[t]his 'Road' leads nowhere." Chiarella praised the environment of the film as a "quietly seething dream" and effused that "there was not a single stupid choice made in turning this book into this movie." Nonetheless, he notes, "You won't want to see this one twice." Todd McCarthy insisted that you shouldn't even see it once. It's "very, very far from the film it should have been"—which is to say, it's not "harsh and daring," and neither is it "shocking, haunting, and, at the end, deeply moving."

But even good reviews noted the bleak storyline, the grayness of atmosphere and tone, and the filmmakers' curatorial approach to the source text. In *USA Today* Claudia Puig called the film "grimly faithful" to the book, and A. O. Scott of the *New York Times* said that the script "follows the novel as faithfully as a hunting dog." Christopher Kelly called the film one of the worst of the year, in part because Hillcoat is so "excruciatingly literal" in the way that he "translat[es] McCarthy's grim panoramas to the screen." Kelly said that Hillcoat ends up "suffocating the audience," who don't have recourse to McCarthy's lyric prose to leaven such visual despair.

McCarthy himself saw an early cut of the film in February 2008, and much to Penhall's and Hillcoat's relief thought that it was "really good" and insisted that he "didn't drive all this way [to Albuquerque] just to blow smoke up your ass" (Penhall). One still wonders if he was just being polite, but around the time of the film's release in 2009, he sat down with John Jurgensen of the *Wall Street Journal* for a lengthy interview and included John Hillcoat in the conversation; Jurgensen noted that the two men "showed easy affability in their friendship, despite what could have been a prickly collaboration." McCarthy reiterated his admiration for the adaptation, which he said absolutely "caught the spirit of the book," and also noted that like the Coens, Hillcoat "didn't need any help from me to make a movie." He emphasizes here that an adaptation is its own, independent artwork, and that "[y]ou don't embroil yourself in somebody else's project"—clearly desiring credit for the film to go to Hillcoat. It's also true, however, that after that 2008 screening in Albuquerque, Penhall and Hillcoat received four typed pages of notes from McCarthy that Penhall called "generous" and "extraordinarily useful." "Notes, at the best of times, are one of the world's great arse pains," said Penhall. But this was different: "Those four pages I should have framed." Though he wasn't involved to the extent he was on other projects, he was interested enough to trade thoughtful ideas with the filmmakers.

In that conversation Jurgensen also asked him what he thought of Thornton's adaptation of *All the Pretty Horses*, and McCarthy's verdict was that "[i]t could have been better." He goes on:

> As it stands today it could be cut and made into a pretty good movie. The director had the notion that he could put the entire book up on the screen. Well, you can't do that. You have to pick out the story that you want to tell and put that on the screen. And so he made this four-hour film and then he found that if he was actually going to get it released, he would have to cut it down to two hours.

McCarthy understands the curatorial approach as misplaced fidelity and criticizes that method of adaptation with regard to *Pretty Horses*. He doesn't discuss *The Road* in the same terms—though many critics did—and indicates that Hillcoat's film demonstrates the selectivity or interpretation that adaptation requires. Certainly *The Road* demonstrates that old stories are powerful—hence their appeal as well as their danger. They can drag the father back into the past but also propel the son into his future while providing him with a way to navigate those new experiences. It is the mother's story, however, that is narratively enlarged and yet philosophically impoverished in the film, a problem that is heightened, I think, when *The Road* is set against *The Sunset Limited*, in which the arguments for a commitment to a world with others and with God (as articulated by Black) and for the necessity of self-annihilation in the face of an absurd, violent, and isolating world (as articulated by White) are given full rhetorical and dramatic consideration.

In the end, *All the Pretty Horses* and *The Road*, which were made with such reverence for the original novels, seem to be haunted by them—though at the same time, neither film is quite as haunted as it should be. Both, after all, are stories about loss—of the West (or at least the idea of the West), of loved ones, of the world that once was. Deprived of that mythic long shot as a final scene, *All the Pretty Horses* ends rather prosaically. And *The Road* ends with a fairly clear sense of optimism for a restored world, tempered only by that minor tone overtaking the sounds of children playing during the final credits—an optimism that feels a bit false after the film has spent some one hundred minutes emphasizing the difficulty of survival. Both cinematic narratives flirt with tragedy but avoid it in the end.

In *The Road* the boy is a character whose personality—and perhaps even his divinity—is defined by his insistence on taking risks on people, on daring to reach out in even the bleakest of circumstances. McCarthy celebrates this quality even as he delimits it—the boy will probably not save all of mankind, like the protagonists of so many apocalypse films, as there are some things that really can't be made right again. Hope, however, is a sustaining force, even (or perhaps especially) in Hollywood, and adaptations of *No Country for Old Men* and *The Sunset Limited* would prove to be much more positively received interpretations of McCarthy's work.

CHAPTER FIVE

Tragic Success Stories

NO COUNTRY FOR OLD MEN AND
THE SUNSET LIMITED

*D*URING THE OPENING CREDITS OF TOMMY LEE JONES'S 2011 adaptation of *The Sunset Limited* for HBO, a train's headlights flash as it comes into a station, and the camera lingers on an apartment door's many locks, on an open window, a worn armchair, a beat-up refrigerator, a crucifix. Turn on the DVD's commentary track, and you can hear what those involved in the making of the film have to say about it. They introduce themselves. "Hello, my name is Tommy Lee Jones. I directed this little movie, and I play a character called White." "My name is Samuel L. Jackson, and I play a character named Black." Then comes the third—and rather surprising—contributor to this conversation: "And this is Cormac McCarthy, and I'm the playwright."

McCarthy allows Jones to take the lead in the conversation that ensues, listening to Jones's thoughts about camera selection and color processing and Jackson's about how people in backwoods Georgia told stories when he was a kid. For his part, McCarthy asks the others questions, muses a bit about hunting, Mozart, and chitlins, and notes that it's the four-hundredth anniversary of the King James Bible. The three make a good team, evidenced by their comfortable banter, but McCarthy is no last-minute addition. He was present for the shoot as well, one of only four people allowed in the room: Jones, Jackson, a script supervisor, and McCarthy (Hinckley). Together, with Jones in the director's chair, they took the story that McCarthy began as a novel and reworked as theater, and they turned it into film. (Note that McCarthy unambiguously calls himself the playwright despite the published play's equivocating subtitle "A Novel in Dramatic Form," which, as I noted in chapter 3, was probably not McCarthy's idea.) Once again, McCarthy played a significant role in the adaptation process and the result was a made-for-television film that, like *The Gardener's Son*, was praised by critics and considered a quiet success.

Nonetheless, that success was dwarfed by the sensation that was *No Country for Old Men*, a runaway hit that garnered four Oscars, three British Academy of Film and Television Arts awards (or BAFTAS), two Golden Globes, and recognition by the American Film Institute as a "Movie of the Year." More than any other project, this was the film that cemented the association of McCarthy and adaptation for the general public as well as for scholars and critics. These two film adaptations of *No Country for Old Men* and *The Sunset Limited* differ in their setting and their scope, though they share an iconic actor—Tommy Lee Jones appears in both—and they each engage with McCarthy's ongoing theme of male forays into unfamiliar territory. Unlike the films discussed in the last chapter, these were fruitful and celebrated projects with production histories unmarred by the kind of newsmaking disagreements that plagued *All the Pretty Horses*. Rather than that film's largely curatorial approach, these adaptations can be best described as superimpositions, to use another of Thomas Leitch's terms—films that "superimpose more or less explicitly identified coauthors on the material it borrows from literary sources" (100). And as I've explained in previous chapters, both are based on texts that can be understood as tragedies. The Coens' *No Country* in particular emphasizes that tragic arc, though like *The Sunset Limited* it also suggests the possibility of hope at the end of narratives suffused with considerable devastation and suffering.

NO COUNTRY AND ADAPTATION: THE CHARACTERS FAIL, BUT THE COENS SUCCEED

When McCarthy's novel *No Country for Old Men* was published in July 2005, many readers noted that both the style and storytelling seemed quite cinematic and that the book was a notable departure from his earlier novels. This is due at least in part to its own source material, McCarthy's original screenplay from the 1980s, though as I explained in chapter 2, McCarthy made drastic changes to plot, characterization, tone, and even genre when he adapted his own material from screenplay to novel. When he reviewed the Coens' adaptation in *Variety*, Todd McCarthy (the same critic who blasted the film versions of both *All the Pretty Horses* and *The Road*) noted that the novel has "built-in cinematic values" that the Coens used it "respectfully but not slavishly . . . cutting for brevity and infusing it with their own touch" (T. McCarthy, "*No Country*").

But although some film reviewers saw an inevitable progression from cinematic novel to literary film, some reviewers of the novel specifically denied its ties to cinema, perhaps because they wanted to claim it more definitively as literature. Adam Begley was careful to say that the novel is neither "an airport page-turner nor a screenplay in the making," and Patrick Beach noted—amusingly, in retrospect—that McCarthy writes rural and small-town folk so well, and without any condescension, that he's "not likely to write a screenplay for the Coen brothers anytime soon." McCarthy doesn't end up writing *for* the Coens, of course, but the Coens do end up writing *from* McCarthy. Even given all these associations, setting the novel and film against one another shows how well each works in its own medium—the novel *as* a novel and the film *as* a film.

Despite the Coens having worked with previously existing material before—most notably in *O Brother, Where Art Thou?* (2000), a cheeky reworking of Homer's *Odyssey*—they called *No Country* their "first adaptation," and told Charlie Rose, "Why not start with Cormac? Why not start with the best?" Their respect for the author is clear, though they exaggerate it to comic effect in another interview when they describe their process of writing the adaptation by saying that "One of us types into the computer while the other holds the spine of the book open flat" (Patterson). They joke that their adaptation is so devotedly curatorial they quite literally have altered nothing. Though much of the dialogue is indeed taken directly from McCarthy's novel and alterations to the plot are relatively few, the Coens' adaptation is more productively discussed as a superimposition. As an example of this kind of film, Leitch mentions the 1940 adaptation of *Pride and Prejudice*, which as he notes is less of a "Jane Austen film" (especially since there had been no previous adaptations of her novels for cinema) than "an Aldous Huxley film, a Jane Murfin film, even a Robert Z. Leonard film, and especially an MGM film," as that studio dictated a particular style that was characterized by "beautiful actresses, lavish but not necessarily historically accurate costumes and sets, expressive music, bright and even lighting, clear enunciation, and a tendency toward declamation" (101). *No Country for Old Men* provided ample material for the Coens to exercise their interest in eccentric characters, regional patterns of speech and behavior, an often dry humor, and eruptions of brutal violence, as well as their technical mastery of dramatic mise-en-scène. Of all the Coens' films, their adaptation of *No Country* has the closest ties with their first film, *Blood Simple* (1984), which is set in Texas and engages the neo-noir and crime thriller genres, and with *Fargo* (1996), which features a law officer pursuing criminals whose capacity for violence she finds mystifying. Despite their own joke about extreme fidelity, there are more viewers who would identify *No Country* as a Coen brothers film than as a Cormac McCarthy adaptation, and the finished film works as a superimposition of their interests, style, and narrative practice onto McCarthy's plot, characters, dialogue, and themes.

As was the case with *All the Pretty Horses* and *The Road*, the rights to *No Country* sold fast. When the novel appeared in July 2005, Scott Rudin immediately bought the film rights (Begley). By August the Coens had signed on to write and direct (Fleming, "Rudin Books"). Rudin arranged a production partnership between Paramount and Miramax, under which Paramount's specialty division would handle domestic distribution and Miramax the international release. By early 2006 Tommy Lee Jones was in negotiations to star, and Heath Ledger had been interested in a role—presumably that of Llewelyn Moss—but withdrew himself from consideration in favor of taking "some time off" (Thompson). Javier Bardem and Josh Brolin had joined in by April 2006, with Woody Harrelson and Stephen Root (a Coen brothers regular) rounding out the big-name gets in June (Fleming, "Coens"; Siegel, "Coens").

Jones and Bardem were cast without much fuss. Jones took the role of Sheriff Bell, not a considerable stretch given his West Texas roots and his previous acting choices. "I suppose I have played several Texas law enforcement officers," he reflected—likely thinking primarily about Woodrow Call in *Lonesome Dove* (1989)—"and actors live in constant fear of being typecast, but the attraction of working with Cormac McCarthy's material was overwhelming" ("Making of *No Country*"). How to cast Anton Chigurh was less clear, given McCarthy's deliberate ambiguity regarding the character's appearance and origins. Javier Bardem had already been eager to work with the Coens; when his agent asked him with whom he would most like to make a movie, the sibling team was his first choice. "I knew that never was going to happen," he said, "because the Coens always play these deeply profound American stories." As it turned out, the enigma that is Chigurh within this particular American story was a good fit for Bardem. "And then when they came to me and asked me to do this, I was really pleased and really surprised," Bardem remembered ("Working with the Coens").

Finding someone to fully embody Llewelyn Moss, however, was a more difficult task. "There was a somewhat lengthy search," commented Robert Graf, an executive producer on the film. "You need someone who seems ruggedly competent in a way, a real person who understands the country and really seems like they're from the country." "We thought it would be really easy," added Ethan Coen, "because in our minds it's kind of the regular guy. We thought, well, you know, we just need a good clean kid. It turns out that it's really not that easy to embody that without either being dull or not being of the region, which is a bad thing" ("Making of *No Country*"). Brolin heard about the role and sent in an audition tape that was definitely attention-getting—it was filmed by Quentin Tarantino and Robert Rodriguez, with whom Brolin was working on *Grindhouse* (2007). But it didn't make the impression he hoped for: "They watched it and their response was, 'Who lit it?'" Brolin commented. His agent kept trying to convince the Coens that he was the right one for the part and managed to get Brolin an in-person audition, which finally landed him the role (Murray). Once cast, everyone thought he was the "perfect choice," as Graf put it, and Brolin was happy he could draw on his childhood experiences growing up on a ranch ("Making of *No Country*"). Finally, the Scottish actress Kelly McDonald was an unusual choice to play Carla Jean Moss, given the directors' desire to choose actors who could authentically portray West Texas characters. Joel Coen noted that he was "very skeptical" about the idea but conceded that "[e]very now and then you come across someone who just has that facility with accents and who's that good an actor" ("Making of *No Country*"). With the principal actors in place, filming began in late spring of 2006 in New Mexico and Texas. The feature opened in November of the next year, a speedy production schedule compared to the delays experienced by *Pretty Horses* and *The Road*.

No Country for Old Men is a network of predators and prey. When Moss is introduced, he's hunting, and in the book he hikes past ancient pictographs, "[t]he men who drew them hunters like himself"—although being a hunter is no guarantee of survival, since of those hunters there is now "no other trace" than the fading images (11). The characters move among big, rough dogs, hawks, even cats scavenging some spilled milk from the scene of a shooting, and are hunted as much as they hunt others. Early in the film an unsuspecting motorist is confused when Chigurh approaches him. "What is that?" he asks. "What is that for?" Chigurh responds, "Would you hold still, please?" as he places the barrel of a captive bolt pistol—Chigurh's weapon of choice—on the man's forehead. Then he fires. The scene cuts to Llewelyn Moss painstakingly aiming his long-range rifle at an antelope on the plain below. "You hold still," he intones before pulling the trigger. Unlike Chigurh, Moss misses—he injures, but fails to kill, the animal he shoots. This repeated line of dialogue, shared between the two antagonists-to-be and not included in McCarthy's novel, emphasizes a number of things for the viewer: Chigurh's ruthlessness, Moss's impressive but still ineffective level of skill, and the two men's shared use of violence in a world of moving targets.

Moss's missed shot draws him down into the plain, tracking the animal he injured in order to kill it and relieve its suffering. When he sees another blood trail, it leads him eventually to the circle of shot-up cars and bodies, and then, with a bit more tracking on his part, to the money left over from the drug deal gone bad. That missed shot gets the plot moving, but it also prefigures the tragic arc his life will take. Richard Gilmore, who calls *No*

Country for Old Men a "tragic Western," argues that the introduction of Moss is in fact a "Greek tragedy in miniature" (62). Moss is clearly a very competent, patient hunter with a high level of expertise. All the details of the scene are "signs of his knowledge, his ability, his power, but the scene also shows his ultimate hubris, literally and figuratively. Instead of killing the antelope, he only wounds it, the worst possible outcome for a responsible hunter." As noted in the introduction, Gilmore writes that the Greek term hamartia is "derived from archery and literally means 'off the mark,' signifying that one's aim has been slightly off." In this case, when Moss takes his long shot, "[a]ll the elements of the movie are here, Llewelyn's talents as well as his misjudgments, as well as certain implacable facts of nature, distance, heat, the movement of the antelope.... His aim is good but not quite good enough" (62). Like Oedipus, also smart, competent, and well-intentioned, Moss is a "good but flawed man [who becomes] enmeshed in events that will prove to be his ruin" (60). And so when the antelope won't hold still, when Moss can't fire an effective shot, his tragic destiny is set.

Tragedy, however, isn't what most viewers bought tickets to see. Instead, the film initially looks like a combination of Western and thriller, genres built around the competent masculine protagonist. The opening of *No Country* immediately draws our attention to Western generic markers with shots of the landscape: all open spaces, slanting sunlight, and a lone windmill turning lazily. Sheriff Bell's voice-over narration complements these images with a history of local law enforcement in the region and his own family's history serving as sheriff. And as Robert Jarrett has noted, a series of what can ultimately be considered "false signals" also set up the film as a thriller: "Moss's initial escape in the arroyo, his ability to dress his own wounds, his ability to solicit medical help across the border, his canniness in concealing and then recovering the money, his arming himself with a cut-off shotgun. Perversely," Jarrett adds, "the narrative thus allows Moss to be misread as the American action hero" (62). Perverse, because although McCarthy's original screenplay of "No Country for Old Men" affirms the ideals of masculine confidence, endurance, and risk-taking, the ensuing novel and film do not. Ben Walters and J. M. Tyree have written that *No Country for Old Men*, and particularly Bardem as Chigurh, "[fit] satisfyingly into the Coens' ongoing interrogation of American manhood, which they present as always problematic and often absurd." The narrative's avoidance of conventional validations of masculine skill and resourcefulness may well be precisely what appealed to the Coen brothers.

Each of the three male leads embodies a different version of the masculine ideal and displays traits that, in thrillers and Westerns in particular, are celebrated markers of manhood—traits that, in a typical genre film, pay off in the end. Moss is the consummate opportunist, ready to seize good fortune when it comes by and (literally) run with it. He is clever and backs up that resourcefulness with formidable determination and optimism. Though Chigurh displays a similar ability to improvise and make productive use of his surroundings, his own character is more appropriately described as rational. His actions are not motivated by optimism, pessimism, or indeed by any emotionally inflected view of the world. He begins with his principles, and his actions follow in what he considers an entirely reasonable manner. Finally, before we even see him, Sheriff Bell's opening voice-over makes clear his respect for and adherence to tradition, particularly the tradition of Texas law and leadership. He laments, however, the changing times and what he sees as the general erosion of that respect. Bell, then, also wants things to "hold still."

Stories of masculine adventure and risk-taking often end with a protagonist bloodied and beaten but victorious over adversity. Think of *Shane* (1953), *Lethal Weapon* (1987), or even *In the Valley of Elah*, a film released the same year as *No Country* that follows Tommy Lee Jones as a father trying to uncover the circumstances of his son's death. His discoveries are horrific and painful, but they still enable him to piece together precisely what happened. In the end he prevails—he uncovers, untangles, and solves the mystery of the murder of his son. *No Country*, however, gives us a different kind of masculine portrait. Here, the three main characters are indeed variously bloodied and beaten down during the narrative, and yet in the end they do not prevail. Each of the three models of masculinity fails in his attempt at mastery. By its conclusion, however, the film has gone further than the novel and presented us with an alternative mode of engaging with the world, one that doesn't rely on the need to take control with the use of cleverness, stubbornness, rationality, tradition, or lethal force. The tragic hero, after all, always thinks he's in control until he realizes just how badly things are going. The alternative practice suggested by the film in the wake of the tragic events is based instead on renunciation and the surrender to those forces that are beyond one's control rather than repeated attempts at mastery.

In his opening voice-over, Bell reveals his strong nostalgia for the "old timers," and thus from the outset the film raises a lingering question about what constitutes this modern West. To a greater degree and more consistently than the thriller—a genre defined most basically by the emotional reaction it evokes and one that includes a number of types and subgenres—the Western leads us to consider the representation of masculinity and the assignation of power, since the genre is perhaps the ultimate venue for the display of male power as evidenced by the ability to overcome the wilderness as well as the bad guy. A number of critics have commented on this association, including Steve Neale, for example, who notes in his discussion of "masculinity as spectacle" that the male protagonists of the Western often rely heavily on narcissistic fantasies of power, omnipotence, mastery, and control; Neale draws our attention to icons like Clint Eastwood in *A Fistful of Dollars* (1964) and *The Good, the Bad and the Ugly* (1967), Tom Mix in his Westerns, and even Mad Max, a futuristic Australian Western hero (11). Framing her claim against those of scholars like John Cawelti, Will Wright, and Martin Pumphrey, Wendy Chapman Peek has argued that postwar Westerns celebrate a variety of masculine behaviors and character types rather than a single masculine ideal, just as long as the character in question is a) male and b) successful: "In Westerns, then, the most important thing is to be a man. The second most important thing is to be successful. Ideal masculinity matters only to the extent that it supports the other two, which may be not at all" (211). Control matters. *Winning* matters, and the ability to achieve that victory becomes the Western hero's defining characteristic, regardless of how—or even *if*—you wear your gun, hat, and boots. Men in Westerns are made of variously tough stuff. They get the job done and they do it with flair, to such a degree that their stories often have the qualities of myth and epic. They are fun to watch but perhaps more difficult to imitate. The Coens, however, are after something different.

Though *No Country* begins with Sheriff Bell's voice-over and soon shows us Chigurh, Llewelyn Moss (the third man to be introduced) seems to be our protagonist. His actions, and particularly his theft of the money from the drug deal, drive the film's plot and propel the two other men into pursuit. When Moss finds the circle of cars and bodies where a drug deal was to have taken place, he moves carefully through the scene with his gun at the ready, calm and unruffled by the carnage. When he finds one man barely alive and begging for "*agua,*" Moss asks him curtly about the "*último hombre,* last man standing." Moss finds the drug money by tracking that last man, who took the satchel that contains it to a stand of trees before dying from his wounds. From a distance, Moss crouches and watches patiently for any movement, then approaches with caution. When he opens the satchel and gets his first look at the money—a considerable amount, even at a glance—he remains largely unaffected. "Yeah," he grunts under his breath, thoughtfully affirming that the money isn't really too much of a surprise. Later, he returns home and hides the satchel under his trailer. His mood, as he sits next to his wife Carla Jean on the sofa, is light and confident. He deflects her questions about the satchel, the pistol he also took from that last man, and where he's been all day. "You don't need to know everything, Carla Jean," he chides her, and emphasizes his role as the head honcho when he warns, "You keep running that mouth of yours I'm going to take you in the back and screw you." But later that night, he makes the decision to return to the circle of cars to give water to the wounded man who had begged him for it. He admits to Carla Jean that he's about to do something "dumber'n hell," but that he has to do it anyway. Moss has demonstrated his opportunism as well as his caution, and here he shows himself to be principled, even though putting those principles into action conflicts with his highly developed pragmatism.

Moss, a Vietnam-era sniper, is no stranger to difficult territory, but when he's discovered returning to the scene, he finds himself on unfamiliar and dangerous ground. The erstwhile hunter has to take off in desperate, scrambling flight, eventually getting away but getting shot in the process. The Coens get the shot, too, filming that pursuit in a predawn darkness with a distant thunderstorm slashing the sky, and the camera shakes and jostles as it follows Moss's wild footrace in front of faceless pursuers in a pickup, its headlights and headlamps reaching out for him. As Moss stumbles over a ridge and down toward the river, the men stop the truck to continue firing at him and a pit bull vaults past them and over the ridge, launching itself into the river after Moss. Moss escapes the men as the day breaks, but the dog is still coming. After Moss swims downstream and exits the water, he has just enough time to ready and fire his gun before the dog attacks, knocking them both to the ground, the embrace of two figures who are predator and prey both. It's a sequence that exemplifies the superimposition of the Coens' sensibilities on McCarthy's narrative, as the Coens take a Hemingwayesque two pages describing Moss's flight to and down the river and create one of the set pieces of the film: the sky shifts subtly from thunderstorm to dawn just as Moss goes over the ridge; we can hear but just barely see his pursuers; and the tension is counterintuitively heightened by the near absence of a score (just a barely perceptible low tone underneath the gunshots, truck engine, and Moss's desperate breathing and footsteps). And then, of course, there's the dog, an addition that makes the scene simultaneously scarier and absurdly comic while also underscoring just how tenacious Moss's predators are going to be.

When Moss returns to Carla Jean, he is bloody and beaten up yet unrepentant about these new developments. "Baby, things happen. I can't take them back," he tells her. Moss is dismissive of the past, but he does have a plan for the future. On the bus, as he sends Carla Jean along to her mother's, he remains optimistic, telling her that his "good feeling" ought to balance out her bad one. "I shall return," he says with a smile, echoing that most masculine of military icons Gen. Douglas MacArthur speaking of his leadership in the Philippines in World War II. At this point in the story, Moss is still confident he can remain on top, eluding his predators to return to Carla Jean in triumph. Carla Jean wants to believe him. When Bell speaks with her, she tells him that "Llewelyn can take care of himself," that he never quits, that he

Llewelyn Moss (Josh Brolin) tries to escape the men pursuing him from the scene of a drug deal gone wrong in the Coen brothers' No Country for Old Men *(Miramax and Paramount Vantage, 2007).*

can "take all comers." But as the sheriff notes, Llewelyn has gotten involved with some "pretty bad people," notably Anton Chigurh.

Chigurh indeed poses a threat, and once he enters the scene, Moss's confidence begins to waver. In Eagle Pass, Chigurh follows the signal of the transponder hidden in the satchel of money to Moss's hotel room as Moss waits tensely on the other side of the door. Chigurh fires his captive bolt pistol to blow out the lock, Moss responds by firing his shotgun, and there ensues a running gun battle between the two men that wreaks havoc on the quiet town. Neither man makes the kill, but each manages to wound the other seriously. Moss suffers a debilitating wound in his side that gradually slows his movement from quick but considered action to literal unconsciousness. The wound is emasculating—Moss can no longer act with his characteristic speed and cleverness. Instead, he is reduced to bribing a trio of young men for a jacket to cover his bloody torso on the bridge into Mexico, and later he weakly offers a bloodstained bill to some surprised mariachis serenading him at dawn in exchange for "*médico*," or help finding a doctor. Instead of operating with masculine efficacy and power, Moss now has to rely on money as his only currency.

As a result of that wound, Moss is forced to spend valuable time recovering in a Mexican hospital and eventually crosses the border back into the States in his hospital gown. The border guard asks him how he "come to be out here with no clothes," and when Moss returns to the boot shop in Del Rio that he had recently patronized, he sheepishly asks the clerk, "You get a lot of people come in here with no clothes on?" The clerk affirms that it is, in fact, unusual. Moss is, of course, wearing clothes—he's just not wearing the utilitarian shirt and jeans that would mark him as a proper Texas man. He wears what is effectively a dress, and an insubstantial one at that. The imposed femininity of his outfit is so glaring in the masculine ethos of the Western that the border guard, Moss, and the clerk all refuse to refer to it as any kind of garment at all. His predicament is played for a joke, but the implications for Moss's masculinity are serious. As Peek notes, Western heroes may indeed have recourse to a range of variously domestic, intellectual, and violent abilities in order to achieve success and thus don't necessarily need to wear a particular masculine costume and behave in a particular masculine way, but here Moss's attire signals his loss of control—over his body, his clothes, and his appearance. If, as the title of Peek's article suggests, Westerns are a "romance of competence," Moss's gown does not indicate his proficiency. According to Moss's own way of seeing the world, he has been subtly coded as feminine in this highly masculinized environment. This, Moss seems to sense, is a bad sign.

When Carla Jean speaks to Bell again, her estimation of Moss has changed. This time, she tells Bell that "Llewelyn would never ask for help. He never thinks he needs any." She implies, of course, that he does need help now, and he needs it badly. But he doesn't get it. Before Bell can track him down, Moss is shot down by an anonymous gang of pursuers while waiting for Carla Jean in the El Paso Desert Sands Motor Hotel. Bell arrives at the scene, and the camera frames the aftermath of the shooting from Bell's point of view. We see a seriously wounded Hispanic man crawling on the ground, and then we see Moss's body, inert and bloody, inside a hotel room door. It comes as a shock, to Bell and also to the viewer. We are not accustomed, while watching Westerns, action movies, or masculine adventures of any kind, to seeing a scrappy, clever underdog succumb to his pursuers, especially not without a long, dramatic showdown. Here, Moss dies inelegantly, late in the story (though his is not the final death in the film), and because the exchange of bullets happens offscreen, he is not permitted to utter any memorable final words. Neither does the film allow him a *Butch Cassidy*-style freeze-frame glorifying his passing. He just ends up as a staring, broken corpse, one among others. Whether the fault was hubris, fate, his morally motivated but pragmatically misguided attempt to bring water to a dying man, or some combination of all those factors, his life ends tragically—a death that would surprise any viewers still believing they were in the theater for a Western thriller.

Most American viewers had not heard of Javier Bardem, who plays Anton Chigurh, before this film, although he became much more recognizable after he won the 2007 Academy Award for Best Supporting Actor for his performance. Bardem was, in fact, previously nominated for Best Actor for his role in *Before Night Falls* (2000) as the gay Cuban poet and novelist Reinaldo Arenas, and he received accolades for his performance in *Mar adentro* (*The Sea Inside*, 2004) as a quadriplegic who fights a twenty-eight-year campaign in support of euthanasia and the right to end his own life. That film won the Oscar for Best Foreign Film. Considering these roles, and inasmuch as American audiences recognized Bardem, he is cast against type as Chigurh, a coldly principled—some would say merciless—killing machine. That sense of intertextual juxtaposition, however, suits the role well, as Chigurh is a character who is in many ways unknowable. He presents himself as strictly rational, someone who plays by the rules of the game as he sees them. Those rules, however, are lethal. In the opening minutes of the film, a deputy takes him into custody. Back at the station, the deputy makes a phone call, assuring the sheriff on the other end of the line that he has things under control. He may think so, but as is so often the case, that control is just an illusion. Immediately after the man puts down the phone, Chigurh approaches him from behind and wordlessly strangles him with his handcuffs. The two fall to the floor, Chigurh struggling with the flailing deputy in a perverse and physically intense embrace. After a climactic spurt of arterial blood, the deputy goes limp and Chigurh slumps postcoitally, apparently pleased at his successful domination. This is one of the very few hints of emotion that we see on Chigurh's face during the film.

When he kills an unsuspecting motorist a few moments later, he does so with as few words as possible. He is laconic, effective, self-sufficient, and even principled—many characteristics that Robert Warshow identified as central to the Western hero, though Chigurh's propensity to shoot first, and often, clearly disqualifies him for that role. In a subsequent scene, Chigurh speaks more and reveals how he sees the world. He enters a gas station and speaks to the middle-aged proprietor standing behind the counter. Chigurh seems uninterested in that proprietor until the man asks in passing if he's been "gettin' any rain up your way." He further indicates that he has noticed Chigurh is from Dallas, gesturing at his car. When Chigurh responds that his whereabouts are none of the man's business, the man apologizes, but Chigurh does not accept the apology and extends the discussion in hostile and challenging terms to such a degree that the proprietor grows more and more uncomfortable. The man, clearly anxious to be rid of Chigurh, says he needs to close for the day. He admits, however, that he usually closes "about dark, at dark," though outside the sun still shines brightly. This prompts Chigurh to comment, "You don't know what you're talking about, do you?" He probes the man on his bedtime, his house, his marriage, and the details of his ownership of the station, and then suddenly asks, "What's the most you ever lost on a coin toss?" Chigurh insists the man call the toss and pick heads or tails. In explaining the value (or the necessity) of the coin toss, Chigurh emphasizes the coin's agency, the fact that "it's been traveling twenty-two years to get here. And now it's here. And it's either heads or tails." Indeed, the coin works as a proper divining tool because it *is* either heads or tails, and the man is free to choose either outcome. Regardless of this equal probability, one of those choices is clearly the better one for Chigurh. "Heads," or the use of reason, is far superior to "tails," the reliance on baser or more "animal" motivations, like emotion, passion, or desire. The proprietor's fear leads him to speak as if he "didn't know what he was talking about," and that earns Chigurh's disrespect. When the man calls "heads then," Chigurh uncovers the coin and responds, "Well done." Heads is the right answer—it keeps the man alive, but it also symbolizes rationality. Other characters call him crazy, though Chigurh clearly sees himself as reasonable and reasoning.

Chigurh operates largely unopposed for much of the film, although Moss manages to wound him with his shotgun during the battle in Eagle Pass. Chigurh pursues Moss into the streets, and when cornered behind a car, simply disappears. We next see him methodically gathering the resources he needs to attend to his wound. He steals medicine and first aid equipment from a pharmacy, rents a hotel room with a television for audio "cover," and lays plastic sheeting on the floor. Then we watch as Chigurh methodically cleans and disinfects the gaping wound in his leg. The camera lingers on it, making sure that we notice its severity. Chigurh is naked and perforated, clearly experiencing pain, and yet remains in total control. His expression is one of concentration, with perhaps a scant amount of irritation at having to attend to himself in such a way. Bodies, like emotions, are simply secondary to the mind and the will. He expresses the same kind of irritation with the Houston businessman whom he summarily dispatches in his office. The man gave the tracking receiver to two "executive types" who were also hunting Moss and whom Chigurh also shot. "That's foolish," he says of the decision to employ others and to give them the receiver. "You pick the one right tool."

Chigurh, as played by Bardem, is not conventionally coded as masculine by his physical appearance. He wears a denim jacket and jeans that would seem to be an attempt at Western attire, but their newness and neatness stand out in a region where well-used boots and broken-in clothes are more common. The oddity of his Prince Valiant haircut has, of course, been commented upon extensively in reviews and elsewhere, but its exacting arrangement makes sense on a man who has everything under control—emotions, employers, coiffure. Yet despite these deliberately off-center masculine tags, and despite the associations Bardem brings from his previous roles, Chigurh is nevertheless a hypermasculine figure. The emphasis on his rationality in all situations, his emotionless responses, and the impressive exertion of his will make this possible. His kill ratio, of course, doesn't hurt either, especially in a genre built on the fetishization of guns and their skilled use. Chigurh does indeed have the biggest gun.

Of course the Coens (and Cormac McCarthy before them) delight in surprising us with the moment when Chigurh's will is simply not sufficient, when he can't keep everything in front of him. As he drives away from presumably killing Carla Jean—implied in the film by a shot of Chigurh fastidiously checking his boots for blood after exiting her house—his car is unexpectedly slammed by another car running a red light. We see him checking his rearview mirror to monitor the position of two boys on bicycles as he proceeds through an intersection with a green light. The camera shoots Chigurh in profile from the right, and so when the other car smashes into his passenger side, the viewer is as surprised as Chigurh. No one sees it coming. Chigurh is clearly shaken as he exits the vehicle and must negotiate with those same two boys for a shirt to conceal his (very) broken arm. He offers money, just as Moss offered money for a jacket on the U.S.-Mexico bridge, because he seems to have run out of options. Though Chigurh limps away from the scene, down the sidewalk, and into an uncertain future, he has been reduced to being the object, rather than the subject, of violent action. The boys comment no less than three times on the bone sticking out of his arm. "Look at that fuckin' bone," one of them marvels, awestruck at the pitiable spectacle that is Chigurh, bleeding on the sidewalk. Even Anton Chigurh, whose masculine will to power is so formidable, is vulnerable in this world, and even the staunchest will is no guarantee of lasting mastery.

Though Moss and Chigurh are by no means one-dimensional, the third male character, Sheriff Bell, is the most complex of the three. He is by turns laconic and introspective, wryly humorous and deeply somber, dedicated to his job and doubtful about it. Bell is played by Tommy Lee Jones, a native Texan and the biggest star of the film, one who is imbued with Western masculine presence. An actor as well known as Jones brings with him associations of his previous roles (as film theorists like Richard Dyer and John Ellis have explained), and Jones himself noted the similarity of Sheriff Bell to characters like the steadfast and long-suffering Woodrow Call in the television miniseries *Lonesome Dove* (1989). Further, his parts in films like *The Fugitive* (1993) and *Men in Black* (1997) clearly traffic in that reputation of a rough man with deep but hidden feelings. More recently, his roles in *The Three Burials of Melquiades Estrada* (2005), which he also directed, and *In the Valley of Elah* (2007) show Jones portraying men steeped in masculine traditions—ranching in *Burials* and the military in *Elah*.

For audiences Jones brings associations with Texas and the Western, the idea of tradition and a longstanding method for accomplishing goals, the aura of leadership, and the qualities of a paternal figure. In *No Country*, however, he proceeds to ironize these associations by playfully making reference to them onscreen. While preparing to take two horses to investigate the scene of the drug deal, Bell and his wife Loretta (Tess Harper) exchange what seems to be an oft-repeated bit of conversation. "Be careful," she says. "Always am," he replies. "Don't get hurt," she adds. "Never do." And finally, "Don't hurt no one," she insists. Bell appears amused, and responds, "Well. If you say so." He mocks the very idea that he could be dangerous, much less lethal. Only if Loretta verbally forbids him, he jokes, will he refrain from actions better suited to a cowboy, a gangster, an action hero.

He also refuses to echo the language of Deputy Wendell (Garret Dillahunt) as they explore the scene of the crime, which Wendell introduces by saying that the "OK Corral's just yonder." As they examine the circle of cars and bodies, Wendell characterizes one set of killings as executions and the other as "Wild West." Bell will only acknowledge that if it's not a mess, "it'll do till the mess gets here." The scene, in his language, is sufficient, but he is reluctant at this early stage to allow for its excess. He certainly refuses to associate it with anything like a romantic or nostalgic Western atmosphere. When they later arrive at Moss's trailer and see that the lock has been blown out, Wendell gets excited. "We goin' in?" he asks, and Bell answers in the affirmative: "Gun out and up." Wendell complies, but seems confused by Bell's amused refusal to follow suit. "I'm hiding behind you," Bell whispers. Bell mocks the very masculine codes that his character summons up as a Texas lawman.

And yet as the film continues, that attitude toward his own role as a sheriff, a citizen, and a man slides from gentle self-mockery and amusement to real regret, even grief, as the killings escalate beyond his ability to curtail them. Those dead bodies eventually include Moss and Carla Jean, though Bell also laments the state of the world generally, as evidenced by young people's general lack of respect for their elders; he sees this in the abandonment of common conversational terms of courtesy, and, in more extreme fashion, in news items about serial killers preying on the elderly for their Social Security checks. Bell's sense of failure is most prominently emphasized in the film's denouement. After deciding to retire from law enforcement, Bell goes to visit his uncle Ellis and comments to the older man that he feels "overmatched." He regrets, he says, that God never came into his life as he got older. "I don't blame him," he adds. "If I was him I'd have the same opinion of me that he does." Here, Bell's self-assessment is openly damning, leading Ellis to chide him that "you don't know what he thinks." In the screenplay and the finished film, the Coens elect to cut a significant exchange that occurs between

The final two shots in No Country for Old Men. *In this, the penultimate, Bell's wife Loretta (Tess Harper) listens attentively and sympathetically as Bell describes his dreams.*

Bell and Ellis in McCarthy's novel. In it, Bell tells a story about his past that further emphasizes his sense of failure and his regret at not living up to his potential as a sheriff, a citizen, a man, and in the excised anecdote, a soldier.

In the novel, Bell introduces the topic with a question to Ellis: "Did you ever do anything you was ashamed of to the point where you never would tell nobody?" (272). He talks about receiving the Bronze Star for fighting off a group of German soldiers in World War II. He adds, however, that after repelling their initial attack, he waited until dark and then ran away, leaving behind a group of wounded fellow soldiers. Although he notes that he almost certainly couldn't have helped them, and further that if he had stayed he almost certainly would have been killed himself—and even further that he attempted to refuse the commendation—he still feels that his flight has tainted his entire life:

> If I was supposed to die over there doin what I'd give my word to do then that's what I should of done. You can tell it any way you want but that's the way it is. I should of done it and I didnt. And some part of me has never quit wishin I could go back. And I cant. I didnt know you could steal your own life. And I didnt know that it would bring you no more benefit than about anything else you might steal. I think I done the best with it I knew how but it still wasnt mine. It never has been. (278)

He and Ellis agree that Bell's father would have stayed at the scene, and Bell says that he thinks that makes his father the "better man." Ellis doubts that notion, but it does little to comfort Bell. McCarthy's novel takes pains to couch Bell's failure to catch Chigurh and prevent Moss's death within a

And in the final shot, Bell (Tommy Lee Jones) gazes pensively back, having absorbed the weight of his experiences.

much longer history of personal failure and loss, a level of detail that is more fitting for a novel than a film. Bell interprets this earlier inability to prevent the deaths of his comrades as a failure of his life as a whole—or, at the very least, as the rendering of his life as inauthentic, as something that he hasn't fully owned. He failed his community of brothers-in-arms, and despite the impossibility of saving them, he can't forgive himself for breaking their union by surviving. McCarthy's Bell sees the more recent events as a reinforcement and reminder of his ongoing weakness and inauthenticity—it's a level of repetition that echoes that of John Grady's and Billy's losses in the Border Trilogy and that gives the final loss additional resonance. In the film, however, we are encouraged to read Bell's weary posture and expression as primarily reflecting the burden of Moss's death alone. (In an additional departure from the novel, the Coens place Bell's conversation with Ellis before, rather than after, the scene between Chigurh and Carla Jean, and so presumably Bell is unaware of her impending murder.) Here, the death of one man is presented as more than enough to rouse feelings of inadequacy and to knock the wind and the spirit out of Bell.

The film ends with Bell in his sunny kitchen on one of the first mornings of his retirement, and this final scene provides an opportunity to consider the damage Bell's spirit has suffered as witness to these tragic events. He tells his wife about two dreams he had the night before, both of which also reflect a feeling of regret and loss. In the first dream, he meets his father in town. His father gives him money, which he loses. In the second, he and his father are on horseback at night, in the cold and the snow, riding through a pass in the mountains, like in "older times." His father rides by him, carrying fire in a horn "the way people used to do." Bell says that in the dream he knew that his father was going on up ahead to make a fire, "in all that dark and all that cold," and would be waiting for Bell when he arrived. "Then I woke up," he finishes. The scene lingers on Bell and Loretta's faces for another moment, and then cuts to black, the quiet sound of a ticking clock easing slowly into the music that will run over the credits.

Certainly it's an ambiguous ending, as various confused and outraged comments in theaters attested. But as Steven Frye and Benjamin Mangrum have argued with respect to the novel, I do think it indicates the presence of hope even in the wake of devastation and Bell's perception of his own failure. Bell and his wife sit in their sunny kitchen, and despite the taciturn quality of their back-and-forth banter, she is a patient and empathetic listener. If Bell is a witness to Moss's tragic fall, as Billy is to John Grady's, Loretta is a witness here to Bell's own suffering, echoing the woman Betty at the end of *Cities of the Plain*. Further, in the dreams that Bell relates, he recognizes what's of value—a connection with his father and the need to "carry the fire" through the darkness and cold, a sentiment directly reflected by the father and son in *The Road*. In the first dream, when his father gives him money, he loses it— he knows, as Moss didn't, that money isn't a worthy object of one's care and attention. Walters and Tyree aptly note that with the Bells' marriage generally "the Coens once again suggest that human connection trumps Hollywood-style man-alone heroism." Bell may fail at his task, but as a tragic witness, he may also learn a way of being in the world that values quite different qualities.

Noticeably lacking from the film is the climax we might expect from a story set in the West that employs the chase as a central element of the plot. There is no showdown between any of these men. Moss is killed by auxiliary drug employees, Chigurh's plans are thwarted by an anonymous driver, and Bell is either not quick enough or not motivated enough to keep himself in the game at all. Earlier in the film Moss and Chigurh do engage in the destructive gun battle in Eagle Pass, but the two men never face off, never exchange a line of dialogue, and neither kills the other. In fact, except for one brief shot in which the camera looks over Moss's shoulder at Chigurh diving behind a car, the two men never even appear in the same frame. If this can be considered a showdown of sorts, it is both unsatisfying and incomplete.

In fact, perhaps the most impressive showdown of the film occurs not between two of the male characters but between Chigurh and Carla Jean. In a film that hews so closely to McCarthy's source text, this scene marks the most notable change from the novel. There, Carla Jean initially resists calling the coin toss that Chigurh offers as a chance at staying alive. "God would not want me to do that," she says, but when Chigurh insists that "[t]his is your last chance," she submits. "Heads" (258). The coin is tails, and so she loses. She tries to argue, however, that it isn't the coin that makes the decision, that in fact Chigurh is the mover, "the one" here. Chigurh counters with a long explanation, arguing that in fact Carla Jean's death is both necessary and, in its own way and under Chigurh's principles, just. "You can say that things could have turned out differently," he says, "That they could have been some other way. But what does that mean? They are not some other way. They are this way. You're asking that I second say the world. Do you see?" (260). And, as the scene ends, Carla Jean answers in the affirmative. "Yes," she says, sobbing. "I do. I truly do." "Good," Chigurh responds, and shoots her.

In the book, Carla Jean is convinced by Chigurh's argument—she says that she understands. She assents to those principles that demand her death. But the Carla Jean we see in the film has quite a different reaction to her impending murder. She enters the bedroom where Chigurh is waiting, and the two are briefly framed in the same shot. Like the shot that framed Moss and Chigurh together, if only for a moment, this one looks over Carla Jean's shoulder at Chigurh. But unlike that earlier scene, no one runs away. They both sit and calmly discuss the situation. "You got no cause to hurt me," Carla Jean asserts. "No, but I gave my word," Chigurh responds. "That don't make sense," Carla Jean tells him, taking the rhetorical position more often held by Chigurh. Chigurh explains the necessity of killing her, but offers a coin toss as a chance to defy death. "This is the best I can do," he tells her. "Call it." Carla Jean once again responds by identifying what she sees as his fundamental irrationality: "I knowed you was crazy when I saw you sitting there. I knowed exactly what was in store for me." "Call it," Chigurh insists. "No. I ain't gonna call it," she counters. "Call it," Chigurh says, for the third time. But Carla Jean refuses, and sticks to her guns, so to speak. "The coin don't have no say. It's just you." Though Carla Jean dies, she admits no assent. She may be killed by Chigurh's bullet but she remains unmoved by his assertions of principle—her staunch and moral resolve uncompromised even in the face of what she recognizes as the darkest evil and at the cost of her life, a heroism that McCarthy celebrates elsewhere in characters like John Grady Cole. But McCarthy didn't write her resolve—the Coens did, their narrative superimposition here echoing the strong female characters who face down other villains in *Blood Simple* and *Fargo*.

Chigurh consistently proves formidably intimidating to the men he encounters. Even Carson Wells (Woody Harrelson), who is somewhat flippant about their association and Chigurh's character, reveals real fear when Chigurh finds him in the Eagle Pass hotel. Carla Jean, however, refuses to wilt, as does another woman in the film—the large, festively bouffanted woman working in the office of Moss's trailer park. When Chigurh comes looking for Moss, he hits what appears to be a literal and figurative brick wall. "Did you not hear me?" she asks in irritation. "We can't give out no information." When Chigurh pauses, considering the sound of a toilet flushing and thus the possibility of a witness, the woman watches him in consternation that threatens to escalate into physical action. For all Chigurh's skills at intimidation, they don't seem to work on these two women.

The real message of the story is perhaps provided by another young woman as well as an old, wheelchair-bound man, who are certainly nothing like traditional figures of masculinity. Near the end of the film, Moss waits for his wife at a motel in El Paso, and a girl by the pool tries to charm him into sharing a few beers. Does he keep looking out the window, she asks, because he's watching for that wife of his? "Lookin' for what's comin'," he replies. "Yeah, but no one ever sees that," she playfully chides him. Ellis echoes her a few minutes later when he talks to Bell, in a repetition that mirrors the two imperatives to "hold still" at the beginning of the film. When Bell comments that he feels overmatched by the things he's up against, Ellis responds that "You can't stop what's comin'." He further adds that to think you are in control of events in the world is not only incorrect but relies on the false assumption that you are more important than you actually are. "It ain't all waitin' on you," he says. "That's vanity." Instead, Ellis suggests that the proper course is to recognize the formidable forces that are beyond your power to shape, which are in fact "nothin' new" after all. "All the time you spend trying to get back what's been took from you more's going out the door. After a while you just have to try and put a tourniquet on it." Masculine mastery, he intimates, is not only an illusion but a dangerous one at that. In trying to hold on to what you feel is yours by right, you may be losing other aspects of your life: relationships, beliefs, some modicum of peace of mind.

No Country for Old Men reveals a particularly masculine dread, one that the structure of tragedy feeds and exacerbates—that you can't always keep things in front of you and under your control. Life won't hold still, waiting for the assertion of mastery. Danger approaches from all directions—in Chigurh's case, it comes from the side, and in a split second transforms a confident assassin into something like roadkill. You can't see it, and you can't stop it. Masculine doggedness will just get you into trouble. The film seems hostile to masculinity in animal form as well, as no fewer than three rough, tough pooches all get shot before the narrative has progressed very far. Moss sees one wounded pit bull as he approaches the site of the drug deal, another lies dead at the scene, and the third memorably gives chase when Moss returns that night. Despite this—well, this *doggedness*—all these animals suffer. The cats in the film, animals generally associated with feminine qualities rather than masculine, fare much better. A number of them swarm over and around Ellis, who is arguably the moral center of the film, and seem to have the run of his small shack. Perhaps more notably, in Eagle Pass, just about the time that Moss is figuring out what kind of trouble he's really in, he returns to the hotel lobby and sees that the man at the hotel desk has been killed. In front of the desk, a small cat happily laps at the milk that has spilled from its dish, presumably as a result of all this "fracas," as Deputy Wendell might have put it. But the cat—the feminine—makes a nice meal out of that spilled milk, no tears of regret in sight. In the end, the Coens' Western thriller emphasizes the renunciation of attempts to achieve and maintain masculine control. *No Country for Old Men* takes us from opening shots of wide open spaces to a final, close-up portrait of loss and, perhaps, acceptance.

Reviews of the film were almost universally positive; *No Country* has a 94 percent positive rating on Rotten Tomatoes. In their piece for *Sight and Sound*, Walters and Tyree called it "a pitch-perfect thriller that delivers the pleasurable fear and suspense expected of the genre even as it sends its conventions to the shredder." They go on: "It is masterfully designed and shot, with brilliant sound editing and perhaps the subtlest score in film history." A. O. Scott similarly praised its "tight editing, nimble camera work and faultless sound design," and called it "pure heaven." He noted the fidelity to the novel but made a point to praise the film as a film, saying that "the pacing, the mood and the attention to detail are breathtaking, sometimes literally" ("Hell to Pay"). David Denby, writing for the *New Yorker*, objected to the defiance of convention that so pleased other critics and was particularly disturbed by Moss's death. The Coens, "however faithful to the book, cannot be forgiven for disposing of Llewelyn so casually," he writes. After all our investment in his character, "[h]e doesn't get the dignity of a death scene." But as Dennis Rothermel has argued, "It could not be other if the story is to leave the trivial plot gratifications behind, among them the expectation that likeability guarantees virtue, which guarantees victory, which guarantees redemption, which guarantees affirmation of meaning and purpose" (193). It's an equation that McCarthy tried out in his 1980s screenplay and later definitively rejected in the novel, a rejection that the Coens embrace and superimpose with their own sensibilities.

As skilled as all these hunters are, there are simply no guarantees in this story that engages a number of genre expectations before turning them on their head. One of those expectations—so common to Hollywood films and so anathema to tragedy—is that even as they move amid new environments good men, or men who are mostly good, will prevail through a combination of skill, luck, and the support of a plot that is effectively rooting for them. But these men don't. Llewelyn runs alone and dies alone, Chigurh walks off bloody and alone, and Bell, despite his survival, can't help but feel responsible for the deaths of others. Each of them, in some way, fails—though on the other side of that failure, Bell seems to find some consolation in renunciation, an alternative way of engaging with the world and the suffering it in-

evitably causes. It's a kind of hope, though it's far from the victory and closure that Hollywood typically offers (and that McCarthy does as well in his
original screenplay). This is, rather, the promise of some small comfort in a
cold, harsh world.

THE SUNSET LIMITED: THIS TIME, THE CHASE IS ALL TALK

Like *No Country for Old Men*, *The Sunset Limited* is also a cat-and-
mouse story. But while the characters in *No Country* flee from and pursue
each other throughout the open landscapes of West Texas and Mexico, the
two men in *The Sunset Limited* are confined to a small, spartan apartment,
though their own various flights and pursuits are even more wide-ranging,
figuratively speaking. After McCarthy's play *The Sunset Limited* premiered
with the Steppenwolf Theatre Company in May 2006, it was produced and
performed in a number of different locations in the United States and abroad.
Then in the summer of 2009, Tommy Lee Jones signed with HBO to direct
and star with Samuel L. Jackson in a film adaptation of the play for that
network. Jones told David Carr that after he read the play, he and his wife
were having lunch in Santa Fe and talking about it. Jones commented to
his wife that he wished he could talk to Cormac. "[S]he looked up over my
shoulder and said, 'Hello, Cormac,' and there he was." That was the beginning of Jones's interest in adapting *The Sunset Limited* for film, and after that
conversation with McCarthy, "the first thing I did was send a copy to Sam"
(Hinckley). Samuel L. Jackson had been on McCarthy's mind as well—as
I noted in chapter 3, the author scribbled Jackson's name along with John
Malkovich's on a folder holding an early draft. Given that connection as well
as Jones's deep engagement with the project, the roles of Black and White
were easily cast. Despite the differences between Jones and Malkovich as
actors, McCarthy was pleased with the choices. "Tommy is a talented man,
and he's smart," he said. "That's really about all it takes for me, plus having
a genuine interest in the project, which I sensed right away" (Carr). Jones's
pitch-perfect performance as Sheriff Bell in *No Country* was likely an asset
as well.

And so Jones got to work, thinking of ways to make the film "visually
interesting" while keeping the focus on the two men and their conversation. "You can't shoot exteriors," he said, indicating his desire to keep the
entirety of the story inside Black's apartment, without recourse to prologue,
flashbacks, or other additional material. "[T]hat would simply kill it," he
explained (Hinckley). Instead, Jones took McCarthy's play—which has no
divisions into acts and scenes and no intermission—and broke it down into

fifty-two components in order to create a structure for the film. He then helped design a set with walls that could "fly" out of the cast and crew's way, so that the camera would be free to move around the two men (Carr). "We moved the camera a great deal," said Jones, "but only in service of the language and the actors. I had to keep the camera moving, but I didn't want to move it for its own sake. I didn't want it to be a shot that's about a camera. I wanted to make it a shot that was about Sam as he moved around the room" (Hinckley). The two actors' interactions, then, would provide the dynamism rather than an artificial inflation of the story with more characters or locations; the sole exceptions to the film's restriction to the apartment are seven shots of a train and train station that run during the opening credits, culminating in the film's title.

With those plans in place, Jones, Jackson, McCarthy, and the script supervisor moved in to a sound stage at the College of Santa Fe and closed the door behind them (Adams). Their work together went particularly well, Jones remembers. "[T]hose were some of the happiest, most creative days of the process. There was no argument, no dissent, no friction at all. We knew what we were doing, and we knew what we were going to do" (Hinckley). They shot the entirety of the play in sequence, though the film was later cut to ensure that its length was no longer than ninety minutes, a requirement from HBO; Jones estimated that about twenty minutes, taken from different places in the story, ended up being cut from their finished footage, and regretted having to lose even that amount (*Sunset Limited* commentary). Though the film does succeed in creating what Jones called "visual interest" with this kind of camera movement and mise-en-scène, and it avoids the static camera placement that would make the piece seem more like recorded theater, Jones still thought of the film as drama. "With just two actors, see this as a play," he said. "Performed by players. Pretty much of a single mind, we worked well together. There's a certain rhythm and careful thought in the performance. I hope Sam sees that in me. I see that in him" (Adams). In his interviews about the film, Jones emphasizes the seemingly conflict-free cooperation between himself, Jackson, and McCarthy, making a point to note that McCarthy was involved but not dictatorial about the way the story was performed. "He listens, and talks a little bit about each scene," Jones says in the "making of" short included on the DVD. "He simply collaborates with us." That sense of an enjoyable, simpatico relationship is an ironic mirror of the story itself, pitting as it does two men of vastly different life experiences and worldviews against one another in a rhetorical contest that is part dance and part boxing match.

Jones had previously directed just one other film, *The Three Burials of Melquiades Estrada*. As such, the superimposition that occurs with his adaptation of *The Sunset Limited* has less to do with Jones's directorial style than with the associations and interpretations that Jones and Jackson bring to their roles as actors. Jackson is best known for playing smooth-talking urban criminals in Quentin Tarantino's *Pulp Fiction* (1994) and *Jackie Brown* (1997), for taking the title role in the remake of *Shaft* (2000), for headlining the so-bad-it's-good phenomenon *Snakes on a Plane* (2006), and more recently for appearing as Ultimate Nick Fury in a number of movies based on Marvel comics, like *Iron Man 2* (2010) and *The Avengers* (2012). (In fact, Jackson and Jones both appeared in 2011's *Captain America: The First Avenger*, Jackson as Fury and Jones as Col. Chester Phillips.) Because of his choices and how often he works, in 2011, the year *The Sunset Limited* premiered on HBO, Jackson became the highest grossing film actor ever (Powers). As an actor, then, he is a familiar presence, and audiences would tend to associate him with verbal dexterity and physical grace. Here, his appearance is similar to his apartment—worn but tidy—and his short hair and beard are going substantially gray. He wears a work shirt labeled "Lennox Ave Industries," suggesting his blue-collar status, though neither the film nor the play ever makes clear exactly what Black does for a living. The label, which is not included in McCarthy's description of Black in the play, may be an oblique reference to Lenox Avenue in Harlem, which is named for the philanthropist James Lenox and since 1987 has also been called Malcolm X Boulevard. The street is in an area that was central to the Harlem Renaissance and home to many different groups of immigrants, precisely the kind of place that might inspire Black to make the stew that he heats up for White in the middle of the film.

Tommy Lee Jones, as I mentioned earlier in this chapter, is known for playing Western heroes—tough, laconic men whose experience is communicated more by the lines on their faces than by any words they might say. Though as an actor Jones appears to have spent more time outside than your typical professor might have, White certainly begins the film laconically, and in his rumpled, unkempt state does look like someone who's been suffering quietly for a long time. He has a scraggly, mostly gray beard and wears baggy trousers and a black jacket over a maroon long-sleeved polo shirt, a slight departure from the white T-shirt and matching running pants and jacket that McCarthy describes in the play (3). Instead of looking worn but tidy, as Jackson does as Black, Jones as White looks worn and wilted; everything about his appearance and clothes seems to sag, though it's clear that his intelligence is sharp as ever. For much of the film, Jackson as Black displays a confidence and mastery of rhetoric that viewers would find familiar from his other roles, and Jones a dour terseness that he's played before in films like *Lonesome Dove* and *The Fugitive*. By the end of the film, however, those associations have been undone and in some sense reversed—one of the pleasures of the film is watching these two Hollywood icons play on their own associations as actors in order to embody characters whose familiarity to the audience recedes as the film goes on.

The two characters are introduced in close-up, each gazing pensively—Black at White, and White rather vacantly off to Black's right. A close-up of White's hand, flexing slightly as it rests on the table, emphasizes his quiet discomfort. Black speaks the first line of dialogue—"So what am I supposed to do with you, Professor?"—and from there the conversation begins. As Jones directs the film, the majority of Black and White's interaction happens at the kitchen table—an echo of that table in *The Road* that hosted the mother and father's conversations about the justification for suicide. As I noted in chapter 3, at least one theatrical production of the play rose to the challenge of confining the actors to the table for the entirety of the story, allowing the dialogue to be the central—in fact the only—place where the action was happening. But Jones doesn't take quite so restrictive an approach, and in the film the two characters also move around the apartment, rising to look out a window, make coffee, or sit on the red sofa and green chair, also in the same room. When Black asks White what his father did for a living, Jones slumps down on the sofa while Jackson sits in the chair behind him like an analyst querying his patient—though of course none of White's previous attempts at therapy have ever done him any good.

The center of the two men's engagement, however, and the center of the apartment generally, is the table that they joust around, eat off of, and occasionally strike to make a point. The table is, notably, round—a difference from most, if not all, of the previous stage adaptations—a feature that allows Black and White to move, by degrees, closer to one another or farther apart. At times the two sit directly opposite one another, but White scoots closer to Black when he entreats Black to let him go home, promising not to kill himself en route, and Black scoots closer to White when he wants to make his point about White having "more elegant reasons" for suicide than the general rabble. As the discussion ebbs and flows, Jones allows the camera to cross the axis of action, which is generally verboten in the classical Hollywood style. As a result, neither character is continuously on the same side of the frame and neither is always "in the right" either literally or figuratively. And as they drift around the table, their faces frame different parts of the apartment—the locked door, the sink, a bare wall.

That round table allows Black and White to drift into each others' rhetorical spaces as well. Black is a person who reaches out to others, and White is in retreat, or outright recoil, from everyone. Black says that the truth he knows is that "you must love your brother or die," while White wishes, longs for "No community . . . Silence. Blackness. Aloneness. Peace." Yet their conversation reveals that the two aren't so philosophically distant as they might suppose.

White (Tommy Lee Jones) and Black (Samuel L. Jackson) are close together but still far apart in Tommy Lee Jones's The Sunset Limited *(HBO Films, 2011).*

Black fulfills White's request for a "jailhouse story" and tells about how his fight with a fellow inmate left the man horribly and permanently injured but also led to his own religious conversion. As Black, Jackson stands and gives the story its full dramatic heft, even pantomiming striking White as he tells about "wailing on this nigger's head" with a table leg. It's a performance, and it even leaves him somewhat out of breath—as a monologue, it holds its own against similar Jackson set pieces in *Pulp Fiction* (1994) and *The Hateful Eight* (2015). Speaking as the director, Jones says that he was aware that the original Steppenwolf production chose to perform this sequence in quite an understated fashion, but that he wanted "a different approach," something closer to "commedia dell'arte, a narrative that is performed." He compliments Jackson on his ability to make this a one-man show: "One of my favorite moments in the jailhouse story is when Sam changes points of view instantly, just with his own body. He points and looks up at the guard up on the rail, and then he becomes the guard, and points the shotgun down. With one [camera] shot that doesn't move, the narrative point of view is changed, it's demonstrated. It's a reverse that doesn't cut" (*Sunset Limited* commentary).

Jackson infuses the story with all the anger and violence of the moment—and yet, after all, this is ultimately a story about finding God, a point that White latches onto quickly. It's a "strange kind of story," he says, one in which "a fellow prisoner became a crippled one-eyed halfwit so that you could find God." It's not an easy claim to dismiss, and in fact Black never directly addresses it—how his understanding of the human community and the divine stemmed from a moment of literal and figurative destruction. In a similarly paradoxical fashion, White would seem to be a person who hates people, and yet his desire for suicide is at least partially based on the crushing pain the world has had to endure. His lament takes as its premise the value of human life—all of it. If everyone matters, then everyone's pain adds up, and that sum is devastating both for the world and for White. As the story reaches its conclusion, White is finally convinced by Black to articulate his view of the world, and he does, describing the world as a "forced labor camp" and confessing how he yearns for the darkness and release from the "torment, betrayal, loss, suffering, pain, age, indignity, and hideous lingering illness." As White, Jones delivers these lines in a more understated fashion than Jackson, speaking them as if he is slightly amused by them but also as if he recognizes the rhetorical power they will certainly have. Just as some of Black's more forceful statements of faith are underlined by a subtle, sustained tone in the film's score, White's statements here are similarly scored, emphasizing their importance and highlighting that force. The force builds. When Jones makes the point that "if that pain [human pain] were actually collective instead of simply reiterative then the sheer weight of it would drag the world from the walls of the universe and send it crashing and burning through whatever night it might yet be capable of engendering until it was not even ash," he performs a bit as well, raising and then lowering his hand as if to illustrate the physical weight of that collective pain. The score echoes him, and it reaches a subtle crescendo at the end of his statement that reflects the power of his words and their effect on Black.

As different as they are in their backgrounds, lifestyles, and chosen responses to suffering, Black and White do share some important qualities: the performative nature of their engagement with each other, their ability to both see the humor in the other and to take the other's points very seriously, and their enjoyment of the meal they eat together. Even their worldviews aren't entirely separable—one man is dedicated to loving others but had to hurt someone in order to realize that dedication. And another man is "disgusted" by his fellow man and yet so deeply empathizes with the suffering of others that he can't stand to keep drawing breath. Despite that overlap, however, as the film ends the two men's irrevocable disagreement is clear. Their roles have reversed: White has taken over as the rhetorical master, and Black is now the quieted one. *The Sunset Limited* becomes a Jones and Jackson film as well as a Cormac McCarthy adaptation through those two actors' engagement with and then upending of their own typecasting.

White finally wrests himself away, and Black has nothing to do but unlock the locks of his apartment door and allow him to leave. "Thank you," Jones says pleasantly. "Goodbye." He exits, leaving Black shaken and grieving and angry at God. Jackson shouts, physically very agitated, asking God why He didn't give him the words to save White. He stumbles to his sofa and moves to sit, only to collapse down to the floor. He gathers himself, assuring God that it's all right, that he'll keep His word and his faith. The scene, which had focused on Jackson from a slightly elevated angle, then cuts to a more strikingly composed shot. Jackson is centered in the frame, the camera at about the level of his heart, his hands resting on his knees and his eyes turned upward. Behind him, dawn is visible through the window. After the agitation of the final confrontation between the two men and Black's anger and sadness, this shot has a sense of stillness. Jackson speaks the film's final lines: "Is that okay? Is that okay?" And then the camera slowly zooms over his right shoulder and out the window, all the way into the rising sun, as the film fades to white and the credits begin to roll.

As I discussed in chapter 3, William Quirk has called McCarthy's play a minimalist version of a Nietzschean tragedy, as it sets the Apollonian character of White against the Dionysian character of Black, a tension that Nietzsche argued defined tragedy and is finally resolved in the annihilation of the Apollonian and the ascendance of the Dionysian spirit of unity and revelry. Jones's interpretation of the play hews to this sense of closure, as White disappears, lost to Black, but the rising sun counters what might otherwise be a final emphasis on isolation.

Because "the most widespread symbol of the deity over the centuries has been the sun," Jones notes, "I thought that's how we would go out—we would just watch the sunrise and move into it." He calls Black's final words "the most important speech of the play" (*Sunset Limited* commentary) and has said that he thinks it's a "pretty happy ending [for Black] as far as I'm concerned" (Carr). Uplifting music plays over the credits, which Jones says is "about different notions of God" and has a final effect that is "harmonious." Jones is clear in his emphasis on hope in the wake of devastating loss. The music in the credits, however, finally fades out and is subsumed by the sound of a ticking clock that increases in volume, as well as the sound of a train. Final aural reminders, perhaps, that time and death—in the form of a clock and the Sunset Limited—are always waiting for us. It's a moment of final ambiguity echoing that in Hillcoat's *The Road*, where the sounds of children playing heard over the credits fade into a low, sustained tone.

Reviews of Jones's adaptation were positive, and several noted the challenges of filming a story like this one. Two separate reviewers in the *Washington Post* and *Variety* used the word "stultifying" to describe what it's usually like to watch a two-person stage play put to film, though they then go on to call this one "beautiful," "thought-provoking," "eminently watchable," and "hypnotic" (Stuever; "*Sunset*"). Bill Brownstein noted the essential hybridity of Jones's approach and suggested the kind of resistance that such hybridity can engender: "Theatre folk may feel that it plays more like a film," he writes, "and film folk may feel it plays more like theatre. Both factions are right: *The Sunset Limited* plays like filmed theatre, which is what most would label a piece driven by dialogue and performance and bereft of car chases and apocalyptic eruptions." Jones's film, Brownstein implies, successfully avoids the easy lures of action-movie magic and instead manages to tell a real human story.

At the end of the Coens' *No Country for Old Men*, Bell and his wife Loretta sit at their breakfast table, and in the face of the darkness of the world, Bell conjures his dreams as she listens. Black and White sit at a different table in *The Sunset Limited* and find momentary flashes of understanding in their shared meal and storytelling. In both films, the Apollonian ideal of order, reason, control, and individualism fails, but instead of resorting to nihilism, each also suggests the possibility of community and hope as responses to tragedy. Human relationships may be the source of much of our suffering—that suffering being both the effect and the very substance of the changing world around us—but they are also sustaining, a glimmer of light in the encroaching darkness.

CHAPTER SIX

Great Expectations

THE COUNSELOR AND *CHILD OF GOD*

*A*S I'VE NOTED IN PREVIOUS CHAPTERS, CORMAC MC-
Carthy's career has seen a number of dramatic turning points:
1992's *All the Pretty Horses* made him both rich and famous; 2006's *The Road*
won him a Pulitzer and an appearance on *The Oprah Winfrey Show*. In 2012 he
became an executive producer on a film for which he had written the screenplay, a story that I'll tell in this chapter. McCarthy's engagement with film
and media culture, however, didn't go so far that he sought out additional
interviews or opportunities to talk about his work. Nonetheless, in 2014 his
name was repeatedly mentioned on the talk-show circuit, as James Franco
advertised his adaptation of McCarthy's third novel, *Child of God*—a short,
lyrical character study of Lester Ballard, a man whose eviction from his family
home and shunning by his community leads him first to petty crimes and
eventually to necrophilia and serial murder.

Franco had long been a fan and student of McCarthy's writing and
worked hard to raise the profile of his low-budget film featuring admittedly
challenging subject matter. He wrote several pieces for the web site *Vice* about
McCarthy, one of which discussed "Wake for Susan," a little-known short
story that McCarthy wrote in college, and he released a twenty-five-minute
test reel that he had made years earlier for an adaptation of *Blood Meridian*—
all with the goal of stoking interest in McCarthy generally. He did a number of interviews on television and in print, including an appearance on *The
Tonight Show* in which he joked around with host Jimmy Fallon about how
to take a proper selfie, of which Franco has been a prominent practitioner
and proponent, defending the creation and dissemination of these digital
self-portraits in the *New York Times*.

Franco then appeared on *The Colbert Report* on 30 July 2014, two days
before his film was to premiere in New York. Stephen Colbert, hosting the

satiric news show in his usual persona of a self-important right-wing pundit, began by noting Franco's many different pursuits, evidenced (to list only a few) by the film, his recently published book of poetry *Directing Herbert White* (2014), his intermittent appearances on the soap opera *General Hospital*, and the classes he teaches at UCLA and USC: "Well, James, you're an Academy Award–nominated actor, you're a poet, author, photographer, painter, you're a conceptual artist, teacher ..." Franco acknowledged his busy schedule, and Colbert responded, "This is what worries me. Do you have time for a family?" The concerned comment was appropriate for Colbert's conservative guise, but it also reflected an observation that many stories about Franco tend to include: the ambitious, nearly frenetic pace of his professional and artistic life.

Franco responded with some ambivalence and then, at Colbert's prompting, proceeded to talk a bit about *Child of God* and Lester, its protagonist. "He becomes a murderer and he's a necrophiliac," he says. "It's really an exploration of what it is to be human and need intimacy with another person so badly, and that if you are a person who is incapable of doing that because you're so strange, or you're an outsider ..." Colbert then jumped in: "Or so busy teaching and doing movies and books and that kind of thing that you can't actually allow yourself to have that kind of relationship and get married and have children."

Franco laughed, of course, but Colbert had just unwittingly demonstrated both the strength and the weakness of this *Child of God* adaptation. As I'll discuss and as Franco indicates in this brief comment, he sees Lester as human but also as someone whose strangeness sets him apart in a fundamental way, who is irreparably Other. As interpreted here by Franco and by Scott Haze, the actor playing the lead role, Lester certainly declines during the course of the story, but he's fairly crazy to begin with, too. Lester's really not like you and me, Franco suggests.

But Colbert upends that assumption by linking Lester's lack of intimacy with his playful recognition of Franco's own. For Colbert, Lester's not so different after all—and that view is more in line, I think, with the character that McCarthy describes in his novel. Franco brings a multitude of talents and abilities to an adaptation like this—and that is a great strength—but his film misses the point that Colbert pounces on here, that Lester really *is* "much like yourself perhaps," as McCarthy writes.

Their discussion of *Child of God* was brief, as it tended to be in Franco's television appearances. In fact, this particular interview made the news not because of the film but because of two unrelated exchanges between the host and the guest. Colbert asked Franco to take a side concerning the recent scuffle between actor Orlando Bloom and pop star Justin Bieber; Franco noted his opinion and the gossip columns duly reported another vote for

"Team Orlando." Then, as Colbert began to close out the segment, Franco leaned in and pressed the host on one last point. "I will see you on the new show," he said, referring to Colbert's upcoming replacement of David Letterman on *The Late Show*. "Now, are you going to go Democrat when you go to the new show?" He was curious, as many had been, what it would be like to see Colbert out of his conservative persona, doing "straight" comedy instead of constant satire. "Now, here's the interesting thing," Colbert responded without missing a beat. "I don't know what the fuck you're talking about."

It was a great moment for Colbert, who has made a career out of spinning surprisingly complex layers of performance with lightning-fast retorts, but I also like the interview as a whole for its fascinating addition to a consideration of McCarthy, adaptation, and interpretation: two actors, each of whose career has been defined by keeping people guessing when their mask is on or off, talking about a character (or, more precisely, an interpretation and performance of a character) that, more than any other in McCarthy's oeuvre, has provoked discussions of community and of personal adaptability. And in the last few years, James Franco, for better or for worse, has probably done more to champion McCarthy's status as a great American writer than anyone else.

McCarthy's place in American culture in the second decade of the twenty-first century, however, is also defined by *The Counselor* (2013), his most recently published work and a film directed by Ridley Scott. On the surface, *Child of God* and *The Counselor* couldn't be more different—Franco's a low-budget production with an art-house aesthetic and Scott's a big-name extravaganza with plenty of studio firepower behind it. Both films, however, followed a similar trajectory: a great deal of media attention for each project followed by generally negative and sometimes even vituperative reviews, followed again by cautious reconsideration. Even when the films' quality was in question, the projects' connection to McCarthy made them interesting enough to be the subject of extensive, considered, and ongoing discussion.

As I've noted, McCarthy has directly identified *The Counselor* as a tragedy: "The counselor is a classic figure in tragedy," he said. "He's a decent guy who gets up one morning and decides to do something wrong. And that's all it takes" ("The Counselor" commentary). Even more than Llewelyn Moss, the counselor fits the generally Aristotelean model of a man of status whose hamartia (which McCarthy implies is an error, or bad choice, though in this case it could also be productively understood as a character flaw) sets him on a path that leads to his downfall. But as Russell Hillier has argued, *The Counselor* is more than the Aristotelean tragedy of the title character. As written, it's also Malkina's revenge tragedy, though the elements of that revenge are then eliminated from the film. Similarly, James Franco's adaptation of *Child of God* blunts the force of Lester Ballard's tragedy—which, like Robert Mc-

Evoy's in *The Gardener's Son*, can be understood (in René Girard's terms) as the result of exile from his community. Here, Franco skirts tragedy by emphasizing Lester's difference rather than his ostracism and also by ending the film on a triumphant note. *The Counselor* and *Child of God*, then, can be compared to the film adaptations of *All the Pretty Horses* and *The Road* in that they dilute the source texts' tragic content, though certainly *The Counselor* still presents a devastating plot and resolution. That in itself doesn't explain why the films haven't been considered successes, however. While neither film appears to have been bound by the restrictions of a curatorial approach—as *Pretty Horses* and *The Road* were, at least in part—neither achieves a productive superimposition of the kind that works well for *No Country for Old Men* and *The Sunset Limited*. Most particularly, the presentation of Lester Ballard in *Child of God* and Malkina in *The Counselor*—the result of a combination of directing, casting, acting, and costume design—has the effect of making those characters less rather than more interesting and, in Malkina's case, even openly offensive.

THE COUNSELOR: DROPPING A BOMB ON HOLLYWOOD

In January 2012 Amanda "Binky" Urban, McCarthy's literary agent, was expecting him to deliver his new novel, reportedly called *The Passenger*. Draft materials of the book date back at least to 1999, and the rumor was that it would be a long and substantial opus. She was surprised, then, to instead receive a screenplay called *The Counselor*. The story is reminiscent of *No Country for Old Men* in that it follows a man who buys into a high-stakes drug deal, though this time the story is set contemporarily rather than in 1980, the plot is even more labyrinthine, and a female character plays a major rather than auxiliary role. The word was that McCarthy had taken a bit of a break from the novel and written the screenplay in about five weeks as a kind of palate cleanser (Tonkin).

To say that Hollywood was excited by the news is an understatement. Almost immediately, Nick Wechsler and Steve and Paula Mae Schwartz, who were also producers on *The Road*, bought it in what was described as "a sizable deal" (Fleming, "Pulitzer Prize"). When Ridley Scott saw it, he thought it was "one of the best screenplays [he had] ever read," and arranged to meet with McCarthy and make a pitch for the job of directing it (McClintock). The meeting happened in Albuquerque within thirty-six hours, and Scott said that a handshake sealed the deal (Dean).

In February Michael Fassbender signed on to play the leading role, reuniting with Scott after their previous film together, *Prometheus* (2012). Then began a host of speculation about which big-name stars would fill the remaining roles. News items appeared mentioning Javier Bardem, Jeremy Renner, Brad Pitt, Angelina Jolie, and Penélope Cruz, with reporters duly noting that the list of possibilities included two of Hollywood's most famous couples, Pitt/Jolie and Bardem/Cruz (Fleming, "Top Actors"; Pulver, "Brad Pitt"; Pulver, "Penelope Cruz"). By July, Jolie had dropped out of consideration, but Pitt, Bardem, and Cruz had all been confirmed along with Cameron Diaz and Rosie Perez for a small role (Kroll). The high-flying cast had ten Oscar nominations among them. Mike Fleming called these developments "a most charmed path" for the film. Scott also noted the speed with which he was able to complete the casting—"in a matter of weeks"—and attributed that luck to McCarthy's screenplay: "You would not get this level of cast in one film, so it would have to do with the quality of the script" (Fleming, "Top Actors"; "Scott: I Love"). The film began shooting in London and Spain in the summer of 2012, but was halted briefly in August when Tony Scott, Ridley's brother and the director of a number of films, including *Top Gun* (1986), *The Last Boy Scout* (1991), *True Romance* (1993), and *Unstoppable* (2010), committed suicide in California. Ridley Scott later dedicated the film to his brother, although the dedication is uncredited. Production then continued with the film slated for release on October 25, 2013, a finish line less than two years after the screenplay had first appeared in Hollywood.

As he had been with *The Gardener's Son*, McCarthy was heavily involved in the making of *The Counselor*, unlike his relatively minimal influence on *All the Pretty Horses*, *No Country for Old Men*, and *The Road*—which makes sense, given that he didn't write the screenplays for those three adaptations. He signed on as executive producer of *The Counselor*—no small commitment—and also approved Scott as director, weighed in on casting as well as final edits, and was on set for about forty days of filming overseas. "He was there every day," remarked Fassbender, "and if I was getting something wrong, he'd let me know." This was all quite deliberate, noted producer Nick Wechsler: "Cormac wrote it with the intent of being involved from beginning to end" (Alter).

All the big names, not least McCarthy's, made *The Counselor* seem like a sure bet for some, and in the early fall the film began to appear on "must-see" and "Oscar watch" lists ("2013 Must-See"; Lacey; Odam). Writing for *The Guardian*, Michael Hann predicted that the film would be a contender in "[a]ll the major categories, probably. A script by McCarthy—unless it proves to be an unspeakable mess—will surely be a shoo-in for a best original screenplay nom, which would then open the door for best picture and a fourth best-director nomination for Scott. How the actors divvy up the supporting and lead nominations is likely to be the main point of doubt."

In addition to trailers and standard advertising, Scott commissioned what he called a "viral video" to be released before the film's premiere. Directed by Johnny Hardstaff, who did similar pieces for *Prometheus*, the two-and-a-half-minute vignette shows the counselor buying lingerie at an upscale boutique from a saleswoman played by Natalie Dormer, who appears in the film as a different character, a blonde hired by Malkina to seduce Westray ("Johnny Hardstaff"). The vignette is unsettling, as Fassbender plays the scene with an intensity that hints at a predatory nature—he instructs the saleswoman on the provenance of good silk and tells her that "you should wear stockings" instead of pantyhose. The interaction is flirtatious but scored with an insistent, sustained minor tone. As he leaves the shop, the audio is taken over by what sounds like an exchange on police radio about the victim of a crime. In this scene, which was never intended to be included in the film but merely to stoke interest in the character, the counselor comes off as knowledgeable, charming, and rather dangerous. As he leaves the shop, the saleswoman watches him go, her smile faded into a slightly troubled expression, as if something just happened that she can't quite assimilate.

A different kind of teaser was published by the *New Yorker* in its 10 June 2013 issue, a piece credited to McCarthy and described as a selection taken from "the screenplay for the forthcoming movie." The excerpt, titled "Scenes of the Crime" and which includes sections taken from several scenes early in the screenplay, has no dialogue—it consists entirely of action descriptions that follow the progress of a septic tank truck holding fifty-five-gallon drums of cocaine and a motorcycle rider who is decapitated by a wire strung carefully across a deserted road. Gathered together like this, the descriptions are dense and not easy to follow, though they do serve as a detailed, technical introduction to the methodology of smuggling drugs in septic trucks and decapitating a speeding biker.

This action-only excerpt was an interesting contrast to the way that those working on the movie perceived the story—the *New Yorker* piece focused totally on work and movement, while the film itself was seen to have a much heavier emphasis on dialogue than is the norm. It was that quality that "riveted" Fassbender, he said: "It was unusual that it was so dialogue-heavy, especially in the industry these days, and just the way he unraveled material, the information, how much he gave to the reader and how much he held back. I thought it was exquisitely done" (Lewis). Penélope Cruz concurred, remembering that when she read the first scene, she was surprised at how long it was. "[T]he opening scene between Michael and I, it was 15 pages long," she noted. "It was really interesting for me to have that much material because there's no rush. It's like doing a play in every scene" ("*Counsellor* Cast"). Bardem made the same point: "As an actor, it's a gift to have that dialogue and long scenes with great partners" (Dean). *The Counselor* seemed to be a winning project, given the combination of its well-known author and crime-centered plot, the famous director and stars, and the luxury that all that dialogue afforded the cast. Ten days before the film opened, Vintage published the screenplay, the first new work by McCarthy since 2006's Pulitzer Prize–winning *The Road*.

The Counselor *on the Page: McCarthy Amplifies Tragedy*

McCarthy's screenplay of *The Counselor* begins with a veiled encounter. Unlike the hidden confrontation between the judge and the kid that is the narrative climax of *Blood Meridian* and that is likely violent, possibly sexual, and certainly unpleasant, this one is definitely sexual and very pleasurable indeed. Laura and the counselor, who like the kid and the characters in *The Road* is not otherwise named for the whole of the story, linger in bed, enjoying each other after a two-week separation and before Laura is due to travel again that evening. The description indicates drawn curtains, a dark bedroom, and figures under the bedcovers. The dialogue, then, is to appear in subtitles (3).

The counselor ignores Laura's suggestion that they recuperate from their energetic lovemaking with conversation—"[w]e could talk," she says, presumably about nonsexual topics—and instead urges her to "[t]ell me something sexy" (4). At his instigation, she responds with requests for him to touch her, to give her oral sex, and to "finger fuck" her, to "stick your finger up me and find my spot and push on it" (9). They tease each other: Laura asks how he knows how to do such things ("From hanging out with really nasty girls" is his answer), and the counselor tells her that she's "reached a whole new level of depravity" (7, 9). The scene ends with Laura calling out in pleasure, using the religious phrase "Oh my God" that the counselor had just noted women always say in such situations, along with "Jesus Christ" (10, 8).

It's a striking scene, and not entirely unlike the outhouse scene in *Blood Meridian*. The sex is to be heard but not seen, and though it certainly includes a level of detail that's completely lacking in that earlier novel's encounter, it's still clearly supposed to be left largely to our imagination. The scene is one of mutual pleasure and admiration, and the two lovers are clearly playful and comfortable with each other, but there are unsettling elements in their dialogue as well. Do they in fact have nothing else to talk about but sex? *Has* the counselor been hanging out with a questionable crowd? (And the answer to that one is quickly provided in the affirmative by subsequent plot developments.) Might Laura, a practicing Catholic, later regret taking the Lord's name in vain in precisely the same way that the counselor told her his previous lovers did? Finally, the counselor's diagnosis of Laura's "whole new level of depravity" ironically foreshadows what will eventually become of her — and more particularly, her corpse.

Despite these hints of darkness — which really only become clear in hindsight — the scene as a whole features happily shared sexual pleasure, a rarity in McCarthy's works. But that lightness is quickly darkened by the subsequent action descriptions of a welder working on a septic tank truck in a Mexican garage and a well-dressed woman watching intently as a cheetah chases and kills a jackrabbit in a Southwestern desert grassland. Descriptive vignettes of each of these activities are intercut with those describing the counselor consulting with a diamond dealer in Amsterdam, which is the subject of the next full scene.

The counselor and the dealer discuss different types of diamonds, the counselor clearly eager to purchase an excellent stone. The dealer, however, advises him, "The truth is that anything you can say about a diamond is in the nature of a flaw. The perfect diamond would be composed simply of light" (15). Even so, when the counselor, displaying his knowledge of the appropriate terminology for parts of a cut diamond, examines one stone that the dealer suggested, he notes an imperfection — that "[t]he crown and pavilion don't fit. The girdle comes out crooked" (17). This prompts the dealer to answer in another way. Rather than reassuring the counselor of the diamond's quality and the ability of the slightly crooked joining to reflect additional light, he instead remarks on the inability, essentially, to do anything about it:

> Yes. The crown and the pavilion may be well cut each in itself and yet stand alien to one another. Once the first facet is cut there can be no going back. What was meant to be a union remains forever untrue and we see a troubling truth in that the forms of our understandings are complete at their beginnings. For good or for ill. (17)

The dealer begins by talking about diamonds, which are beautiful because their cut surfaces come together imperfectly and thus sparkle, reflecting more light. But as a metaphor for, say, human knowledge or relationships, this is instead a "troubling truth," that "untrue unions" may be set in place by "the forms of our understandings" and thus can never be avoided or changed. The first cut, so to speak, determines all that follows. It's a statement that is similar to ones made in *No Country for Old Men* by Moss and Chigurh — two other characters who have ample opportunity to think about the different ripples in the world that a single decision can set in motion. As Moss tells the young hitchhiker, not long before he's killed by Mexican drug dealers, "You dont start over. That's what it's about. Ever step you take is forever. You cant make it go away.... You think when you wake up in the mornin yesterday dont count. But yesterday is all that does count. What else is there? Your life is made up of the days it's made out of. Nothing else" (227). Likewise, Chigurh tells Carla Jean, "Every moment in your life is a turning and every one a choosing. Somewhere you made a choice. All followed to this. The accounting is scrupulous. The shape is drawn. No line can be erased" (259). These characters describe a tragic determinism in which every choice has consequences.

Reviewers writing about *The Counselor* were attuned to its tragic elements. Alexandra Alter said that the story "unfolds as swiftly and relentlessly as a Greek tragedy," and another reviewer described the "Shakespearean consequences of one man's irrevocable act of avarice" (*"Counselor* Real Thriller"). David Sexton wrote that the characters talk about fate "in terms a Greek chorus might envy," and Manohla Dargis noted the "radiant intimacy" of the opening scene between Laura and the counselor by comparing it to "'the world of light' of Mount Olympus described by Homer in 'The Odyssey,' that place where 'gods live their days of pleasure.' Gods fall, though few as mercilessly or memorably as those in 'The Counselor,' a tale of good and evil, but because it was written by Cormac McCarthy, mostly evil."

In *No Country for Old Men* Llewelyn Moss makes the fateful decision to take the money from a drug deal, setting in motion a chain of events that eventually leads to his own death as well as the death of his wife and dozens of other people. In *The Counselor* the title character has also made a bad choice involving drugs and money, though we don't actually see him do it the way that we see Moss find the case of money and consider it, "[h]is whole life ... sitting there in front of him. Day after day from dawn till dark until he was dead" (18). The counselor's decision, in contrast, has either already been made or occurs offscreen, though his two immediate partners in the deal warn him about it even after he's already thrown his lot in. When his friend Reiner asks him if he knows why women like him, he responds, "I'm a good fuck?," glib and crass as ever. No, Reiner says. It's because they can "sniff out the moral dilemma"—or the quality of his character and/or his choices that results in vexed moral circumstances, the things that lead the counselor to the crossroads (33). Reiner elaborates on what this hamartia could mean in the context of the deal they are entering into: "You pursue this road that you've embarked upon," he says, "and you will eventually come to moral decisions that will take you completely by surprise. You wont see it coming at all" (34). Moral decisions like killing someone, he adds. Reiner then describes a killing machine called a *bolito*—an esoteric instrument not unlike the captive bolt pistol that Chigurh carries in *No Country*—that operates by retracting a steel cable in an ever-tightening noose that's placed around someone's neck. Once it's engaged, there's no way to stop it, an unfortunate corollary to the counselor's own experience and the "untrue unions" described by the diamond dealer.

The counselor then meets with Westray, his other partner, and they talk business. The counselor asks him about the "buy-out for the whole deal," and Westray responds that although it's hard to "put a cold dollar on it," "[i]f the whole deal were to go tits up in a ditch the papers would put the street value at a hundred mil" (53). He then says to the counselor, "If you're not all in, you need to tell me." The counselor answers in the affirmative, though in a casual way that suggests he doesn't take the deal quite as seriously as he should: "I'm all right" (54).

And so the counselor gets another warning. Westray notes the number of people killed in Juárez the previous year—three thousand, most of them young girls—and drug lords' use of kidnappers to provide subjects for snuff films. Westray says that he "cant advise" him, although of course he's doing just that, as the counselor notes (59). "Maybe I should tell you what Mickey Rourke told what's-his-face," Westray adds, making reference to the film *Body Heat* (1981) and a scene in which a bomb maker named Teddy (Rourke) advises the lawyer Ned (William Hurt) not to use the incendiary device that Teddy just made for him: "That that's my recommendation anyway. Dont do it" (59–60). The counselor smiles at the reference and quotes the next line: "Because I'll tell you something, Counselor. This arson is a serious crime" (60). He then remarks to Westray that he's surprised by the "cautionary nature" of the conversation, though he would do well to think not only about the warning but also the plot of the film to which Westray just alluded. In *Body Heat*, a lawyer blinded by desire and greed ends up being double-crossed by a femme fatale who is ultimately the "last man standing," to use the words of Llewelyn Moss. Neither does Westray, who seems to have thought of everything, consider the full implications of his allusion. Those in the cartel are indeed dangerous associates, but they're not the only ones who constitute a threat.

Westray then explains to the counselor why he's been intent on warning him about a business deal to which the counselor has already committed. He gives a short speech that reads like a condensing of both White's and Black's views in *The Sunset Limited*. He begins by pointing out that "everything that exists will one day vanish," including explanations of the world as offered by people like Newton, Einstein, Homer, Shakespeare, and Michelangelo (61–62). In *The Sunset Limited*, White sees that process as already occurring, that the "foundations of civilization" have lost their value and that "[t]hat world is largely gone" and soon will be "wholly gone" (25). But then Westray moves more into Black's perspective and says, "Everything that perishes is but a likeness," which he realizes sounds like "Plato on wheels" (62). (It's actually a translation of a line from Goethe, which Westray also gives in the original German.) Though White is the one who calls the prospect of eternal life with his family and other associates "Kafka on wheels" (135), the change of referents here is significant. For Westray, "seizing the day wont quite do it"—that is, it's not enough just to seek pleasure even if everything's on its way out. Instead, "the only thing ultimately worth your concern is the anguish of your fellow passengers on this hellbound train" (62). This is one of Black's last points to White, that if he "get[s] in the right line" with his "fellow commuter[s]" and maybe even nods at them or says hello, he might find some kind of solace, a sense of community that would "save you a trip you'll be thankful you didnt take" (133–134). And Black himself, of course, is desperately trying to save White. "It's little enough," says *The Counselor*'s Westray, but it's "not nothing." "You have to help Tom Gray up off the barroom floor," he adds in another allusion, this time to the poem "Tom Gray's Dream" by Retta M. Brown, which is often used at Alcoholics Anonymous meetings. Tom Gray, drunk on the floor, dreams he's on the hell-bound train but wakes to pray desperately for salvation. As dirty as Westray's business dealings may be, he does seem to have a moral sensibility, one that dictates he should attempt to dissuade the counselor from such involvement. Choose your associates with care, he says. He's almost like a Greek chorus here as he articulates the conservative, community-minded view of things while being fascinated by the world he's skirting, the threat of upheaval, of violence.

Westray seems to be speaking generally, but in the context of this "cautionary" conversation, it's the counselor who's on the hell-bound train. Despite the warnings, however, the counselor remains blithely confident—at least until word comes that the septic tank truck containing the drugs has been stolen. "We've got a problem," Westray tells him. "Let's say pretty bad. Then multiply by ten" (104–105). That's indeed bad news, but worse news is that a man holding the keys to the truck as well as cables needed to start it has turned up dead, and he can be coincidentally linked to the counselor. "Now the shipment is missing," Westray says when they meet in a coffee shop, "and the only thing they have to go on is that he was a client of yours" (109). That dead man was actually the son of one of the counselor's clients, a woman named Ruth who asked the counselor as a favor to bail out her son, in jail for speeding. He did, and once the man was back on his motorcycle, carrying the septic truck keys and cables in his helmet, he was decapitated by a wire strung across the road at precisely the right height. The biker died, the truck and the drugs are gone, and the counselor has been linked to the biker. The counselor's willingness to help Ruth was a good deed, but coupled with his decision to throw in with a drug deal, it's proved to have very bad consequences. The combination of bad and good impulses, just like Moss's decisions to take the money and then return to bring a wounded man some water, situates both characters in the moral liminal space that Aristotle felt was essential for a tragic hero (and makes any discussion of their hamartia an appropriately complex one).

"They cant hook me up to this," the counselor insists to Westray. "What do they think I would *do* with the stuff?" (111). But Westray knows that there's no explaining or clarifying that the counselor can successfully do. "Because they"—the cartel—"dont really believe in coincidences," he says. "They've heard of them. They've just never seen one" (109). The waitress arrives and asks for the counselor's order. His answer is glib, but appropriate for his oncoming downfall: "Hemlock," he says (110)—famously the poison that Socrates was said to have drunk after being condemned to death by Athens. Lest the counselor doubt the seriousness of the situation, Westray clarifies both the problem and the stakes: "It's always later than you think, Counselor ... I've known this was coming for a long time. For all my sins I still believe in a moral order. I'm not so sure about you. And it's not that you're going down, Counselor. It's what you're taking down with you" (114, 115). Westray does everything but mention Laura by name, but again, the counselor isn't really hearing him.

The consequences of the botched deal are indeed quick in coming. Reiner is killed trying to flee with his two pet cheetahs. As for the counselor, he travels to Boise, Idaho, and arranges to meet Laura there, but she is seized by two men in the airport parking lot (140). When she doesn't show up at the hotel they agreed on, the counselor then goes to Juárez and contrives to speak to "Jefe"—or "Boss"—a powerful man with the unnamed cartel in question. The counselor pleads for help, but the man only reiterates the statements of the diamond dealer, of Moss, and of Chigurh: one must accept the fate that one's choices have dictated. "I only know that the world in which you seek to undo your mistakes is not the world in which they were made. You are at a cross in the road and here you think to choose. But here there is no choosing. There is only accepting. The choosing was done long ago. . . . In any case, to prepare a place in our lives for the tragedies to come is an economy few wish to practice" (147). He asks if the counselor would "take her [Laura's] place upon the wheel," and the counselor says yes—but the question was about the counselor's character, not about a trade that could actually take place. The jefe reiterates that the world that plagues the counselor is "a thing which you have created, no more, no less" (150). He ends by saying that he has other calls to make, "and then, if there is time, I will take a little nap" (151). The juxtaposition—of his serious and thoughtful consideration of the counselor's situation with his refusal to be at all exercised about it—is devastating. Steven Knepper has noted, however, that the jefe's fatalistic statements "obscure that he chooses to uphold the cartel's punishment in this instance," thus reflecting "a classic Brechtian critique that tragedy uses the universal and immutable to veil the particular and contingent"—that it deflects what could be channeled as appropriate political outrage and reform (43, 42).

And as Knepper further points out, the counselor doesn't do what the jefe recommends. Rather than accepting the world that he has made for himself, he goes to Juárez to move "*among the mourners*" of the city, all of whom are seeking loved ones lost or disappeared (153). He thus "evinces the higher hope of the penitent," which "raises the possibility of a different sort of tragic recognition. If the jefe offers a pessimistic recognition, the trip to Juárez offers something like moral recognition." Contra the Brechtian critique, the counselor's actions show how "tragedy, as it often does, draws new attention to the downtrodden and even to the artifice of class" (Knepper, 44–45). Here is the glimmer of hope that so often tempers McCarthy's tragic narratives, and that hope is, as in other works, evinced in the recognition of a human community, in this case one of which the counselor was previously either unaware or utterly dismissive.

For the counselor, however, that glimmer of hope doesn't last, and his final scene is one of the bleaker moments of revelation in McCarthy's oeuvre (perhaps rivaled only by Culla's witnessing of his child's fate in *Outer Dark*). A boy delivers a package to the counselor's room, which he opens to find a DVD. He "*sits looking*" at it until he realizes that it must be a snuff film of the kind that Westray described to him earlier, in which young girls are decapitated and their bodies used to sexually satisfy the person who paid for that privilege (165). A few pages later, a bulldozer working a landfill briefly uncovers the "*headless body of Laura in her red dress*," which appears briefly only to then disappear "*in the trash and garbage*" (174). When the counselor realizes what he's been sent, he "*clutches at his face, his hands clawed*" and repeats Laura's words from the opening scene, this time in a different kind of paroxysm: "Oh God. Oh God. Oh God" (165). The counselor holds a visual record of her death, but just like that first scene, the event is veiled, its power evident only from the character's cries to God.

At this moment the counselor's tragedy is effectively over, but the screenplay isn't. Like *No Country for Old Men* after Moss's death, the plot keeps moving and refocuses our attention on the remaining characters, who are more important than is initially apparent. As the counselor has fumbled in his flight away from and back toward the cartel, the drugs and money from the deal have been up for grabs. The septic truck containing the drugs, driven by "Wire-Man" (the man who set up the wire that decapitated the biker), is ambushed by the cartel, and Wire-Man is killed. Malkina—who, it turns out, had employed Wire-Man to kill the biker and steal the truck—speaks to someone on the telephone, assuring the caller that she's "not out" and that she "know[s] where the truck is" (134). But in fact she's not interested in the truck. She wants the money, which Westray keeps in offshore accounts, as he mentioned to the counselor (52). Westray also told the counselor that he "can vanish. In a heartbeat," and that in fact the only reason he doesn't just walk away from everything altogether is his own weakness, "[w]omen" (60–61). Knowing this, Malkina tracks Westray to "*a major hotel in a world city*," where she pays a "*very attractive blonde*" to seduce Westray and lift information from him: his social security number, driver's license information, and, crucially, passwords presumably related to his accounts (161–163). Malkina then sits in a cab and oversees Westray's murder by an assassin, who slips a *bolito* around his neck and steals the small canvas bag that he's carrying (166). As Westray is slowly decapitated by the device, Malkina takes the bag from the assassin and transfers its contents to her own, contents that include a laptop, a jump drive, passports, and papers. She then pays the assassin and the cab driver and disappears into the crowd (167).

But her work isn't done. In a scene dense with specialized terminology, Malkina then meets with a man named Lee to work out how to access the accounts and take the money. "I've got the routing numbers and the account numbers," she tells him. "I've got the source code but we'll have to have a compiler to translate everything into machine-readable code. It's all doable" (169). She wants to ensure that the theft is as foolproof as possible, and she quizzes Lee on how "clean" his toolkit is. As she puts it, "a remote access Trojan Horse like Zrizbi or Torig is not for keeping track of your household expenses"—that is, when the authorities find out that someone's using hacker programs like these, they "keep looking" (170). She continues, ever cautious: "You can clone your cell phone with a SIM writer but the bills keep going to the number you're cloned off of so you cant use it forever" (170). The theft will require four encrypted calls, and when it's done Malkina will walk away with "[e]verything I need to take with me" on a USB stick (172). She says that if they manage to access all four accounts, the profit will be about $22 million, and Lee negotiates $400,000 as payment for his services. The scene isn't necessary for the plot, as most readers would be unfamiliar with these terms and processes, but it demonstrates Malkina's intelligence, her efficiency, and her ability to bring all the threads of a complex plan together.

And the plan works. In the screenplay's final scene, Malkina enters a penthouse restaurant with "*a tall and elegant man*," who is called an "escort" in the screenplay (176). They chat about where she will go next, and she mentions China as well as carrying diamonds as an easy way to "compress wealth" (178). She is also, the stage directions note, "*about five months pregnant, just noticeable*" (176). The escort asks if the child is Reiner's, and Malkina answers in the negative, adding that Reiner "had had a vasectomy" (179). "The child will have no father," the escort observes, but Malkina disagrees: "Every child has a father. In this case the best kind of father.... The best kind of father is a dead father" (180). She echoes Judge Holden here, who says in *Blood Meridian* that "it is the death of the father to which the son is entitled and to which he is heir, more so than his goods" (145). But while Holden says that a father who dies before the son is born, rather than dying during the son's life, makes himself "an idol of a perfection to which [the son] can never attain" and thus "eucher[s] the son out of his patrimony," Malkina considers instead the damage that a "contentious father" can do and remarks upon the potential for the mother to shape the child's life accordingly: "And the virtues of a dead father—his very identity for that matter—are limited only by the mother's imagination" (181).

Like Holden in *Blood Meridian*, Chigurh in *No Country for Old Men*, and White in *The Sunset Limited*, ancestors of Malkina in the McCarthy canon, she then gives a long speech that reveals, in part, her view of the world and her place in it, both of which are decidedly dark. After telling the escort that the only thing she really wants is her "own life," she adds:

> When the world itself is the source of your torment then you are free to exact vengeance upon any least part of it. I think perhaps you would have to be a woman to understand that. And you will never know the depth of your hurt until you are presented with the opportunity for revenge. Only then will you know what you are capable of. (182)

After talking about the fate of her two cheetahs, Malkina then muses on the hunter's "purity of heart"—as distinguished from the human's—and her last statement ends the screenplay:

> I suspect that we are ill-formed for the path that we have chosen. Ill-formed and ill-prepared. We would like to draw a veil over all that blood and terror. That have brought us to this place. It is our faintness of heart that would close our eyes to all of that, but in so doing makes of it our destiny. Perhaps you would not agree. I dont know. But nothing is crueler than a coward, and the slaughter to come is probably beyond our imagining. Should we think about ordering? I'm famished. (184)

Malkina, then, is very much the focus of the final section of *The Counselor*. Although it's not obvious until the story ends, she's been two steps ahead of everyone the entire time and finally emerges as the "last man standing," ultimately outwitting even Westray. When the Wire-Man that she hired to kill the biker is himself killed and the truck stolen, she's still in the game, as she insists to her unnamed colleague on the phone, and manages the highly technical and complex theft of the funds in Westray's offshore accounts. She ends by explaining how the denial of human violence only leads to its exacerbation and prepares to satisfy her own prodigious appetite.

Malkina, both as written and as performed in the film, is a troubling character. Though she is clearly a descendent of other coldly rational and ruthless figures like Holden and Chigurh, her sexual appetite—and the male characters' reactions to it—make her a kind of exacerbated femme fatale. The story Reiner tells the counselor about staring in fascinated horror at Malkina's genitals as she rubs herself to climax on the windshield of his car and his description of her vagina as "[o]ne of those bottom feeders you see going up the side of the aquarium" reflects Reiner's uneasiness with Malkina and his sense of foreboding; the story serves as yet another warning to the counselor about the people with whom he's now involved (92). It also reads, however, as the simple equation of female anatomy and sexuality with dread and darkness. Likewise, Malkina's visit to a Catholic confessional in which she deliberately provokes the priest with sexual comments is a joke that's largely incidental to the plot and not as funny as Judge Holden's similarly sexual taunting of the Reverend Green in *Blood Meridian* (86).

Malkina's very name, as Russell Hillier has noted, "derives from Medieval and Renaissance English slang and the word malkin. A malkin, the diminutive form of Maud or Mary, denotes 'a lower-class, untidy, or sluttish woman' (OED I.1a) but can also stand for 'the female genitals' (OED I.1b)" ("Nor Hell" 153). In name and in nature, Malkina is a devouring *vagina dentata* whose appetite only increases as the story goes on. Contrast this with Laura, who shares a name with Petrarch's pure and unattainable mistress; despite the evidence of Laura's own sexuality, it creates a McCarthy-inflected virgin/whore dichotomy (153).

Certainly these are elements of the film that critics have rightly taken to task, as I'll discuss. But it's also true that Malkina in the screenplay is more interesting and complicated than she appears in the film. In the screenplay Malkina is Argentinian, and more specifically "pura Porteña" ("pure Buenos Aires"), as she tells Lee (169). This helps explain her odd comment to the priest that she never knew her parents because they were "thrown out of a helicopter into the Atlantic Ocean when I was three" (85). As Boyd Tonkin has noted, Argentina's military dictatorship of 1976–1983 did precisely this to dissidents, and "their children were often forcibly adopted by military families loyal to the junta." Perhaps, he writes, this serves as partial motivation for a woman bent on exacting vengeance on a world that has tormented her. (Cameron Diaz apparently suggested something of this "exotic" background by speaking her lines with "a soft Barbadian accent"—Barbados, for some reason, serving as a substitute for Argentina—but then "studio executives were so appalled" at the result that she re-recorded all of her dialogue without it [Pulver, "Cameron Diaz"].)

If Malkina did grow up in such a world, that could explain her ruthlessness. And she did so as a woman, as she notes, exacerbating both her vulnerability and the need for that ruthlessness, at least in her eyes. But it doesn't explain what precisely she understands herself to be avenging—nor the enigma of her pregnancy at the end of the story, something the film leaves out entirely. Hillier has argued convincingly that rather than simple greed and cruelty, "Malkina's motivation is more nuanced and the plot is a revenge plot that rivals a Jacobean revenge tragedy in Malkina's ingenuity and method." Further, he notes that the film eliminates these elements, thus simplifying both the story and her character ("Nor Hell," 151).

As Hillier explains, McCarthy's screenplay suggests that Westray is the father of Malkina's child and that she is avenging his disavowal of that child by killing him and seizing his assets. Two subtle though telling exchanges suggest this, the first between the counselor and Westray:

> WESTRAY: I never go in [Reiner's] club. And I miss the bastard. We always shared a taste for exotic women. A few times in fact we shared the women themselves.
> COUNSELOR: That wouldnt include the present one would it?
> *Westray leans back and studies the counselor.*
> WESTRAY: And why would you ask me that?
> COUNSELOR: No reason. Sorry.
> WESTRAY: I see a murky picture forming in your mind. How well do you know her?
> COUNSELOR: Not all that well. Why?
> WESTRAY: Because you dont know someone until you know what they want. Is why. (56–57)

Westray's responses here suggest that he's avoiding the club because of Malkina, perhaps because they had a relationship—a "murky picture" about which he's clearly a bit sensitive. Later, when Malkina talks to the blonde woman who has stolen information from Westray, the exchange suggests what Hillier calls "a vestigial nostalgia for [Malkina's] broken relationship with Westray and a hint of curiosity, even jealousy, at the intimacy the blonde thief has recently shared with him" (155):

MALKINA: I'll have the computer. Were you planning on seeing him again?

BLONDE: What would be the point? He'll be broke.

MALKINA: Smart girl.

BLONDE: Or is it worse than that?

MALKINA: What do you care? (163)

Malkina does, of course, indicate considerable sexual appetite and experience, but the only specific men we hear about her having relationships with are Reiner and, by implication, Westray. If the father of her child is dead, as she tells the escort, then that adds credence to the theory that it was Westray. And she does personally order, witness, and pay for his protracted, gory murder. If the child is not Westray's, then her pregnancy at the story's end would serve no other purpose than for the reader to contemplate a "monstrous mother" in all her triumphal glory. Malkina is indeed identified with her rapacious female body to a disturbing degree, even to the point that she could serve as a good example for Barbara Creed's recognition of the "monstrous-feminine" figures populating horror films—including, perhaps most notably for this analysis, Ridley Scott's *Alien* (1979). But considering her actions against Westray as revenge rather than simply the means to a big payday gives her problematic character a much more interesting motivation.

It gives the story as a whole more resonance as well. Understanding *The Counselor* as a tragedy initially focuses our attention on the counselor himself, a "decent guy," as McCarthy put it, whose greed and arrogance lead him to make some very bad choices indeed and thus be brought low. In an Aristotelean sense, this works nicely, and the paradigm could be applied to Westray as well, whose admitted weakness for women is what leads to his own demise—at the hands of the blonde thief whom he can't resist seducing and Malkina herself, whom he may very well have loved and left, thus enkindling her desire for brutal retribution.

But shifting our focus from the counselor and Westray to Malkina also deepens the way we think about the screenplay as tragedy. Malkina's pregnancy and her actions against Westray are more particularly resonant with Jacobean revenge tragedy, a genre typically characterized by an intricate plot and a contemporary setting. *The Counselor*, of course, boasts McCarthy's most intricate plot and most contemporary setting to date. As Hillier aptly adds, McCarthy has the counselor quote almost directly from Christopher Marlowe's *The Jew of Malta* (1592): when Westray says that a fight he had "was in another country," the counselor responds, "And besides the wretch is dead?" (51–52). In Marlowe's play the Machiavellian Jew Barabas is challenged by a Dominican friar:

FRIAR BARNARDINE: Thou hast committed—
BARABAS: Fornication—but that was in another country:
And besides, the wench is dead. (Marlowe 4.1.40–42)

Hillier has further noted that avengers in tragedies like these often carry around a memento of their wounding: "Hamlet has his mourning weeds and a locket bearing the likeness of his dead father and his horrible uncle; Titus Andronicus has a stump where his hand once was and his raped and mutilated daughter Lavinia by his side; and Vindice [in *The Revenger's Tragedy*] carries about the rotting skull of his betrothed, who was horribly murdered." But Malkina's token is a bit different—it's the child she has inside her womb, a living being rather than something dead or lost. "And we don't even know about it until the very end of the screenplay," writes Hillier—"quite the sting in the tail" (Hillier, personal communication). That child was the motivation for her vengeance and is now, perhaps, a reminder of its success.

Malkina, then, is simultaneously the most fascinating and troubling element of *The Counselor*. While her background, motivation, and declarations don't quite reach the level of Chigurh's or Holden's, they are interesting enough to potentially generate ample critical commentary, not to mention the fact that she is a major character who is also female, a rarity in McCarthy's work. But the ways that she is rendered *as* female reflect a suspicion or fear of female sexuality evident throughout the narrative. Even the staunchest anti-Freudian, for example, would be hard-pressed to deny the association of Westray's decapitation with a long, slow, bloody castration at the hands of a vicious malkin, terrifying in her assurance, her sexuality, and her rapacious appetite. Malkina's characterization amplifies the fascinating, troubling tradition of the femme fatale, like those embodied by Barbara Stanwyck (as Phyllis Dietrichson) in *Double Indemnity* (1944) and Mary Astor (as Ruth Wonderly) in *The Maltese Falcon* (1941). But Phyllis and Ruth both fail in their schemes, while Malkina cleverly skirts considerable danger, achieves her vengeance, and does quite well for herself in the end. A subtle interpretation that underscored Malkina's motivations and tamped down her sexuality could make her the keystone of an intricately rendered tragedy.

The Counselor *on Screen: A Tragedy's Fatal Flaw*

Ridley Scott is no stranger to strong female characters. His films *Alien, Thelma and Louise* (1991), *G.I. Jane* (1997), *Hannibal* (2001), and *Prometheus* (2012) all feature female protagonists who don't shrink from danger or conflict; Ripley in *Alien* and Thelma and Louise in particular have been celebrated as feminist touchstones in cinema. In the same way that the

Coens' *No Country for Old Men* played to the directors' strengths while also making small but significant adjustments to the source material, a film could work well that superimposed Scott's demonstrated ability to direct dramatic stories about women whose sexuality is far from their defining characteristic onto McCarthy's tragic depiction of the intersections of greed, commerce, narcotics, hubris, and extreme violence. Unfortunately, however, Scott's film takes the opposite tack, eliminating Malkina's revenge plot and amping up the representation of her sexual appetite. As a result she becomes more of a caricature than a fully realized character. She is the tragedy's keystone, but a weak keystone that makes the entire structure untenable.

The film begins with shots of a motorcyclist speeding into El Paso, and then the camera pans into the bedroom of a sleek, expensive-looking apartment where two figures are tangled together in bed under a white sheet. They are completely covered, which makes them look a bit like mummies or wrapped corpses until the camera joins them under the sheet in the small, safe bubble of their life together. Because of the camera's proximity, the subtitles that McCarthy prescribed in his screenplay aren't necessary.

As the counselor, Michael Fassbender is attractive and assured and brings an intensity to the role that viewers might recognize from his other performances, especially those in partnership with director Steve McQueen, such as his portrayal of Bobby Sands in *Hunger* (2008), of a sex addict in *Shame* (2011), and of a vicious slave owner in *12 Years a Slave* (2013). The latter earned him an Academy Award nomination for Best Supporting Actor. For much of the film Fassbender is impeccably put together, dressed in well-tailored Armani suits and very much the picture of the cool, successful professional. As costume designer Janty Yates puts it, Fassbender "gives good crisp" ("The Counselor" commentary). But when he breaks into a smile, as he begins to in this opening scene, he can look sharklike, and that hint of danger—or recklessness—is apt for a character who's already made some questionable decisions.

In the theatrical release this scene is edited to remove some of the more sexually explicit language, though it's still clear that the counselor is giving Laura oral sex, and the scene ends with her climax. In an unrated director's cut released on Blu-Ray that is about twenty minutes longer than the version shown in theaters, this scene is one of those extended with more of the dialogue from the screenplay. Those making the film found that the additional dialogue made the scene honest rather than vulgar. "Some of the language that's in the film is kind of very sexy without being rude," said Scott. "It's really good, it's really subtle and real. There were those who were offended by it, so I had to trim some of it out, which I thought was honestly

The counselor (Michael Fassbender) breaks into a dangerous smile in the opening scene of Ridley Scott's The Counselor *(20th Century Fox, 2013).*

pretty straightforward" ("The Counselor" commentary). McCarthy himself weighed in as well: "You get the sense that the people who make Hollywood movies had never had sex," he said. "How many times have you seen a movie where two people who don't even know each other's names run into a room and start ripping each other's clothes off? I've never seen such a thing. And I'm not particularly naïve.... When was the last time I saw a film where two people in love actually made love?" ("Laura" commentary). Both McCarthy and Scott saw the scene as a representation of authentic, rather than Hollywood-style, sexuality.

In both versions of the opening scene, Laura's pleasure is the focus. Played by Penélope Cruz—who, like Bardem and Rubén Blades (playing the jefe), is a veteran of another McCarthy adaptation—Laura is beautiful and a bit girlish, with visible freckles across her nose. And like Fassbender she brings an assurance to the role that is notable in her previous performances, like those for director Pedro Almodóvar in *All About My Mother* (1999) and *Volver* (2006); she was nominated for a Best Actress Oscar for *Volver* and later won for Woody Allen's *Vicky Cristina Barcelona* (2008). As Laura, she is clearly sexual but is also coded as innocent, wearing a short white nightgown and framed by white sheets as the film begins. She is somewhat bashful, covering her face with her hand during some of the dialogue and worrying about the need to "tidy up." Ben Beaumont-Thomas commented on this scene and its effect on Laura's character in a piece that appeared in the *Guardian* titled "Why Is Oral Sex Hard for Hollywood?" Depictions of cunnilingus in film, he argues, still usually result in an NC-17 rating, and within films themselves often appear less as a standard sexual practice than a "weighty stand-in" for something like "po-faced male devotion, or female exoticism." *The Counselor* is "a classic re-

He repeats that sharklike smile as he prepares to propose to Laura (Penélope Cruz). She has just asked him, "Have you been bad?"

cent example," he says, in which the practice is "the ultimate signifier of devotion and masculinity." "Look," writes Beaumont-Thomas sarcastically, "he even goes down on his lover, and he's not emasculated! The woman receiving this kind of film pleasure is not having fun, but being blessed and anointed somehow." He sums it up: "In Hollywood, if a woman receives oral sex, she's a Madonna; if she gives it, she's a whore."

Laura is indeed put on a pedestal by the counselor and by the film itself, which builds to the sight of her headless body consumed by garbage as the ultimate in loss and pointless degradation. And despite the surprise of a sex scene that occurs even before the film's opening credits, the relationship of Laura and the counselor is a believable one, largely due to Fassbender's and Cruz's performances—performances that suggest both their love for one another as well as a sense of disquietude, as when the counselor breaks into his shark smile while proposing to her, or when Laura gives the counselor a concerned, appraising look after they are vaguely menaced by his former acquaintance at a polo club.

If the sexuality of the film was limited to the dialogue and oral sex of the opening scene and the suggestion of phone sex between Laura and the counselor that happens later, the film could be considered progressive in this regard—after all, showcasing a woman's pleasure is still something of a rarity in mainstream Hollywood film, and despite Beaumont-Thomas's concerns it can be seen as refreshing, as Scott and McCarthy say they intended it to be. But it's the character of Malkina that makes the film's treatment of female sexuality problematic. Cameron Diaz was cast against type for this role, as she is more generally known as an attractive, athletic, and slightly goofy comedienne from roles in films like *My Best Friend's Wedding* (1997), *There's Something About Mary* (1998), and two Charlie's Angels films (2000,

2003), though it should be noted that she's also been recognized as a dramatic actress in *Being John Malkovich* (1999), *Vanilla Sky* (2001), and *Gangs of New York* (2002). Diaz understood the character as "basically a sociopath," and Scott summed up Malkina as a "black widow" ("Malkina" commentary). The filmmakers carefully crafted her appearance to make her as animalistic and predatory as possible. She has close-cut black hair visible through longer blonde layers, chrome-colored fingernails, and a tattoo of cheetah spots running from her back over her shoulder and onto her neck. She is wardrobed in designs by Paula Thomas of the Thomas Wylde label, a lesser-known designer who received a good deal of press coverage for her work on *The Counselor*. Malkina's outfits are heavy on animal prints, skintight cuts, and stilettos. Janty Yates was eager to make Malkina's clothes as extreme as her character: she's "such a powerhouse" that "we could get away with anything, really," Yates said, and so went for an "out there, slightly Goth, slightly aggressive, fabulous design" ("Malkina" commentary). It's a departure from the screenplay, which describes Malkina wearing expensive riding clothes, a business suit, *"elegant fitted clothes,"* and even *"an ankle-length black pleated skirt"* at various points—hardly the sexually feral couture that we see in the film (11, 162, 167, 176).

But the most notable thing about the way that Malkina is seen in the film—other than the fact that she's not pregnant at the end—is that she appears at all in its most notorious scene, when she climbs on Reiner's car and has an orgasm with him watching. In the screenplay this disturbing equation of female anatomy and desire with horror does serve to reveal Reiner's doubts—that Malkina "scares the shit out of me," as he puts it, and that being in love with Malkina is like being in love with "[c]aseful death" (in a nod to Keats) (95). Regardless, the scene makes Malkina into a devouring vagina—one who will, in fact, kill you with pleasure. Its status as an unset-

Malkina (Cameron Diaz) is the essence of feral sexuality in The Counselor.

tling memory that Reiner relates to the counselor at least relegates it to narrative, a story told between two men whose reactions to it are as significant as the event itself.

Scott, however, chooses to dramatize the story as flashback, unable to avoid the temptation of *seeing* such a thing. As Reiner, Javier Bardem's gawping expression is played for laughs, and the audience is invited to ogle Malkina—played here by a body double and costumed in a short dress printed with cheetah spots—as she performs a full split on the windshield and then moves up and down, shot from above to obscure the double's face. It's not clear what McCarthy—an executive producer, after all—thought about the decision to film this scene rather than having one character report it to another. When Scott speaks about it, he says that his only concern was whether or not it was realistic:

> This is kind of the scene that mostly brings down the house in most people. They can't believe what they're seeing. I didn't think it was possible until I met the acrobat, and she said, "Yeah, it's possible." So I stood in this Ferrari garage with all the mechanics standing there gawping while this girl—this acrobat—climbed up on the screen and did her thing. That's good, that's cool. She's a good double. I think it makes her [Malkina] dangerous. It makes her a bit frightening. ("The Couselor" commentary)

In asking an acrobat to "do her thing" in front of a group of mechanics, Scott essentially reproduces the moment from the film: a woman's intimidating sexuality as display for a man, or a group of men. Scott doesn't mention the acrobat's name, nor does this woman appear to be listed in the credits. The credits do list a stuntwoman named Zarene Dallas, who doubled for Diaz in the shots of Malkina riding a horse, but her work apparently did not extend to the car scene ("She's Just"). As a character Malkina may indeed be using the male gaze against itself, but in this staging Diaz and the nameless acrobat are merely spectacle. "That's good, that's cool."

This sexist attitude is echoed in other statements made in the film's DVD commentary track. In speaking about filming the party at Reiner's house that occurs early in the story, executive producer Mark Huffam says that it was "a kind of fabulous day. Fast cars, fast cats, and we won't say anything about the women that were there." His comment is heard over a shot of a woman's buttocks, clad in a skimpy bikini. During the scene in which the counselor borrows a woman's cell phone to call Laura, Scott talks about the actress, Giannina Facio, offering up his version of a conversation with her: "She says, 'What am I gonna do in *Moses*? [referring to Scott's next project, *Exodus: Gods and Kings* (2014)] Who am I gonna be?' I said, 'I thought you would be a con-cubine or a slave girl.' She said, 'Oh, jolly good.' She likes it." According to Scott, the representation of sexual service is no problem for her, because "she likes it," as he says. (Partners for over a decade, Scott and Facio were married in June 2015.) And finally, immediately before the car scene, Scott is com-menting on some people's reactions to the film's depictions of sex, in the con-text of a scene that suggests phone sex between the counselor and Laura. He disparages those who object to the depictions: "It's extraordinary how prudish some people are. In the [screening] room, or one of those rooms, there could easily be three hundred people, and a high percentage of women would react. Absolutely extraordinary. I couldn't understand it. That's beyond—it's pass-ing beyond prudish. It's ridiculous." Scott doesn't seem to consider that these female viewers might be reacting instead to the description of their genitals as "one of those catfish things," "one of those bottom feeders you see going up the side of the aquarium," or that their objections could be to the oversim-plified, oversexualized depictions of women rather than merely the result of prudishness or an inability to deal honestly and openly with sex.

Scott is less generous to his female characters as well as his female audi-ence. Both the theatrical and extended versions of the film eliminate the scenes with Lee that highlight the depth of Malkina's intelligence, and both also eliminate her Argentinian background and her pregnancy at the story's end. She is merely a predator in stilettos, a sexy, dangerous vamp who de-stroys for no other reason than greed, and she is able to do so because she completely lacks the stereotypically feminine softness and empathy displayed by Laura. In a film with undeniable strengths, like Fassbender's portrayal of the counselor's gradual disintegration and Rubén Blades's thoughtful and musical performance of the jefe's conversation with the counselor, the film's handling of Malkina tarnishes the whole. It may not be a tragic flaw, exactly, but it undoes what might have been an impressive achievement and an effec-tive superimposition of Scott's previously demonstrated facility with strong, interesting female characters; of the skills and star power of actors like Fass-bender, Cruz, and Blades; and of McCarthy's intricate revenge tragedy.

Many reviewers honed in on exactly this problem. David Sexton summed up the film's treatment of its female characters as "nasty stuff about women [and] male sexuality as a fatal weakness." Three separate reviews compared the film, and the car scene in particular, to Paul Verhoeven's *Showgirls* (1995), a "so-bad-it's-good" romp through the sex and ambition of Vegas entertain-ment that eventually became a cult classic. Joe Neumaier called Malkina's encounter with Reiner's car "a bad-sexy moment to rival anything in 'Show-girls,'" but others note that *Showgirls* differs from *The Counselor* in that the former's excess was in some sense deliberate. Whether intentionally or not, however, *Showgirls* achieves the level of camp, whereas reviewers agree that *The Counselor* does not. "Even counting the already infamous scene in which Cameron Diaz humps the windshield of a Ferrari, while Javier Bardem stares at her genitals, goggle-eyed and disbelieving, from the passenger seat—it's like an outtake from a suppressed Jerry Lewis porn film—this isn't a work of miscalculated camp excess, after the fashion of 'Showgirls,'" writes Andrew O'Hehir. Tony Dayoub concurs: "'The Counselor' is a special kind of awful," he says. "If it weren't so crass, it would be kind of funny. Is it meant to be deliberately nasty in the way Paul Verhoeven's 'Showgirls' was?" For Neumaier, O'Hehir, and Dayoub, *The Counselor*, though bad, is not quite bad enough to be good.

Dayoub also wrote about the possible influence of Ridley's brother Tony Scott on the film, arguing that it really feels more like a Tony film than one by Ridley. Noting particularly the film's treatment of women, which he calls misogynistic, he says that quality is

> associated less with Ridley Scott, who gave the world Ripley, Thelma and Louise and G.I. Jane, than with Tony. Notwithstanding the resilient women of *The Hunger* and *Domino*, Tony's films were more often called out for abusing or demonizing women (*Beverly Hills Cop 2*) when they weren't excluding them from the action (*Crimson Tide*) or treating them as martyrs (*Revenge*) or prizes (*Top Gun, Days of Thunder*).

Dayoub ends by wondering if *The Counselor*'s lack of a satisfying ending is "perhaps an acknowledgment of the filmmaker's own unresolved feelings concerning the premature end of his close relationship with Tony," and invites comparison with Roman Polanski's first film after his wife's murder by the Manson family, a grisly, nasty *Macbeth* (1971) that was hard to take "even by that tragedy's usual standards."

Most critics simply thought the film wasn't any good. Reviews appeared with titles like "Appeal Denied," "'The Counselor' Is Guilty," and "This Guidance Not Suggested" (Neumaier; Sragow; Lumenick). Many noted that the dialogue felt stilted and went on way too long—Neumaier called the film a "lethally pretentious, talky, lethargic drama," and Claudia Puig's review in *USA Today* was titled "Be Glad This Talky 'Counselor' Doesn't Charge By the Word: It's a Crime to Waste Such a Talented Cast in This Implausible Thriller." That such A-listers were behind the project led many reviewers to pan it further. Mary Pols, writing for *Time*, called it "portentous [and] emotionally vacant," and said that it "plays like a parody of a Cormac McCarthy adaptation."

Andrew O'Hehir went furthest, and he caused a minor stir with his essay about the film on *Salon.com* titled "Meet the Worst Movie Ever Made." For O'Hehir, *The Counselor* is bad in all the wrong ways. He compares the title character's suffering to that of Job, "with about the same level of explication but less drama and worse writing. Way worse writing." He sums it up as "a mumblecore movie about a bunch of Sarah Lawrence philosophy majors, made by coked-up rich people for 100 bajillion dollars," and ultimately calls it a prime example of the lure of "devil's candy," that perfect combination of art, timeliness, and success that everyone in Hollywood chases. Because *The Counselor* couldn't miss, in other words, it ended up missing in a huge, expensive, and embarrassing way.

But like other "devil's candy" disasters that O'Hehir mentions, including D. W. Griffith's *Intolerance* (1916) and Joseph L. Mankiewicz's *Cleopatra* (1963), other critics stepped up to praise the film, or at least to temper some of the blazing critiques. In the *New York Times*, Manohla Dargis praised the plot's speed and "unobvious" nature, its "thrill-free" violence, and how "all the ellipses, as well as the eccentric, mesmerizing poetry of his dialogue" made her think that "McCarthy appears to have never read a screenwriting manual in his life"—which, she says firmly, is a compliment. Dargis clearly appreciated how thoroughly the screenplay and the film avoided the simple, unrealistic pleasures of the crime genre and how the result rendered the world "unrecognizable [and] unsettling."

Dargis's review appeared early, before the onslaught of negative criticism, though other essays appeared later and in response to the negativity. Doug Dickinson published a piece titled "In Defence of *The Counselor*," and Scott Foundas, the chief film critic for *Variety*, explained to readers "Why 'The Counselor' Is One of Ridley Scott's Best Films." *Blade Runner* (1982), he noted, also received poor initial reviews, and though *The Counselor* isn't quite like that earlier film, it is, Foundas argues, "bold and thrilling in ways that mainstream American movies rarely are, and its rejection suggests what little appetite there is for real daring at the multiplex these days." The fault isn't with the film, he says; it's with a lazy, spoon-fed audience who can't handle a more confronting, difficult story. *The Counselor* as a whole, he effuses, is "a ravishing object—a triumph of mood and style, form as an expression of content, and dialogue that finds a kind of apocalyptic comedy in this charnel-house existence." When the Blu-Ray edition of the film was released, which includes a 220-minute extra, combining a director's commentary on the film with deleted scenes and making-of documentaries, Amy Taubin praised that "fascinating extra" as well as the film itself, which she called "the most underrated and indeed ridiculously maligned film of 2013."

The Counselor was certainly criticized—wrongly for its lengthy dialogue sequences and complicated plot and rightly for its treatment of women. Malkina in particular is a strong, intelligent woman whose most interesting qualities are overshadowed by her status as black widow, *vagina dentata*, a castrating and devouring horror. That sexual rapacity and danger is evident, though less emphasized, in the screenplay, and though here I've attributed the film's portrayal largely to Scott, McCarthy's role as both screenwriter and executive producer indicates his own responsibility in originating and then exacerbating this interpretation of the character. Malkina should be the unseen machinery of this tragedy and its triumphant if villainous avenger, but she emerges as its greatest flaw. Unlike the Coen brothers, who took McCarthy's portrait of Carla Jean Moss and made her a wounded but worthy rhetorical opponent to Chigurh, Scott's film aggravates rather than ameliorates the problems of Malkina's character. The end result isn't exactly the "slaughter beyond imagining" that Malkina envisions and tragedy dictates, but the overwhelmingly bad press is likely to give other filmmakers pause when they consider future film versions of McCarthy's works. As of this writing in 2016, none are slated for production.

CHILD OF GOD: MUCH LIKE YOURSELF, OR MAYBE NOT

In 2013 McCarthy was everywhere in entertainment news. James Franco's adaptation of *Child of God* didn't get nearly as much press as *The Counselor*, but relative to the size of the production, the coverage was robust. In the lead-up to the two films' releases, McCarthy was starting to seem like a can't-miss name in Hollywood—though like *The Counselor*, *Child of God* would prove to be an association of mixed value for the author. If Malkina is oversimplified in Scott's film, Lester Ballard is also made less interesting and less tragic through Franco's direction and Scott Haze's performance. Franco is, as I've noted, one of McCarthy's most prominent champions, a writer and student of literature himself and demonstrably engaged in the ways that cinema and literature can intersect; he played Allen Ginsberg in Rob Epstein and Jeffrey Friedman's *Howl* (2010), and he has written, directed, produced, and acted in two adaptations of Faulkner: *As I Lay Dying* (2013) and *The Sound and the Fury* (2014). He became famous with a role on the well-regarded television series *Freaks and Geeks* (1999–2000) and since that time has appeared in an eclectic combination of Hollywood blockbusters like *Spider-Man 2* (2004), comedies like *The Pineapple Express* (2008), and character-driven dramas like *127 Hours* (2010), while still pursuing his own independent projects like *Interior. Leather Bar.* (2013), a "docufiction" film about an attempt to re-create lost footage from the 1980 film *Cruising*. As such, Franco certainly has the range to attempt the kind of difficult or eso-teric film that an adaptation of *Child of God* would necessarily be—and he also has the star power to sell it. Like *The Counselor*, however, the adjust-ments Franco made in his adaptation serve to lessen rather than emphasize the story's impact, in this case by portraying the protagonist as freakishly tri-umphant rather than sympathetically tragic.

At the 2011 Toronto International Film Festival, James Franco announced that he was setting aside plans to adapt *Blood Meridian* in favor of *Child of God* (Dew, "Franco to Direct"). By January of the following year, it was re-ported that filming would begin in West Virginia by the end of the month, and actor Scott Haze, a longtime friend of Franco's, announced on his Twitter feed that he would be playing Lester Ballard. Additional cast was reported to include Tim Blake Nelson, Jim Parrack, and Brian Lally, and Haze released a brief video of himself firing a rifle, an image of a rifle propped against a chair, and a photo featuring a battered copy of a paperback *Child of God* with some notes in the foreground and a young woman's scantily clad body visible in the background (Dew, "Franco's *Child of God*"). The provenance of the latter photo is unclear, but it fits the way that Franco traded on his brainy–movie star, "books-and-babes" image to bring attention to the film as production continued. As for Haze, he took the opposite tack and decided to find out more about what it would be like to live in some of the conditions that Lester does. He stayed in a friend's cabin deep in the Tennessee woods and even lived in a cave ("James Franco Courts"). He claimed to have lost forty-five pounds "subsisting on apples and fish" and recognized the tendency to invent friends to talk to when you're deprived of the usual distractions of everyday life (Garvey et al.).

Hearing about his Method efforts to prepare for the role, some citizens of Sevier County, where the novel and the film are set, were unenthused about their region's forthcoming portrayal on the big screen. "I have a bad feeling about this," wrote Jason Davis in the *Mountain Press*, the Sevierville news-paper. Noting Haze's time in the cave, Davis sarcastically wondered, "Perhaps he rode a bear and ate some 'possum too?" The fact that the film was shoot-ing in West Virginia didn't help matters. "If the studio has to show the Sevier County countryside being plundered by a serial-killing lunatic, couldn't they have at least shot the thing here?"

Films about serial-killing lunatics often sell lots of tickets, though they rarely add necrophilia to the mix. Knowing the film's content would be a challenge for more viewers than just those in Sevier County, Franco patiently shopped his project around to a number of audiences before its official re-lease. *Child of God* opened first at festivals in Venice, Toronto, New York, Austin, and Virginia in the fall of 2013, and then in spring 2014 it played at

Lester Ballard (Scott Haze) menaces the camera in James Franco's Child of God *(RabbitBandini Productions, 2014).*

festivals in Dallas and San Francisco. On 1 August 2014 it was released in selected theaters in the United States, at which point Franco commenced the blizzard of publicity that I described at the beginning of this chapter.

The film begins with an emphasis on McCarthy's name and quotations from the novel, suggesting that it will take a curatorial approach to its source material—though that initial impression is not borne out by the remainder of the film. An intertitle announces prominently that this is "[a] story by Cormac McCarthy," and a voice-over by Tim Blake Nelson, who plays Sheriff Fate Turner, reproduces McCarthy's titular statement from early in the novel: "He was of German and Irish bloods. His name was Lester Ballard, a child of God much like yourself perhaps." The screen cuts from black to a close-up of Haze as Lester—he has a full beard and short brown hair, and he looks a bit gaunt though not emaciated. He sucks his teeth and works his mouth, looking off to the right as the camera moves in unsteadily to an even closer view. An intertitle appears that reads simply "I.", as in "part 1," and then a close-up of Lester reappears. This time he's looking straight at the camera, his head angled forward as he glares out with his eyes tilted slightly upward. The effect is menacing, and the banjo music that begins playing is appropriate for the region, of course, though its repetitive riff would remind many of *Deliverance* (1972), another film featuring backwoodsmen with violent sexual practices. The handheld camera moves yet closer to Lester, its trembling suggesting nervousness in Lester's presence.

Another intertitle appears, this one a quote from the novel's opening sentence: "They came like a caravan of carnival folk up through the swales of broom straw and across the hill in the morning sun ..." The music becomes fuller and then diegetic as a group of musicians is seen riding in the back of a truck to what turns out to be the auction of Lester's family property. A crowd gathers as the camera finds Lester watching through the slats of an old barn, his head still tilted forward and his eyes dangerous. He exits the barn with his rifle, and the camera follows him up the hill to the crowd, where he cocks the rifle and starts screaming. "Move, move, move, move, move! This is not your property! Move, move, move, move, move, move, move! You're on my property!" The auctioneer and another man confront him, telling him that it's not his property, and Lester looks surprised. "This ain't my property? The hell it ain't." He continues to protest with labored, somewhat slurred speech, and the auctioneer makes clear what's at stake if Lester keeps brandishing his gun: "They're going to lock you up and put you in that rubber room—now, this is not your land." Lester is even more infuriated and approaches the auctioneer with his rifle, demanding that he leave. The crowd gasps, but the other man comes up behind Lester and hits him hard on the head with the blunt edge of an axe. Lester falls to the ground in a paroxysm of pain and anger; he bares his teeth and screams as if he is also sobbing. Superimposed over his image is the movie's title, *Child of God*.

The opening of the film announces Franco's debt to the novel—McCarthy's name is prominent as it begins, and Franco includes prose from the novel in intertitles and in voice-overs from members of the community, the latter taken from chapters in the novel that constitute townspeople telling stories about Lester and about the region. Franco even takes care to have the camera pass under an old rope hanging from a barn rafter, much as McCarthy mentions the same thing briefly without comment, a detail that only becomes significant many pages later when a townsperson talks about how Lester's father hanged himself in the barn (4, 21). Much of the rest of the film makes relatively minor adjustments to the novel's plot, adding, for instance, a scene of Lester accusing the stuffed animals he wins at the fair of conspiring against him and then shooting them repeatedly with his rifle. Franco does make significant alterations, however, to Lester's characterization and to the narrative's ending.

Haze plays Lester as menacing and seemingly unhinged right from the beginning, which led some reviewers to praise his interpretation of the role and some to criticize it, as I'll discuss. It's an interpretation that can be justified by the novel, which does describe Lester's jaw working "as if he were chewing but he is not chewing," and which early on says that he "looked half crazy" and calls him "a misplaced and loveless simian shape" (4, 15, 20). But the novel also notes Lester's small size—McCarthy introduces Lester by calling him "small, unclean, unshaven," and near the novel's end when his kidnappers give him clothes to wear, he puts them on and "there was room inside for a whole Ballard more" (4, 180–181). He is in some sense childlike, as the title also suggests. Additionally, his motivation for the crimes he eventually commits is multifaceted. He isn't, in fact, just crazy. As Dianne Luce writes, "his later turn to murder is prompted by a complex mixture of his despair of making human contact, his distrust of others, his recognition of his role as pariah, his conflicted sense of attraction to and disapproval of his sexually tempting victims, and his pent-up rage" (*Reading* 135).

As Luce has noted, McCarthy based Lester in part on serial killer Ed Gein, who was also the inspiration for Alfred Hitchcock's 1960 film *Psycho*. Like Lester in McCarthy's novel, Anthony Perkins's Norman Bates is slight and lean, hardly a menacing masculine figure. Given that *Psycho* was released well before *Child of God*'s publication in 1974, it's possible that Perkins's portrayal as well as the story as a whole influenced McCarthy's creation of Lester as a character. Luce also reminds us that the contrast between the titles of Hitchcock's film and McCarthy's novel "is a telling one. Always McCarthy insists on the mystery and the humanity of Lester Ballard—on the mystery of humans' dark capabilities and muffled spirituality" (151). Even critics who acknowledge that Lester may be in some way mentally unstable tend to argue that his instability develops gradually as a result of his ostracism by the community. Jay Ellis writes that "whatever the mental insufficiencies and psychological deformities of Lester Ballard, the plot is launched by this action of unhousing; every subsequent action of Lester Ballard—including necrophilia—follows from that initial scene. Ballard is a child of god without a home because it has been auctioned away from him" (Ellis, *No Place* 70).[1] Lydia Cooper notes that one of the townspeople tells a story about Lester as a child hitting another child suddenly and without provocation—seemingly as an example of Lester's violent tendencies—though the narrator ends his story with the odd equivocation, "He never done nothing to me" (*COG* 18). "This narrator is part of a community that has absolutely rejected Ballard," Cooper writes, "evicting him from his ancestral home and refusing him even an abandoned shack for lodging. This is a communal rejection that occurs even though, according to this particular narrator, '[h]e never done nothing to me'" (*No More Heroes* 42).

As portrayed by McCarthy, Lester is certainly capable of brutal acts in his exile, but that exile must be considered a significant causal factor. Like Graniteville abandoned Robert McEvoy to hang in *The Gardener's Son*, the community here seems to regard Lester as a "sacrificeable victim," to use the term of René Girard, a scapegoat to be killed or exiled in order to serve as "the repository of all the community's ills" (77). Girard explains how these scapegoats are both a part of their society and separated from it—they can't be so different that they are unrecognizable, but they can't be like everyone else, either. They are, then, "exterior or marginal individuals, incapable of establishing or sharing the social bonds that link the rest of the inhabitants" (12). Even a king like Oedipus, Girard notes, is both at the center of his community and isolated from it. Because the social link is missing, the sacrifice can be undertaken as "an act of violence without the risk of vengeance"—thus purging the community of its violence and (temporarily) ceasing it (13). Cooper notes how even the townsperson telling the story about Lester "emphasizes both Ballard's uniqueness—how he demonstrated unprovoked and disproportionate violence—and his *non*-uniqueness. . . . This narrator thus describes Ballard's extraordinary behavior while recognizing in a bald statement that Ballard's unprovoked violence is, in many ways, only an extreme version of that which all humanity is capable of committing" (*No More Heroes* 42). Lester's violence was unprovoked—but then Lester "never done nothing" to the narrator to deserve the violence of his ostracizing, either. Christopher Jenkins makes a similar point about the novel's association of sexuality with violence and dehumanization, which is hardly limited to Lester; Jenkins notes, to cite just one example, the dump keeper who chases away his daughter's lover and then beats her with a stick, only to then have sex with her himself, cursing her after his climax (*COG* 27–28; Jenkins 92–93).

In Girard's terms, Lester is a tragic hero, a "child of God much like yourself perhaps." The community, speaking as a kind of chorus, identifies him as irrevocably Other even as their own statements and the town's history bely that difference. But because they do speak and act in unison where Lester's exile is concerned, he has nothing to do but fall. The tragedy is our recognition that he *is* a scapegoat—that he is, in fact, somewhat like us. Our sympathy is evoked even as it is complicated by the increasingly more extreme acts he commits.

Franco's adaptation, however, offers a different portrait of Lester as well as a happy ending. While Scott Haze aptly portrays Lester's haplessness when he shoots someone else's cow for no reason or stumbles in a cold creek while carrying his mattress, he can also appear large, dominating, and dangerous, as when he finds a half-naked woman in the woods and leaps on top of her, screaming "Don't move! Don't move!" The score emphasizes the threatening sense with a sustained minor tone that makes the scene less of a blackly comic encounter than a real assault. Similarly, Lester's first act of necrophilia is a physically violent, explosively feral action that gives him an outlet for his sexual aggression rather than meeting his need as an isolated person to connect; there's no indication here that Lester "poured into that waxen ear everything he'd ever thought of saying to a woman," as McCarthy describes in the novel. After all, McCarthy adds, "[w]ho could say she did not hear him?" (88–89).

In the film Lester's sequential "un-housing" and descent into necrophilia and murder seem more the inevitable result of Lester's already compromised mental state than a fate that he is driven to by his losses and his community's ostracism, as many have understood the novel. If the intent is to portray the suffering and eventual triumph of a person who is already different, then the film works, and that's certainly an apt approach. But for me, it's less powerful than a story about a man whom we observe being driven to such difference, a story in which our own sympathies with him turn back on us when we watch him doing things that are, eventually, quite horrific. But Haze, glaring and sucking and mumbling, doesn't seem very much "like us" at all. Franco does, I should add, create real sympathy for Lester later in the film with Lester's "date" with his first "girlfriend," the corpse of a woman he discovered dead from carbon monoxide poisoning in a car. He dresses her in pretty clothes and talks to her, finally having sex with her and crying out, "I love you! I love you," as sweet music plays on the score. When Lester wakes to find fire engulfing the cabin he's been squatting in, his despair at not being able to "rescue" the girl is real, and moving. But it's one of the few times, I think, that the film invites us to contemplate the familiar human emotions that motivate Lester, his "mystery and humanity," as Luce puts it.

McCarthy himself backed off from a more extreme way of portraying Lester in his drafts of the novel. In one, labeled a "middle draft" by McCarthy, two boys out hunting discover the corpse of Lester's wife in the bottom of White Oak Sink. (In the published novel there is no mention of Lester ever having been married.) The sheriff comes to investigate, and "there he found Mrs Ballard lying in a state of repose on a limestone ledge. Her head was resting on a silk pillow that had embroidered hearts and trees and the inscription I Pine For You And Balsam. . . . She was dressed in a houseshift and had shoes on and her face had been caved in with a blunt instrument." (The state of her corpse and the way she is hauled out of the sink with rope are similar to the scene that ends the published novel, when the newly discovered corpses of Lester's victims are hauled up out of the cave. McCarthy transposes some of the language of this scene with Mrs. Ballard—the "adipocere" that covers her and the "gray rheum" that drips from her body—to the description of those more anonymous corpses.[2]) The implication of this scene is that Lester was married, that he did have companionship of a kind, and that he then at least partially brought his isolation on himself by killing her—quite violently, too, and at close range, without the use of his ever-present rifle. His arrangement of her corpse in a funerary position indicates some combination of regret and affection. A Lester capable of marriage and of killing his spouse is a different Lester indeed, one who could be considered more adult, more responsible for his social alienation, and more immediately capable of passionate, deadly violence.

Another episode McCarthy deleted from the novel further reveals his desire to retreat from a portrayal of Lester as more openly violent or insane. In a draft labeled by McCarthy as a "late draft," Lester exits the cave where he has been living, removes his trousers, and castrates himself, cutting his testicles from his body after laying them on a broken tree limb. "Had his hand done it? Been told? He was still holding the pocketknife. Oh god, he said. Oh god almighty." The scene is followed by Lester's assault on John Greer, the new owner of his former property, while wearing "a frightwig and skirts." This draft includes editorial notes likely made by McCarthy's editor Albert Erskine, who objected strenuously to the castration scene. "No! Talk to me about this," he writes, and then adds, "Mac, it seems to me arbitrary; not set up. OK if you motivate it earlier somehow; but as it comes it is unprepared for. He has haunting guilts [sic] for what he did? OK, but foreshadow it, or you'll lose the reader." He does, however, approve of the scene with Greer on the next page: "Mac—O.K. Now from here this is the way it should go; excellent; true in that way beyond ordinary true; but the key is properly motivating that castration scene."[3] McCarthy apparently agreed that a violently guilty (or perhaps just crazy) Lester—disassociated from the hand that did the deed, perhaps hearing voices—wasn't an apt characterization. In the setting copy for the novel, the castration scene is marked for deletion.[4]

In his interviews about the film, Franco emphasized Lester's human qualities as well as his essential Otherness. "I'm trying to explore the human condition," he said at the Toronto Film Festival, and elaborated: "We all want to connect with other people. We all want to love and be loved. We just do. So this character's obstacle is that he is incapable of being intimate with another living person. He's too weird, he's too creepy, he does not have the tools" ("James Franco Courts"). When the film opened in New York, he said that he saw the project "as an opportunity to examine extreme isolation" (Garvey et al.). Franco is clearly thinking about the effects of alienation on Lester, but the film blurs the line between the effects of isolation and simply being weird or creepy. It's the latter qualities that reviewers most often pick up on. In a positive review for *Screen Daily*, Lee Marshall calls Haze's performance "alarmingly deranged," his Lester a "dimwit ... with a feral survival instinct." In another largely positive review that appeared in the *Guardian* after the film's screening at the Venice Film Festival, Xan Brooks described Haze's Lester as "a feral pariah who rails at his oppressors and shits in the woods and whose constant gurning and grunting suggests he's straining at a stool even when he isn't." These reviewers praise the performance as a committed one, and Brooks notes that even though the acting can be "an awful mixed bag," Franco's film "runs wild through the woods in a way that few others manage."

Negative reviews often honed in on the same elements. In a *USA Today* review titled "*Child of God*: Pray You Don't Have to See It," Claudia Puig rejected the portrayal of Lester as a "monstrous lunatic" as well as the "lurid movie that contains him." Puig describes the film's opening, noting the voice-over that calls Lester a "child of God much like yourself perhaps," and then writes that the cut to "a malevolent beady-eyed gaze peering from a ghoulish face . . . immediately belies the universality of this particular heavenly offspring." A review in the *New York Observer* dismissed Haze as "mumbling [and] scabby" and noted that when the film screened at Venice, it required subtitles to counter Haze's "incoherence" ("James Franco Takes"). And writing in the *New Republic*, William Giraldi had it both ways, calling Franco's adaptation "utterly misguided" but also praising Haze's performance as "virtuosic," "imbued with a feral, frightful intensity." He adds, "He'll be nominated for every major award and if there's any fairness left on earth he will win most of them." But Giraldi contradicts himself a bit when he then says that Haze's garbled speaking constitutes "a suggestion of mental impairment," which is an easy out—it serves to "absolve Ballard of his evil," to "explain what must remain inexplicable." If Haze "grunts, growls, and howls in an exacerbated expression of animality, [it demonstrates that] madness plays best in reticence." Finally, Oliver Lyttleton blamed what he saw as the film's faults on Franco's multitude of projects. "The whole thing feels tossed off," he said of *Child of God*, "like it was made by film students over a couple of weekends. . . . [Y]ou feel that if he were able to focus his considerable energies on a single project, then he might be able to come up with something special."

As in the case of *The Counselor*'s Malkina, an alternative interpretation of this central character might have made all the difference here. The film's overcast, rural setting is evocative, and supporting turns by Tim Blake Nelson and Jim Parrack embody the kind of folksiness that turns decidedly cold whenever Lester shows up. Nina Ljeti, as Lester's dead "girlfriend," is a hauntingly lovely corpse who, ironically, telegraphs more humanity than Haze does as Lester. And the interest in exploring "what it means to be human" is certainly something that McCarthy had in mind as well. But like Malkina, Lester here is too predatory and feral, his motivations too simplified, to make the story as tragically compelling as it might have been. Lester as imagined by Haze and Franco ends the film in triumph rather than pitifully dying from pneumonia. Here, Lester is a superb adapter, managing to live through being shot by Greer and targeted by an angry mob, in addition to the many other indignities of his life. The film concludes with Lester emerging exhausted but triumphant from the underground cave system where he eluded his would-be lynch mob. At the end of the novel, however, he voluntarily returns to the hospital where he dies from pneumonia and his body is dissected by medical students; the decayed corpses of his victims are removed from Lester's underground chamber. By ending with Lester's victory, the film appears to celebrate a difference expressed mostly in hostility and violence rather than lamenting the tragic consequences of exile from the human community.

Like *The Counselor*, *Child of God* is something of a mixed bag for those interested in McCarthy. These two films ensured that the author was a frequent news item in 2013–2014, and they provided ample opportunity for commentary and conversation—not least from McCarthy himself, who revealed in *The Counselor*'s Blu-Ray extras a willingness to talk about his work and his involvement in the film. It's a willingness that's certainly more common now than it was before 2007 and *Oprah*, but it remains a relatively rare occurrence. However, despite the interest generated by new work and McCarthy's own extensive involvement in *The Counselor*, neither film is as compelling a cinematic interpretation or adaptive superimposition as *No Country for Old Men* or *The Sunset Limited*.

Bears That Dance, Bears That Don't

THE ATTEMPTS TO ADAPT *BLOOD MERIDIAN*

*I*N ANY DISCUSSION OF CORMAC MCCARTHY AND ADAPTA-
tion, *Blood Meridian* is the elephant in the room. McCarthy's
epic, philosophical, and pyrotechnically violent novel has been taken up by
producers and directors since at least the mid-1990s, with each eventually
passing on the project for someone else to attempt. Many have seen *Blood
Meridian* as excellent material for a compelling film. It's a tale that is epic
in scope, style, and import, and it's in a genre—the Western—with a long
cinematic history. It also has a narrative focus and sweep that is, as Steven
Frye and others have argued, likely influenced by Western films from directors like Peckinpah, and we know from his correspondence that McCarthy
admires Sergio Leone.[1] The novel's language is ineffably literary and, at the
same time, richly imagistic. After all, this is no *Remembrance of Things Past*,
a deeply internal exploration of memory and the streams of consciousness.
Blood Meridian is a story in which action and landscape speak loudest, and
though it may be philosophical, political, historical, and theological, it is perhaps most primarily a vivid, disturbing, haunting spectacle. And spectacle is
the very language of film. Despite those attractions and advantages, however,
the novel has thus far eluded attempts to bring it to the screen.

Harold Bloom has championed *Blood Meridian* as "the authentic American apocalyptic novel" (Introduction, 1). With that designation, Bloom refers
primarily to the overwhelming amount of violence, although an interpretation following Lorenzo DiTommaso's more specifically theological definition
of apocalypticism (which I reference in my discussion of *The Road* in chapter 4) is also possible—and in fact has been the basis for one of the screenplays adapted from the novel, as I'll explain. Bloom goes on to call *Blood
Meridian* "a canonical imaginative achievement," and he understands that
achievement in the terms of tragedy. He categorizes the novel as "both an

American and a universal tragedy of blood," and deems Judge Holden to be "a villain worthy of Shakespeare, Iago-like and demoniac" (Introduction, 1). Leo Daugherty has written about the novel as "Gnostic tragedy," though he is more interested in delineating the influence of Gnostic thought on the novel than in explaining how the novel creates the "'affect' of Hellenistic tragedy" (168). David Williams has identified elements of the novel consistent with those seen in Greek epic, philosophy, and tragedy, following Charles Segal's understanding of tragedy as an exploration of "boundaries and the ambiguity between [political and social] stages" (17). Kate Montague links *Blood Meridian* to Walter Benjamin's discussion of baroque tragedy (seventeenth-century German drama, what Benjamin calls "mourning plays"). "While tragedy is traditionally understood as the narrative mythologization of violence," Montague writes, "baroque tragedy is, for Benjamin, different from other forms of tragedy because instead of refracting its violent narratives through myth, it does so through a more complicated figuration of historical actuality" (5). (Montague also explains how the kid and the judge "occupy the positions of the two principal figures around which baroque tragedy traditionally centers: one is the 'tyrant,' that source of sovereign juridical power; the other is 'the martyr,' a figure who is excluded from the sovereign order" [6].) For Montague in particular, *Blood Meridian* is a tragedy rooted in history rather than myth, much as Russell Hillier sees *The Counselor* as akin to a Jacobean revenge tragedy, engaging the contemporary issues of the day.

These scholars' approaches to *Blood Meridian* as tragedy also suggest the novel's wide range of influences and intertexts, a range that reaches further than that of any other of his works. Steven Frye has written that *Blood Meridian* "blends all the author's influences, recalling Shakespeare, Melville, Faulkner, and Dostoyevsky, echoing the tone of the King James Bible and Dante's *Divine Comedy*" (66). Frye locates the novel primarily in the tradition of American historical romance, noting as well its revisionist approach to the myth of the frontier hero and its significant philosophical content—content that becomes apparent most often in the statements of and reactions to the character Judge Holden, a "distinctive artistic embodiment of darkness" that engages ideas of "Judeo-Christian cosmology, and typology, scientific materialism with its often purely atheist implications, the continental philosophy of Friedrich Nietzsche, philosophical nihilism, and the fascinating conceptions of ancient Gnosticism" (79). A character like Judge Holden is McCarthy's creation, of course, but he's also based on a historical figure, and the novel as a whole is as rooted in historical research as it is in literary and philosophical traditions.

The primary source for the novel is soldier Samuel Chamberlain's memoir *My Confession: Recollections of a Rogue*. In the late 1840s Chamberlain fought in the Mexican-American War and afterwards rode with John Glanton and his gang, who were contracted by the Mexican government to kill and scalp Native Americans—which they did until the gang was finally decimated by Yuma warriors at a ferry site on the Colorado River. Some of Chamberlain's experiences are the basis for the life of the kid, the book's nameless protagonist who from an early age harbors "a taste for mindless violence" (3). *Blood Meridian* follows the kid as he leaves home at fourteen, travels to Texas, miraculously survives a disastrous filibustering expedition into Mexico in 1849, and then joins the Glanton gang, led by the eponymous Glanton as well as by Judge Holden, a figure who appears in Chamberlain's memoir but in no other historical source that has yet been identified.

McCarthy's research, however, went far beyond Chamberlain. He took notes on works like James Hobbs's *Wild Life in the Far West* (1874), William T. Hamilton's *My Sixty Years on the Plains* (1905), and Waddy Thompson's *Recollections of Mexico* (1846); he recorded precise details about the geography and architecture of places like San Diego, Tucson, and Fort Griffin; he discovered it takes seventy-five parts saltpeter, fifteen parts charcoal, and ten parts sulfur to make a passable gunpowder; and he researched currency, population, individual people, and vocabulary. In his notes on Nacogdoches, Texas, for instance, he wrote, "courthouse built in 1840. By 1850 roof leaked so that rain would force the court to adjourn. Also cold—no stove." He made a list of "horse ailments" that includes strangles, sollander, stanquary, sealing, scouring, scurp, and sandcreaks.[2]

This extensive historical and physical detail lends the novel a feeling of authenticity, of course, but also presents what John Sepich has called *Blood Meridian*'s "problem of information": that the historically verifiable characters and events of the novel are not identifiable or immediately apparent to most readers (1). In addition, "McCarthy's devotion to historical authenticity" set against "the audacity with which he tailors sources to his own ends" creates an interesting friction (3). The kid is the protagonist of the novel, the one we are instructed to "see" in the first sentence—and the kid is not Chamberlain—yet the historical accounts of the Glanton gang provide the backbone of the book. Without them, Sepich says, *Blood Meridian* looks like "three hundred pages of grotesque evidence, derived from McCarthy's imagination, to support Judge Holden's claim that war and violence dominate men's lives" (1). Understanding the novel, Sepich implies, requires the recognition of its particular history in order to justify the representation of such extreme violence. Others have engaged *Blood Meridian*'s presentation of history differently. Dana Phillips argues that the novel's perspective is one of natural, rather than human, history and states that McCarthy could be considered "a writer not of the 'modern' or 'postmodern' eras but of the Holocene, with a strong historical interest in the late Pleistocene and even earlier epochs"

(38). I have written about the interplay between the mythic resonance of the text and the religious beliefs of the Yuma tribe ("Yuman"), and in her article about the archetypal myths of the wilderness that McCarthy engages, Sara Spurgeon locates myths inside the history. "It is within the accuracy of historical detail in *Blood Meridian*," she writes, "that McCarthy finds his mythic history, lurking within the liminal spaces of the familiar rhetoric of Manifest Destiny, the taming of the wilderness, John Wayne's famous swagger, and other pillars of the national symbolic" (76). More recently, David Holmberg uses Foucault's idea of a heterotopian zone to argue that *Blood Meridian* is both myth and history or it is neither. "McCarthy's novel *is* history," he claims, "but it is also myth, narratively and stylistically, although the myth he creates runs concurrent [with] and, importantly, *through* the realities of a revisionist West. . . . *Blood Meridian* is not a case of historical *or* mythological *or* theological *or* postmodern, but historical *and* mythological *and* theological *and* postmodern" (142).

McCarthy himself wrote to his editor Albert Erskine in the spring of 1984, providing a bit of historical information about the Yuma ferry massacre and about a large meteorite discovered in the Southwest that, in the novel, Judge Holden lifts and throws. Then he adds his own estimation of how *Blood Meridian* uses historical sources: "The truth is," he writes, "that the historical material is really—to me—little more than a frame work upon which to hang a dramatic inquiry into the nature of destiny and history and the uses of reason and knowledge & the nature of evil and all these sorts of things which have plagued folks since there were folks." He then adds, "I think the Bard would have agreed with me that that's as proper a use of history as any."[3]

In explaining his use of historical material, McCarthy offers a good definition of what tragedy is and does—a dramatic inquiry that explores destiny, the uses of reason and knowledge, evil, and not least, history itself. These are long-standing, even ancient concerns—ones that have "plagued folks since there were folks"—and McCarthy figures himself as an author who uses historical material much as Shakespeare did when he wrote, for instance, *Richard III*. *Blood Meridian* is a rich text indeed for considerations of those areas of inquiry generated by McCarthy's interest in the various forms of tragedy, as I've argued in previous chapters: what constitutes justice (a central question for Westerns in general and this one in particular), the nature (or absence) of the divine, the question of destiny, humanity's place in nature, the proper workings of society, and—most specifically with regard to the judge—the nature of evil, the uses of knowledge, and the function of representation. This is also a novel in which witnessing is a significant and complex theme. The novel instructs the reader to "[s]ee the child" in its first sentence, and the notion of witnessing is repeatedly interrogated by the judge, who tells Webster, in response to Webster's refusal to consent to the judge's sketching him, that "[w]hether in my book or not, every man is tabernacled in every other and he in exchange and so on in an endless complexity of being and witness to the uttermost edge of the world" (3, 141). A few pages later, the narrator describes another statement by the judge about the ubiquity of witnessing, of witnessing as in some sense the fundamental act of humans:

> The posting of witnesses by a third and other path altogether might also be called in evidence as appearing to beggar chance, yet the judge, who had put his horse forward until he was abreast of the speculants, said that in this was expressed the very nature of the witness and that his proximity was no third thing but rather the prime, for what could be said to occur unobserved? (153)

Finally, near the novel's end, when the judge accuses the kid of breaking with the gang's violent community and setting himself apart from it, he tells the kid that "you were a witness against yourself. You sat in judgement on your own deeds. You put your own allowances before the judgements of history. ... If war is not holy man is nothing but antic clay.... Only each was called upon to empty out his heart into the common and one did not. Can you tell me who that one was?" (307).

The judge accuses the kid of failing to fully embrace what the judge sees as the violent, Dionysian revelry of war, which he also calls (appropriately, if one wishes to understand this in terms of Nietzschean tragedy) "the dance." The kid has held himself apart, he says — he has stepped back, witnessed, and judged, which caused him to break with the group even as he remained a part of it. The kid, however, understands the isolated (and perhaps, again following Nietzsche, Apollonian) figure here differently: "It was you, whispered the kid. You were the one" (307). The main action of the novel ends with the judge literally on stage, dancing naked at a great bacchanal, having surprised the kid — now the man — in an outhouse, "gathering him in his arms against his immense and terrible flesh," and shutting the door (333). Like it or not, the kid is ultimately subsumed by the judge, who insists that violent revelry is the only way to be fully alive, to dance. "There is room on the stage for one beast and one beast alone," he tells the kid in their last words together. "All others are destined for a night that is eternal and without name. One by one they will step down into the darkness before the footlamps. Bears that dance, bears that dont" (331). The judge's dominance and his seeming victory over the kid have been enacted in response to the kid's resistance to his all-encompassing violence, to his dance. I associate the kid, then, with other McCarthy characters drawn together by their struggle against forces that are larger, often malevolent, and not entirely legible to them, like Robert Mc-Evoy in *The Gardener's Son*, Black in *The Sunset Limited*, Sherriff Bell in *No Country for Old Men*, or even Lester Ballard in *Child of God*. Even when the conclusion is tragic, the struggle matters.

These are brief observations about a rich text, but they indicate, I hope, how productive it can be to think about *Blood Meridian*'s engagement with tragedy, spectacle, witnessing, and performance, though an adaptation of the novel for cinematic performance has yet to appear. Indeed, attempts to adapt this sprawling, difficult novel have also been defined by struggle, though interestingly, they take differing approaches to the tragic arc of the narrative. After McCarthy became famous in 1992 with *All the Pretty Horses*, producer Scott Rudin purchased the rights to *Blood Meridian*, and by 1994 Steve Tesich was working on a screenplay; his finished version is dated January 1995 (Busch; Tesich). Tesich had previously won the Academy Award for Best Original Screenplay for *Breaking Away* (1979), and he adapted John Irving's novel *The World According to Garp* (1982). *Blood Meridian* was one of his last projects before he died in 1996. Tesich's screenplay diverges significantly from the novel and yet offers an interpretation of it as theological tragedy, an apocalyptic narrative that withholds final deliverance.

The screenplay's opening uses the Leonid meteor shower of 13 November 1833 to frame its approach to the story. While the novel opens with the kid's father speaking briefly about the night the "stars did fall" with such frequency as to astonish those who watched, Tesich begins in a way that is quite literally cosmic:

> EXT. SPACE
>
> We are high above the earth as if in a spaceship. No sound. Nothing but the calm infinity of space. Things hove past us. Chunks of matter. Chunks of rock. Some enormous. Some not. More and more of the objects move past us, spinning as they move. We're watching the great meteor shower of 1833 heading down toward the earth but we don't see the earth yet. The number of meteors now become hundreds. Then thousands. Like an invasion. What had seemed poetic now becomes menacing. More and more of them. Then we see the earth itself. Way down there. It's a tiny thing. We hurtle toward it as if our camera were another chunk of meteorite. Faster and faster we fall among the spinning meteorites falling toward the earth. Faster and faster. The earth grows in size. (1)

Shots then show Native Americans looking up at the sky, slaves and guards on a slave ship watching in fear, and church bells ringing in a town where the townspeople are screaming. In a farmhouse a woman is giving birth, and after the infant appears, she dies. The next scene follows a horse and rider—the kid, now sixteen—and the second shot shows him from above: "We SEE him, a tiny dot, in the vastness of the oceanic space through which he's moving" (2).

The screenplay repeatedly uses overhead shots to emphasize the vastness of the landscape. They suggest, too, that human actions are insignificant at the same time that they have, paradoxically, cosmic import. What that import may be, especially with regard to the kid, is the central question of the screenplay. When the kid first talks with Judge Holden, the judge asks if he's a "runaway" or a "throwaway." He then adds, "I take your silence to mean that one if not both of the above are true, son." "I ain't your son, Mister," the kid responds, which leads the judge to introduce himself formally and to phrase the question in his own way:

> Judge. Judge Holden. The fact is, son, that none of us can state with any degree of authority who our fathers are, spiritual, intellectual or biological. Even Jesus Christ of Nazareth didn't know for sure who His father was when He was your age. And then He thought He did. And then when He was dying, He had His doubts again. Are you saying that you are better informed on the question of your genealogy than He was? (12–13)

Shortly thereafter, the kid explains to Robert, a man who recruits him into a filibustering expedition led by Captain White, that he doesn't even have a name: "See, I've never been baptized with no name of my own on account of what I did," he says. "I killed my Mama is what" (27). Robert says he figures that's no fault of the kid's, but the kid explains, "My Daddy thought otherwise. Said no Christian name was worth ruining on me. Said the only name worthy of my crime was Judas Iscariot, but he couldn't bring himself to use it on account of being a good Christian himself. So he called me nothing" (28). The kid's namelessness in the novel is never explained and could merely be the author's refusal to designate one for him; here, though, the refusal is the father's, and it reflects his indictment of the kid for causing, however unintentionally, his mother's death.

The judge also figures the kid as a betrayer, implicating the kid with another reference to Judas:

> When wolves hunt, there is harmony in the pack. When men hunt wolves or other men, there must be harmony there as well. All it takes is one man who, in his heart, bears witness against the others to dis-

rupt that harmony. One man. That's all it takes. One man who clings, in however tenuous a fashion ... to the notion that good exists, causes by his mere presence the spectre of evil to appear as a complement. Such a man might be here having supper with us in the flesh and yet withdrawing his whole heart from the rest of us. He must either willingly and lovingly commit himself to this collective endeavor, or else he must be exposed as the Judas Iscariot that he is. (73–74)

The judge further makes clear that their collective endeavor is war, and that "war is God," as he also says in the novel (75). Tesich distills the many battles we see the Glanton gang undertake in the novel into a single massacre of peaceful Tiguas, after which both black Jackson and Glanton himself turn against the judge. Glanton, after being shot in the stomach in a bar fight, vows to kill the judge before he dies. As the judge dances with the bride at a wedding in an unnamed Mexican town, Glanton takes aim and shoots, only to hit the bride instead and then die in the ensuing firefight (104). (His demise is more graphically rendered in the novel, where he is killed by a Yuma chief who "mounts into [his] actual bed," raises an axe, and "split the head of John Joel Glanton down to the thrapple" [275].) The gang scalps the dead Mexicans at the judge's behest, since, as he points out, their dark hair will pass for that of the Apaches they have been contracted to kill. When Mexican soldiers later discover the ruse, however, the gang is attacked in Chihuahua City, and everyone is killed except for Tobin, the kid, the judge, and a small child that the judge uses as a human shield to help him escape.

This confrontation, rather than the Yuma ferry massacre, sets up the endgame of the screenplay. As the four ride into the mountains, Tobin urges the kid to shoot the judge, but the kid fears hitting the child instead. Later, he prepares to slip off and leave while the other three are sleeping but sees the child and reconsiders. Will the kid save himself or save the child? Is he Judas, or is he Christ? In Tesich's screenplay the judge is Satan. "It's a comfort having me around," he explains:

> Knowing that in your most ruthless self-assessment of your own wicked ways, there is one who, in your opinion, is even more wicked. And when the word evil rises up in your mind, it's comforting to deflect its meaning away from yourself and upon me. Who else is willing to take on such a job? (119)

In the end, the kid demands the judge hand over the child. The judge moves to do so, but instead he throws the child over a ridge. The kid unhesitatingly leaps after the boy, catching him as they fall together. The screenplay's ending puts him into the cosmic landscape that the repeated overhead shots and theological allusions have suggested all along:

> A brief image of the JUDGE, standing on the edge of the precipice,
>   and then we're FALLING over the edge ourselves.
> CLOSEUP: THE KID AND THE CHILD
> Falling through the mist. Holding on to one another. Falling into
>   SUNLIGHT. The HORSES, *whinnying* terribly, fall past them. Then
>   TOBIN, spinning, *screaming*, falls past them. The CHILD in the
>   KID's arms is strangely composed, but the KID is not. He is *crying*.
> He is *weeping*.
> KID: GOD! GOD, WHERE ARE YOU?
> And so they fall and fall and fall.
> THE END

The screenplay begins and ends with falling bodies. The kid's last line is clunky and belabors the theological allegory—Why *have* you forsaken me, God?—but it serves to culminate this unapologetic interpretation that emphasizes the kid's metaphysical and theological choice, the nature of evil, and the struggle to comprehend the intentions of an absent God. The theological approach also frames the story's violence as Satan's temptation of man rather than as historical reality, or as a dark view of human nature, or as an exciting visual spectacle. The result is an effective way of addressing the particularly cinematic problem of what to do with all that vivid brutality and bloodshed. And in DiTommaso's terms, it's an apocalypse narrative that represents the conflict between good and evil in such a way that it suggests how the world is ordered in service of a transcendent reality. But it doesn't end with redemptive deliverance: at the screenplay's end the kid is still falling—and still waiting.

Tesich's interpretation was only the first of many that would never reach the screen. Many years later, Ridley Scott decided to take on the project, and he even set a release date of 2009 (Thielman). (Scott Rudin was listed as producer and so likely maintained the rights in the interim.) Scott soon abandoned the effort, however, saying that in his case he couldn't figure out a way to handle the extensive violence. In his commentary on the Blu-Ray for *The Counselor*, he reflects back on that decision:

> *Blood Meridian* was one of my favorite reads. And it was . . . on the
> surface, you think, wow, this is going to make a slam-dunk West-
> ern, be fantastic. But it is so bloody and so unforgiving, irredeemably
> dark, that we had it written, it was written by Bill Monahan, a good

screenplay. But the orchestration of death was so endless, continuous, that I had to say, I wonder—should this not remain a book rather than try to make it into a movie? Because I think it's a good question.

Scott was working with a screenplay by Bill Monahan, who won an Academy Award for Best Adapted Screenplay for *The Departed* (2006). Unlike Tesich's version, many people have heard of Monahan's *Blood Meridian*, and it's available for download on some online screenwriting forums. Unfortunately, this is an unauthenticated copy—it doesn't list Monahan's name on the title page and is attributed to him only by hearsay. Like Tesich's, this version makes changes to the novel's plot, though here the effect is more Peckinpah on steroids than Bergman lite. It begins with the kid shooting his drunken, dying father and ends, after a relentless series of battles, scalpings, murders, and orations from the judge, with the confrontation between the kid and the judge in the jakes. This time, though, the kid pulls a bowie knife, and after some sort of fight that is heard but not seen, he emerges injured but alive— no tragic ending for him. In the final scene, the kid takes responsibility for a small boy, the brother of Elrod, whom he killed in a shootout. He promises to take the boy east and raise him, and the two ride off together, leaving the West and its endemic violence behind.

Monahan reflected on his screenplay in 2010, calling it "one of the best scripts I have ever done." The story's violence presented an obstacle in getting the film made, he noted, and added that "no one can quite understand that Glanton is the hero and the boy is the observer, as in more than one Western, not least *Shane*" (Weintraub). Monahan, then, interprets Glanton as the protagonist, a nonstandard reading that could nonetheless work well narratively. Regardless, though Monahan's screenplay was indeed admired by Scott and others, it never made it into production.

After Scott gave up on the adaptation, director Todd Field took the reins, working on a screenplay of his own (Medina). "[McCarthy's] work examines our core," said Field at the time, "the two faces of violence that co-exist in every savage act—brutal strength of purpose holding hands with a desperate and cowering weakness." Many noted how different this subject matter was from Field's other projects as director, the domestic dramas *In the Bedroom* (2001) and *Little Children* (2006). As Scott's originally had been, Field's *Blood Meridian* was also set for release in 2009 (Medina). That version didn't come to pass either, and the next person to publicly take up the challenge was James Franco. But somewhere along the way, Andrew Dominik, Tommy Lee Jones, and John Hillcoat all considered the project as well. In 2009 it was reported that Jones had written an adaptation of the novel at some point in the past and that Hillcoat had thought about trying to direct an adaptation before working on his Australian Western *The Proposition* (Fleming, "Duo"; Bledsoe). In an article for the web site *Vice* about the various attempts at *Blood Meridian*, James Franco writes that of all the scripts Jones's was the "most loyal" to the book and reports that Jones had talked to Jack Nicholson about playing the judge. Franco also says that Andrew Dominik had spoken with him about being part of an adaptation of *Cities of the Plain* and that during that conversation Dominik mentioned that he had also once thought of pursuing *Blood Meridian*. (Dominik's interest in adapting the novel was also reported by Jonathan Dean in 2013.)

The conversations with Dominik spurred Franco himself to give *Blood Meridian* a try. He shot a half-hour test reel that shows Tobin's story about how the gang met the judge (Franco, "James Franco's 'Blood'"). In this sequence taken from chapter 10 of the novel, the judge helps the Glanton gang fashion gunpowder out of saltpeter, charcoal, and sulfur when they have run out and are being pursued by Apaches. Scott Glenn plays Tobin and Mark Pellegrino, whom Franco notes is his old acting teacher, plays the judge (Franco, "Adapting"). Franco later released the test reel as part of his publicity blitz for *Child of God*.

The test was "awesome," reported Franco, and in 2011 he got a green light for the full adaptation from Scott Rudin, who still owned the rights (Franco, "Adapting"; Brooks, "Franco to Direct"). But this would turn out to be yet another false start. In 2014 Franco tells the story of his own failed attempt at *Blood Meridian*, omitting Rudin's name from the narrative: "It was a dream come true," he writes, "but, for various reasons, it fell apart. The unnamed producer got mad at me and took the rights back, so, *bam*, that's it. I don't get to do it" (Franco, "Adapting"). It's not a detailed explanation—bam, that's it—but whatever happened, it didn't deter Franco from turning his attention to *Child of God* by the fall of 2011 (Patch). Then in May 2016, news broke that Franco was indeed going to direct *Blood Meridian*, this time with Russell Crowe in a starring role (presumably as the judge), and also featuring Vincent D'Onofrio and Tye Sheridan. Almost immediately, however, news followed that the adaptation had been scrapped because Franco did not, in fact, have the rights to adapt the novel, and some speculated that the sudden publicity had derailed already tenuous negotiations (Jaafar). This second false start for Franco, then, seems also to have turned on Rudin's lack of confidence in the project.

Given the parade of failed attempts by quite different writers and directors, *Blood Meridian* has developed a reputation as an impossible adaptation, a story with so much blood and bleakness that trying to put it on the screen would result in inevitable capitulation. McCarthy himself, however, disagrees. When John Jurgensen asked him if it would be impossible to adapt for film, he said,

That's all crap. The fact that it's a bleak and bloody story has nothing to do with whether or not you can put it on the screen. That's not the issue. The issue is it would be very difficult to do and would require someone with a bountiful imagination and a lot of balls. But the pay-off could be extraordinary.

As he suggested to Oprah Winfrey when talking about the plot of *The Road*, assuming you know how the story will end is a mistake—better to take a risk and see where the road takes you. The world is suffused with violence and suffering, and none of McCarthy's narratives demonstrates that as amply as *Blood Meridian*. But the kid doesn't succumb to the judge's calls to the dance. He resists, though he does so in a way that is inarticulate and largely ineffective. The old woman he approaches to help, offering to "convey her to a safe place, some party of her countrypeople" turns out to be nothing but a "dried shell," an old, desiccated corpse, and the prostitute he visits before his final confrontation with the judge shoos him out of her room, offering the weak assurance that "[y]ou'll be all right" (315, 332). At the end of the hallway, he turns and looks back at her standing in the doorway, gazing at her briefly before "[descending] into the dark of the stairwell" (333).

These are attempts, at least, at a recognition of and empathy with others, though they pale in comparison with John Grady's relationship to horses, Black's elaborate effort to save White, or Bell's reflections on how his actions have affected those around him. But the impulse is there, even in a character defined on the first page of *Blood Meridian* as harboring "a taste for mindless violence" (3). Ultimately, all the considerations that the violence of the world gives rise to in McCarthy's work and in tragedy generally are underlain by the fundamental significance of our human communities, moral ecosystems, and how we draw together in response to that violence. That union can be fumbling and inarticulate, traversed more often in language between humans rather than in wordless communion with animals or the divine. And representation, as so many of McCarthy's characters worry, can lead one astray as easily as it leads us to one another. But that's a risk McCarthy's corpus suggests we have to take. Bears that dance, bears that don't. The judge uses this statement to call the kid to create violence, but we could also understand it as a metaphor for the rough creatures that we all are, slouching toward some kind of articulation of the relationships we have with each other, doing our best in the glow of the footlights before we all step down into darkness.

Notes

INTRODUCTION

1. Sophocles, *Oedipus the King*, in *The Three Theban Plays*, 230; emphasis added.

2. The most notable tragic effect, of course, is catharsis (the arousing and purging of pity and fear), another term that has been much discussed and debated.

3. Christopher White and Cameron MacKenzie have also written about the Border Trilogy's engagement with language, vision, and "the real." See White's "Dreaming the Border Trilogy"; and MacKenzie's "A Song of Great Order."

4. See Wegner, "'Wars and Rumors of Wars.'"

5. Notes and fragments included with "Whales and Men" materials, but much appears to be unrelated to that screenplay. Typescript with holograph corrections, n.d., Cormac McCarthy Papers box 97, folder 1, n.p., Southwestern Writers Collection, Wittliff Collections, Texas State University, San Marcos (hereafter CMP followed by box and folder numbers, if applicable).

6. "Synopsis—*Cities of the Plain*," n.d., typescript, CMP box 69, folder 3.

CHAPTER 1

1. Bensky to Erskine, 9 July 1963, Albert Erskine Papers box 29, folder 3, Albert and Shirley Small Special Collections Library, University of Virginia (hereafter Erskine Papers, followed by box and folder numbers, if applicable).

2. Erskine to McCarthy, 14 November 1963; McCarthy to Erskine, received December 1963; Erskine to McCarthy, 2 June 1964, Erskine Papers box 29, folder 3.

3. Erskine to McCarthy, 27 May 1977, Erskine Papers box 29, folder 10.

4. McCarthy to Bensky, [n.d.] 1964, Erskine Papers box 29, folder 4.

5. Author's Questionnaire, [1964], Erskine Papers box 29, folder 4.

6. Berkley to McCarthy, 20 March 1967, Erskine Papers box 29, folder 6.

7. Random House memo, Suzanne Baskin for Albert Erskine to Tom Lowry, 28 March 1967, Erskine Papers box 29, folder 6.

8. Kaminsky to Erskine, 22 August 1968, Erskine Papers box 29, folder 2.

9. Erskine to McCarthy, 23 August 1968; handwritten note on letter from Kaminsky to Erskine, 22 August 1968, both in Erskine Papers box 29, folder 2.

10. McCarthy to Erskine, received 11 October 1968, Erskine Papers box 29, folder 2.

11. Erskine to McCarthy, 17 October 1968, Erskine Papers box 29, folder 2.

12. McCarthy to Erskine, received 8 October 1970; Erskine to McCarthy, 30 December 1970, both in Erskine Papers box 29, folder 2.

13. McCarthy to Erskine, received 24 September 1971, Erskine Papers box 29, folder 2.

14. McCarthy to Erskine, received 1 December 1971, Erskine Papers box 29, folder 2.

15. McCarthy to Woolmer, 28 June 1985, Howard Woolmer Collection of Cormac McCarthy box 1, folder 5, Southwestern Writers Collection, Wittliff Collections, Texas State University, San Marcos (hereafter Howard Woolmer Collection followed by box and folder numbers, if applicable).

16. Quotations are taken from the published version of *The Gardener's Son*, which appeared in 1996. The shooting script, which is a later draft than this version, can be found in the Richard Inman Pearce Collection of the South Caroliniana Library, the University of South Carolina.

17. McCarthy to Pearce, [1976], CMP box 18, folder 1.

18. Ibid.

19. McCarthy to Woolmer, 13 December 1976, Howard Woolmer Collection box 1, folder 2.

20. "The Gardener's Son" draft, n.d., typescript, CMP box 18, folder 5, p. 81.

21. Ibid., p. 85.

22. Ibid., p. 86.

23. Ibid., p. 91.

24. McCarthy to Greenleaf, 19 December 1981, Collection 1700, Southwestern Writers Collection, Wittliff Collections, Texas State University, San Marcos.

CHAPTER 2

1. McCarthy to Woolmer, 28 June 1985, Howard Woolmer Collection box 1, folder 5.

2. McCarthy to Woolmer, 16 October 1985, Howard Woolmer Collection box 1, folder 5.

3. Robert C. Clark includes a chapter on *The Road* in his monograph *American Literary Minimalism* and mentions *No Country for Old Men* in the same context (21, 54, 122–137).

4. McCarthy to Woolmer, 12 March 1974, Howard Woolmer Collection box 1, folder 2; "El Paso/Juarez" treatment, 1978, typescript, CMP box 69, folder 2.

5. McCarthy to Woolmer, 26 January 1977, Howard Woolmer Collection box 1, folder 2.

6. "Synopsis—'Cities of the Plain,'" n.d., typescript, CMP box 69, folder 3.

7. "Cities of the Plain" character list, n.d., typescript, CMP box 69, folder 4.

8. The earliest draft of *Cities of the Plain* has irregular pagination but does include a thirty-four-page version of the epilogue. McCarthy labels this one a "1st and early draft," and the first page is dated "Thurs/Nov 3-'88." No dates appear on the epilogue pages, but a previous scene, in which John Grady fights Eduardo, is dated "Aug 3 [1989]," so McCarthy may have been working on the epilogue in late summer or early fall of 1989. *Cities of the Plain* draft, 1988–1989, typescript with heavy corrections, CMP box 71, folder 5. The date is noted on page 1. The epilogue appears on pages labeled 2-1 through 2-33 and 2-x1, 2-x2, and 2-x3.

9. "El Paso/Juarez" treatment, 1978, typescript, CMP box 69, folder 2, pp. 2, 19.

10. The Cormac McCarthy Papers include a number of complete and incomplete drafts of "Cities of the Plain." The complete drafts are: 1) typescript draft with light corrections, n.d., box 69, folder 7; 2) photocopy and typescript pages with heavy corrections, n.d., box 69, folder 9 (a corrected and expanded copy of the previous draft); 3) printout draft, n.d., box 69, folder 10; 4) printout draft, n.d., box 70, folder 1; 5) photocopy draft with corrections, n.d., box 70, folder 2 (a corrected and expanded copy of the previous draft).

11. "Note to the stenographer" regarding "Cities of the Plain," n.d., CMP box 70, folder 4.

12. "Cities of the Plain" draft, n.d., typescript with light corrections, CMP box 69, folder 7, p. 32.

13. "Cities of the Plain" draft, n.d., photocopy and typescript pages with heavy corrections, CMP box 69, folder 9. See, for example, the page labeled "Page 1 (62)." Given that the English lines of dialogue are typed with what looks like McCarthy's Olivetti typewriter and the Spanish lines appear in a different font, it's possible that someone is providing McCarthy with these translations for him to incorporate as he likes into the screenplay.

14. "Cities of the Plain" draft (incomplete), n.d., holograph pages on notebook paper, pp. 18–62, CMP box 69, folder 5.

15. Ibid., p. 20.

16. "Cities of the Plain" draft, n.d., typescript with light corrections, CMP box 69, folder 7, pp. 22, 29.

17. In her article "John Grady's Heroism in *All the Pretty Horses*," Dianne Luce notes reviews by Richard Ryan, Richard Eder, and Earl Dachslager, all of whom say in various ways that John Grady Cole is just too good to be true (67n1).

18. *All the Pretty Horses* draft, n.d., typescript, first draft with heavy corrections, CMP box 46, folder 9, p. 146.

19. "Cities of the Plain" draft, n.d., typescript with light corrections, CMP box 69, folder 7, p. 14.

20. "Cities of the Plain" draft, n.d., photocopy and typescript pages with heavy corrections, CMP box 69, folder 9, pp. 14A–14B.

21. "Cities of the Plain" draft, n.d., photocopy draft with corrections, CMP box 70, folder 2, p. 15; fragments of draft of "Cities of the Plain" and handwritten notes, n.d., photocopy, CMP box 70, folder 4, n.p.

22. *The Crossing* draft, 1987, typescript with heavy corrections, CMP box 55, folder 6, p. 1.

23. McCarthy to Greenleaf, 5 January 1988, Collection 1700, Southwestern Writers Collection.

24. *Cities of the Plain* draft, 1988–1989, typescript with heavy corrections, CMP box 71, folder 5, p. 1.

25. McCarthy to Woolmer, postmarked 8 April 1989, Howard Woolmer Collection box 1, folder 7.

26. Further complicating the question of the composition process is Edwin Arnold's reporting that in 1994 Gary Fisketjon, then McCarthy's editor, remembered McCarthy beginning the Border Trilogy as two books rather than three, because *"All the Pretty Horses* was seen as necessary preparation for the conclusion of John Grady's story outlined in the 'Cities of the Plain' screenplay. If this is so," Arnold continues, "then *The Crossing* and Billy Parham would be later additions to the narrative" (Arnold, "Mosaic" 183).

27. Charles Bailey reads *The Crossing* as a tragedy, noting Billy's similarities to both Hamlet and Oedipus: "Billy is a dispossessed son whose father's murder took place while he was away. Second, out of moral responsibility and guilt, he must reclaim what the dead father, in the son's absence, has been robbed of" (295). Thus the parallels to *Hamlet*, leading Bailey to *Oedipus* as well: "But no sooner does Billy set the traps than he contrives to check them alone. Acting from an Oedipal impulse, he replaces his father, and when he captures the wolf, instead of bringing her back to the ranch as his father had instructed, Billy steals his father's wolf (a female and a mother) and pursues his own course" (296).

28. McCarthy to Woolmer, n.d. [1986], Howard Woolmer Collection box 1, folder 6.

29. McCarthy to Woolmer, 27 August 1986, Howard Woolmer Collection box 1, folder 6.

30. McCarthy to Erskine, 1 December 1986, Erskine Papers box 28, folder 8.

31. "Whales and Men" draft, n.d., photocopy of corrected pages, CMP box 97, folder 2, n.p. (This is how these materials are labeled in the McCarthy Papers, though McCarthy's own label simply reads "NOTES etc." Rather than a draft, this folder of materials appears to be a hodgepodge of notes and fragments.)

32. "Whales and Men" draft, n.d., typescript with holograph corrections in pencil, labeled "First Draft," CMP box 97, folder 1. On the draft labeled "Final Draft," the "Of" in the title is blocked out. "Whales and Men" draft, n.d., printout with no corrections, CMP box 97, folder 5.

33. "No Country for Old Men" draft, n.d., photocopy of corrected typescript, CMP box 79, folder 1, p. 24.

34. "No Country for Old Men" draft fragment, n.d., typescript pages with holograph corrections, CMP box 79, folder 6, n.p.

35. These changes to the plot are evident in the earliest drafts of the novel included in the McCarthy Papers. One that McCarthy labels "ORIG DRAFT" has all the major plot elements of the novel. *No Country for Old Men* draft, n.d., typescript with heavy corrections, CMP box 80, folder 7. However, materials in a folder that McCarthy labeled "Prison + misc (n/useable)," and that consist of notes and fragments, indicate that at some point in the process of writing the novel, McCarthy considered shaping the plot differently. On one page he writes "Bell/Chigurh showdown?", perhaps wondering if he should include a version of the desert showdown scene from the screenplay. Other pages labeled "prison" indicate that McCarthy wrote scenes in which Chigurh is arrested and put in prison. One fragment seems to describe Chigurh being executed: "The cold gray eyes turned once to the gallery. . . . Then they turned away. They did not close. The doctor watched the retreat away into the skull like a brakeman going down a tunnel with his lantern. They flared again for a moment. Then the fire flickered and vanished." (The space between "the" and "retreat" is in the original.) Other fragments portray Bell and Carla Jean shocked by the news that Chigurh has died in prison of no apparent cause. McCarthy, then, toyed with the idea of Carla Jean surviving to see the death of her husband's murderer; on a page labeled "Carla Jean on Chigurh," an official tells her that "I dont believe you have any further interest in this matter," to which she responds that "he needed to think again cause I had a hell of an interest in it." *No Country for Old Men* notes and fragments, n.d., typescript pages with corrections, CMP box 84, folder 4, n.p., and pages labeled "Prison x3" and "Prison x4."

CHAPTER 3

1. "The Sunset Limited" script, notated by McCarthy, 30 March 2006, CMP box 96, folder 5, pp. 81–82.

2. "Longtime stone-fence builder Frank E. Guy Sr, 77, dies," *Lexington Herald-Leader*, CMP box 66, folder 4.

3. "The Stonemason" typescript, heavily corrected early draft with holograph note on first page, "Begun Thurs Feb 14" [1985], CMP box 66, folder 7.

4. "The Stonemason" draft, photocopy, CMP box 66, folder 10, p. 1.

5. The three drafts in screenplay format are as follows: 1) "The Stonemason's Chronicle," typescript with heavy corrections, CMP box 66, folder 7; 2) "The Stonemason" draft, photocopy of corrected draft, CMP box 66, folder 8; and 3) "The Stonemason" draft, typescript with heavy corrections, CMP box 66, folder 9.

6. "The Stonemason" draft, first page dated "10 Jan 86," typescript with heavy corrections, CMP box 66, folder 11, p. 1.

7. McCarthy to Erskine, 25 February 1986, Erskine Papers box 28, folder 8; McCarthy to Woolmer, 25 February 1986, Howard Woolmer Collection box 1, folder 6; McCarthy to Greenleaf, 25 February 1986, Collection 1700, Southwestern Writers Collection.

8. McCarthy to Woolmer, 3 June 1986, Howard Woolmer Collection box 1, folder 6.

9. Ibid.

10. McCarthy to Woolmer, 5 January 1988, Howard Woolmer Collection box 1, folder 7.

11. Woolmer to McCarthy, 11 September 1992, Howard Woolmer Collection box 1, folder 7.

12. Woolmer to McCarthy, 10 March 1993, Howard Woolmer Collection box 1, folder 7.

13. Janice Paran to McCarthy, 13 May 1997, CMP box 66, folder 2.

14. "McCarter—reading," holograph notes, 20 June 1997, CMP box 66, folder 6, p. 1.

15. Emily Mann to McCarthy, 1 July 1997, CMP box 66, folder 2.

16. McCarthy to Mann, n.d. [1999], CMP box 66, folder 2.

17. Mann to McCarthy, 20 April 1999, and "McCarter Theatre Lab rehearsal schedule," 7 May 1999, CMP box 67, folder 8.

18. These fragments in novel format appear in a folder after an irregularly paginated and incomplete draft of "The Sunset Limited" written as a play. "The Sunset Limited" draft fragments, typescript with heavy corrections, n.d., CMP box 94, folder 2, n.p., 2.

19. "The Sunset Limited" copyedited ms., 20 June 2006, CMP box 95, folder 7.

20. "Sell sheet" for *The Sunset Limited*, typescript, 27 July 2006, CMP box 94, folder 1.

21. "The Sunset Limited" incomplete draft in folder, printout with corrections, n.d., CMP box 95, folder 5.

22. "The Sunset Limited" script, notated by McCarthy, 30 March 2006, CMP box 96, folder 5, pp. 32, 92.

23. See, for example, Barbara Vitello, "Too-Long Treatise on Life, Faith Lacks Drama," *Daily Herald* [Arlington Heights, IL] 2 June 2006; and Hedy Weiss, "'Sunset' Debate on Faith, Salvation Grows Tiresome," *Chicago Sun-Times* 30 May 2006.

CHAPTER 4

1. It's worth noting here that religious studies scholars have debated differing definitions of "apocalypse," which tend to apply much more specifically to sacred texts and their particular historical context. See John J. Collins's *The Apocalyptic Imagination* for an overview of these definitions and how they relate to literary genre, historical movements, and eschatology.

2. *The Road* draft, labeled "The Road—1st draft" by McCarthy, and includes the label "The Grail" on typescript pages, CMP box 87, folder 6, n.p.

3. An earlier draft of this final passage appears in a folder of notes and fragments, and as written here it emphasizes loss and finality to an even greater degree: "Brook trout in a teacolored stream that smell of moss in your hand. Polished and muscular

and torsional. Their white edged fins wimple in the slow current. In this deep glen. A world older than man. Humming with mystery. What has come contains the all of what has been. And now it is no more." "*The Road* notes and fragments," n.d., typescript pages, heavily corrected, CMP box 87, folder 3, n.p.

4. *The Road* draft, labeled "The Road—1st draft" by McCarthy, typescript draft, heavily corrected, CMP box 87, folder 6, n.p.

5. Interestingly, in a folder of notes and fragments included in his manuscript materials for *The Road* is a draft of a scene in which the father sees a firefly and wonders at it: "What sort of light could penetrate the shroud of gloom in which the earth turned." This is a literal source of light in addition to the son's metaphorical light. This scene appears neither in other drafts nor in the novel as published, perhaps because it emphasizes the possibility for ecological renewal further than McCarthy wished (or perhaps because the novel was already heavy with imagery of fire and flame). "*The Road* notes and fragments," n.d., typescript pages with heavy corrections, CMP box 87, folder 3, page labeled "The Grail" and "33/183."

CHAPTER 6

1. Ellis notes that the blow to the head Lester receives doesn't help much, either—a reading that Benjamin West has expanded on, speculating on the possibility that one could attribute some of Lester's subsequent behavior to post-concussion syndrome.

2. *Child of God* draft, n.d., typescript draft with corrections, CMP box 16, folder 2, p. 3. This scene is inserted after an irregularly paged draft. On the folder McCarthy has noted dates in 1970 and 1971 and correlated them with page numbers, indicating when he was working on which sections.

3. *Child of God* draft, n.d., photocopy with holograph editorial notations, CMP box 16, folder 5, pp. 136–138.

4. *Child of God* setting copy, n.d., photocopy, CMP box 16, folder 6, p. 137.

CONCLUSION

1. McCarthy to Cumbow, postmarked 9 March 1987, Collection 1700, folder 2, Southwestern Writers Collection, Wittliff Collections, Texas State University, San Marcos.

2. Notes on Hobbs, Hamilton, and Thompson appear in photocopied notebook pages in a folder labeled "OV (West)," CMP box 35, folder 5, n.p. The notes on cities, the gunpowder recipe, and the list of horse ailments appear in a folder of typescript notes with holograph corrections, CMP box 35, folder 7, n.p.

3. McCarthy to Erskine, [March 1984], Erskine Papers box 28, folder 8.

Bibliography

Acting McCarthy: The Making of Billy Bob Thornton's All the Pretty Horses. Dir. Peter Josyph and Raymond Todd. Lost Medallion Productions, 2001. DVD.

Adams, Emily. "Lots of Magic Before 'Sunset.'" *New York Post* 3 February 2011. 14. Print.

Alarcón, Daniel Cooper. "All the Pretty Mexicos: Cormac McCarthy's Mexican Representations." *Cormac McCarthy: New Directions.* Ed. James Lilley. Albuquerque: U of New Mexico P, 2002. 141–152. Print.

All the Pretty Horses. Dir. Billy Bob Thornton. Perf. Matt Damon, Henry Thomas. Columbia Pictures, 2000. Film.

Alter, Alexandra. "Literary Giant Obsessed by Movies: Celebrated Novelist Cormac McCarthy Was Involved with Every Aspect of 'The Counselor.'" *Wall Street Journal* 11 October 2013. Web. 1 September 2014.

Aristotle. *The Poetics of Aristotle.* Trans. Preston Epps. Chapel Hill: U of North Carolina P, 1970. Print.

Arnold, Edwin. "Cormac McCarthy's *The Stonemason*: The Unmaking of a Play." *Myth, Legend, Dust: Critical Responses to Cormac McCarthy.* Ed. Rick Wallach. Manchester: Manchester UP, 2000. 141–154. Print.

———. "Cormac McCarthy's *Whales and Men*." *Cormac McCarthy: Uncharted Territories.* Ed. Christine Chollier. Reims: UP de Reims, 2003. 17–30. Print.

———. "The Last of the Trilogy: First Thoughts on *Cities of the Plain*." *Perspectives on Cormac McCarthy.* Rev. ed. Ed. Edwin Arnold and Dianne Luce. Jackson: UP of Mississippi, 1999. 221–248. Print.

———. "McCarthy and the Sacred: A Reading of *The Crossing*." *Cormac McCarthy: New Directions.* Ed. James Lilley. Albuquerque: U of New Mexico P, 2002. 215–238. Print.

———. "The Mosaic of McCarthy's Fiction, Continued." *Sacred Violence.* Vol. 2, *Cormac McCarthy's Western Novels.* 2nd ed. Ed. Wade Hall and Rick Wallach. El Paso: Texas Western P, 2002. 179–188. Print.

"Author Lives in Blount." *News-Sentinel* [Knoxville, TN] 6 October 1968. F5. Print.

Bailey, Charles. "The Last Stage of the Hero's Evolution: Cormac McCarthy's *Cities of the Plain*." *Myth, Legend, Dust: Critical Responses to Cormac McCarthy*. Ed. Rick Wallach. Manchester: Manchester UP, 2000. 293–302. Print.

Bannon, Brad. "Divinations of Agency in *Blood Meridian* and *No Country for Old Men*." *Cormac McCarthy Journal* 14.1 (2016): 79–95. Print.

Barron, Alexander. "'As Full of Grief as Age': *King Lear* as Tragic Ancestor to *No Country for Old Men*." *Cormac McCarthy Journal* 10.1 (2012): 16–26. Print.

Bazin, André. "Adaptation, or the Cinema as Digest." *Film Adaptation*. Ed. James Naremore. New Brunswick, NJ: Rutgers UP, 2000. 19–27. Print.

Beach, Patrick. "All the Pretty Sentences: Cormac McCarthy Cleans Up His Verbiage—and Gets His Hands Dirty." *Austin American-Statesman* 17 July 2005. K5. Print.

Beaumont-Thomas, Ben. "Why Is Oral Sex Hard for Hollywood?" *Guardian* 28 November 2013. Web. 1 September 2014.

Begley, Adam. "A Taut, Bloody Thriller, Philosophically Inflected." *New York Observer* 25 July 2005. Culture 9. Print.

Biskind, Peter. *Down and Dirty Pictures: Miramax, Sundance, and the Rise of Independent Film*. New York: Simon and Schuster, 2004. Print.

Bledsoe, Wayne. "Literary Knoxville: 'The Road' Film Wins McCarthy's Approval, but Will It Sell?" *Knoxville News-Sentinel* 22 November 2009. Web. 10 August 2014.

Bloom, Harold. *How to Read and Why*. New York: Touchstone, 2001. Print.

———. Introduction. *Cormac McCarthy: Bloom's Modern Critical Views*. New York: Chelsea House, 2009. 1–8. Print.

Bluestone, George. *Novels into Film*. Berkeley: U of California P, 1957. Print.

Body Heat. Dir. Lawrence Kasdan. Perf. William Hurt, Kathleen Turner. Warner Bros., 1981. Film.

Brewer, Mary. "'The light is all around you, cept you dont see nothin but shadow': Narratives of Religion and Race in *The Stonemason* and *The Sunset Limited*." *Cormac McCarthy Journal* 12.1 (2014): 39–54. Print.

Brodesser, Claude. "Inside Movies: 'Horses' Changes Distribs in Midstream." *Daily Variety* 16 August 2000. News 5. Print.

Brooks, Xan. "*Child of God*: Venice 2013—First Look Review." *Guardian* 2 September 2013. Web. 3 September 2014.

———. "James Franco to Direct William Faulkner and Cormac McCarthy Adaptations." *Guardian* 4 January 2011. Web. 19 September 2014.

Brownstein, Bill. "*The Sunset Limited*'s Dialogue and Performances Sparkle." *The Gazette* [Montreal] 11 February 2011. C1. Print.

Busch, Anita. "Rudin Juggles Slates for Stage, Screen." *Daily Variety* 13 September 1994. Web. 19 September 2014.

Byrd, Martha. "East Tennessee Author Talks about His Works and His Life." Unidentified Kingsport, TN, newspaper, n.d., n.p. Albert Erskine Papers Box 29, Folder 1, Albert and Shirley Small Special Collections Library, University of Virginia. [Interview of December 1973]

Carr, David. "'Tis Nobler to Jump in Front of a Train? Discuss." *New York Times* 11 February 2011. C4. Print.

Chabon, Michael. "After the Apocalypse." *New York Review of Books* 15 February 2007. Web. 27 July 2014.

Chamberlain, Samuel. *My Confession: Recollections of a Rogue.* Ed. William H. Goetzmann. Austin: Texas State Historical Association, 1996. Print.

The Charlie Rose Show. "The Coen Brothers." PBS. 16 November 2007. Television.

Chiarella, Tom. "*The Road* Is the Most Important Movie of the Year." *Esquire* June 2009. Web. 27 July 2014.

Child of God. Dir. James Franco. Perf. Scott Haze, Tim Blake Nelson. RabbitBandini Productions, 2014. Film.

Children of Men. Dir. Alfonso Cuarón. Perf. Clive Owen, Julianne Moore. Universal Pictures, 2006. Film.

Clark, Mike. "Slow 'Horses' Saddled with Flaws." *USA Today* 20 December 2000. Life 4D. Print.

Clark, Robert C. *American Literary Minimalism.* Tuscaloosa: U of Alabama P, 2014. Print.

The Colbert Report. Comedy Central. 30 July 2014. Television.

Collins, John J. *The Apocalyptic Imagination: An Introduction to Jewish Apocalyptic Literature.* 2nd ed. Grand Rapids, MI: William B. Eerdmans Publishing, 1998. Print.

Cooper, Lydia. "Cormac McCarthy's *The Road* as Apocalyptic Grail Narrative." *Studies in the Novel* 43.2 (2011): 218–236. Print.

———. *No More Heroes: Narrative Perspective and Morality in Cormac McCarthy.* Baton Rouge: Louisiana State UP, 2011. Print.

"Cormac McCarthy on James Joyce and Punctuation." *Oprah.com.* 1 June 2008. Web.

"The *Counsellor* Cast Praise Scott." *Belfast Telegraph* 4 October 2013. Web. 1 September 2014.

The Counselor. Dir. Ridley Scott. Perf. Michael Fassbender, Brad Pitt, Cameron Diaz. 20th Century Fox, 2013. Blu-Ray.

———. Commentary track.

———. "The Counselor." Extra embedded in commentary track.

———. "Laura." Extra embedded in commentary track.

———. "Malkina." Extra embedded in commentary track.

"*The Counselor* Real Thriller That's First Class Badass." *Hamilton Spectator* [Ontario] 24 October 2013. Web. 3 September 2014.

Creed, Barbara. *The Monstrous-Feminine.* London: Routledge, 1993. Print.

Dachslager, Earl L. "From McCarthy Comes a Wonderful Novel in the Mark Twain Tradition." *Houston Chronicle* 19 April 1992. Zest section, 21, 23. Print.

Dargis, Manohla. "Wildlife Is Tame: Not the Humans." *New York Times* 25 October 2013. C8. Print.

Daugherty, Leo. "Gravers False and True: *Blood Meridian* as Gnostic Tragedy." *Perspectives on Cormac McCarthy.* Rev. ed. Ed. Edwin Arnold and Dianne Luce. Jackson: UP of Mississippi. 1999. 159–174. Print.

Davis, Jason. "Hollywood Portrayal of Sevier County Due Next Month: It Won't Be Pretty." *Mountain Press* [Tennessee] 29 June 2014. 7. Print.

Dayoub, Tony. "Double Vision: Tony Scott's Spirit Possesses Ridley Scott's 'The Counselor.'" *Balder and Dash, Roger Ebert.com* 27 October 2013. Web. 2 September 2014.

Dean, Jonathan. "No Country for Faint Hearts: Films Often Struggle to Capture Cormac McCarthy's Genius. Will the Novelist's First Screenplay Show Hollywood How It's Done, Asks Jonathan Dean." *Sunday Times* [London] 20 October 2013. Culture 8, 9. Print.

Denby, David. "Killing Joke: The Coen Brothers' Twists and Turns." *New Yorker* 25 February 2008. Web. 1 July 2014.

Dew, Blake. "James Franco's *Child of God* Begins Filming Next Week." *We Got This Covered* 25 January 2012. Web. 15 June 2016.

———. "James Franco to Direct Cormac McCarthy's *Child of God*." *We Got This Covered* 15 Sept 2011. Web. 3 September 2014.

Dickinson, Doug. "In Defence of *The Counselor*." *Daily Gleaner* [New Brunswick, Canada] 30 October 2013. C3. Print.

DiTommaso, Lorenzo. "Apocalypticism and Popular Culture." *The Oxford Handbook of Apocalyptic Literature*. Ed. John J. Collins. Oxford: Oxford UP, 2014. 473–510. Print.

Eagleton, Terry. *Sweet Violence: The Idea of the Tragic*. Malden, MA: Blackwell, 2003. Print.

Eaton, Mark. "What Price Hollywood? Modern American Writers and the Movies." *A Companion to the Modern American Novel 1900–1950*. Ed. John T. Matthews. Malden, MA: John Wiley, 2009. 466–495. Print.

Eden, Kathy. "Aristotle's *Poetics*: A Defense of Tragic Fiction." *A Companion to Tragedy*. Ed. Rebecca Bushnell. Malden, MA: Blackwell, 2009. 41–50. Print.

Eder, Richard. "John's Passion." *Los Angeles Times Book Review* 17 May 1992. 3, 13. Print.

Ellis, Jay. *No Place for Home: Spatial Constraint and Character Flight in the Novels of Cormac McCarthy*. New York: Routledge, 2006. Print.

———. "*The Road* beyond Zombies of the New South." *Southern Gothic Literature*. Critical Insights series. Ed. Jay Ellis. Ipswich, MA: Salem Press, 2013. 49–72. Print.

"E.T. Boy to Play Cowboy: E.T. Star Henry Thomas to Portray Cowboy in New Film." *Mirror* 26 September 1998. News 10. Print.

"Film: *The Gardener's Son*." *Village Voice* 16 January 1978. 45. Print.

Fine, Richard. *West of Eden: Writers in Hollywood, 1928–1940*. Washington, DC: Smithsonian Institution Press, 1993. Print.

Fleming, Michael. "Calley's Coup at UA: Pricey 'Penguins' at NL." *Daily Variety* 3 February 1994. Section: The Backlot. Print.

———. "Coens' 'Country' Man." *Daily Variety* 27 April 2006. 3. Print.

———. "Duo Riding into 'Sunset.'" *Daily Variety* 21 August 2009. Web. 3 July 2014.

———. "Pulitzer Prize–Winning Author Cormac McCarthy Sells His First Spec Script." *Deadline.com* 17 January 2012. Web. 1 September 2014.

————. "Rudin Books Tyro Novel." *Variety* 28 August 2005. Web.

————. "Sony, Miramax Horse-Trading for Leo." *Variety* 13–19 April 1998. Inside Movies 2. Print.

————. "Thornton Holds Reins of 'Horses.'" *Daily Variety* 19 August 1997. 1. Print.

————. "Top Actors Lining Up for Villain Role in 'The Counselor.'" *Deadline.com* 24 February 2012. Web. 1 September 2014.

Foundas, Scott. "Why 'The Counselor' Is One of Ridley Scott's Best Films." *Variety* 28 October 2013. Web. 2 September 2014.

Franco, James. "Adapting 'Blood Meridian.'" *Vice.com* 3 July 2014. Web. 19 September 2014.

————. "James Franco's 'Blood Meridian' Test." *Vice.com* 21 July 2014. Web. 26 September 2014.

————. "The Meanings of the Selfie." *New York Times* 26 December 2013. Web. 12 September 2014.

Frye, Steven. "*Blood Meridian* and the Poetics of Violence." *The Cambridge Companion to Cormac McCarthy*. Ed. Steven Frye. Cambridge: Cambridge UP, 2013. 107–120. Print.

————. "Yeats's 'Sailing to Byzantium' and McCarthy's *No Country for Old Men*: Art and Artifice in the Novel." *No Country for Old Men: From Novel to Film*. Ed. Lynnea Chapman King, Rick Wallach, and Jim Welsh. Lanham, MD: Scarecrow Press, 2009. 13–20. Print.

Fuchs, Cynthia. "The Buddy Politic." *Screening the Male: Exploring Masculinities in Hollywood Cinema*. Ed. Steven Cohen and Ina Rae Hark. London: Routledge, 1993. 194–210. Print.

The Gardener's Son. Dir. Richard Pearce. Perf. Brad Dourif, Ned Beatty. *Visions* series. PBS, 6 January 1977. Television.

"'Gardner's [*sic*] Son' on PBS This Week, Written by Louisvillian." *News-Sentinel* [Knoxville] 2 January 1977. G7. Print.

Garvey, Marianne, Brian Niemietz, and Oli Coleman. "James Franco Steals the Scene at Premiere for His 'Child of God' with Scott Haze." *NY Daily News* 1 August 2014. Web. 3 September 2014.

Gilmore, Richard. "*No Country for Old Men*: The Coens' Tragic Western." *The Philosophy of the Coen Brothers*. Ed. Mark T. Conard. Lexington: UP of Kentucky, 2009. 55–78. Print.

Giraldi, William. "James Franco's Utterly Misguided Adaptation of Cormac McCarthy: What Happens When a Selfie-Addicted Celebrity Takes on the Darkest of American Masters." *New Republic* 30 July 2014. Web. 3 September 2014.

Girard, René. *Violence and the Sacred*. Trans. Patrick Gregory. Baltimore: Johns Hopkins UP, 1977. Print.

Gottlieb, Jeff. "Adventures in Rewriting." *Los Angeles Times* 30 June 2002. Web. 13 October 2014.

Groen, Rick. "Playing It a Bit Too Cool: Careful in Its Plotting and Easy to Watch, *All the Pretty Horses* Lacks the Passion that Fuelled the Book." *Globe and Mail* [Canada] 22 December 2000. R8. Print.

Guillemin, Georg. *The Pastoral Vision of Cormac McCarthy*. College Station: Texas A&M UP, 2004. Print.

Hamilton, Ian. *Writers in Hollywood, 1915–1951*. New York: Harper and Row, 1990. Print.

Hann, Michael. "Oscar Predictions 2014: *The Counselor*." *Guardian* 22 August 2013. Web. 1 September 2014.

Haskell, Molly. *From Reverence to Rape: The Treatment of Women in the Movies*. 2nd ed. Chicago: U of Chicago P, 1987. Print.

Hawkins, Susan. "The End of the World as We Know It." *Oakland Journal* 20 (2011): 53–58. Print.

Hedgpeth, Don. *They Rode Good Horses: The First Fifty Years of the American Quarter Horse Association*. Amarillo, TX: American Quarter Horse Association, 1990. Print.

Hegel, Georg Wilhelm Friedrich. *Aesthetics: Lectures on Fine Art*. Vol. 2. Trans. T. M. Knox. Oxford: Clarendon Press, 1975. Print.

Helm, Richard. "Talk Show Goddess Meets Mr. End of the World." *Edmonton Journal* 6 June 2007. Web. 29 September 2014.

Hensher, Philip. "The Play's the Thing ... Unless You're a Novelist." *Guardian* 25 July 2006. Web. 13 October 2014.

Hewitt, Chris. "Cutting 'Horses': The Oscar-Laden Cast of 'All the Pretty Horses' Won't Say Much about How the Four-Hour Film Was Cut to Two." *Saint Paul Pioneer Press* 19 December 2000. 1E. Print.

Hillier, Russell. "'Like some supplicant to the darkness over them all': The Good of John Grady Cole in Cormac McCarthy's *Cities of the Plain*." *Cormac McCarthy Journal* 14.1 (2016): 3–36. Print.

———. "'Nor Hell a Fury': Malkina's Motivation in Cormac McCarthy's *The Counselor*." *Explicator* 72.2 (2014): 151–157. Print.

———. Personal communication. 13 August 2014.

Hinckley, David. "War of Words: Tommy Lee Jones and Samuel L. Jackson Go One on One in a Cormac McCarthy Drama." *Daily News* [NY] 6 Feb 2011. New York Vue 2. Print.

Holmberg, David. "'In a time before nomenclature was and each was all': *Blood Meridian*'s Neomythic West and the Heterotopian Zone." *Western American Literature* 44.2 (2009): 140–156. Print.

Hopewell, John. "Cruz to Take 'Horses' Lead." *Daily Variety* 26 February 1999. News 7. Print.

Hutcheon, Linda, with Siobhan O'Flynn. *A Theory of Adaptation*. 2nd ed. London: Routledge, 2006. Print.

Jaafar, Ali. "Plug Pulled on James Franco–Russell Crowe *Blood Meridian* Project Over Book Rights Issue—Update." *Deadline.com* 5 May 2016. Web. 20 June 2016.

"James Franco Courts Controversy, Again: Actor-Director's New Movie about a Social Outcast Who Becomes a Necrophiliac." *Toronto Star* 12 September 2013. E6. Print.

"James Franco Takes His Directorial Meat Cleaver to Cormac McCarthy's 'Child of God.'" *New York Observer* 30 July 2014. Web. 3 September 2014.

Jarrett, Robert. "Genre, Voice, and Ethos: McCarthy's Perverse 'Thriller.'" *No Country for Old Men: From Novel to Film*. Ed. Lynnea Chapman King, Rick Wallach, and Jim Welsh. Lanham, MD: Scarecrow Press, 2009. 60–72. Print.

Jeffords, Susan. *Hard Bodies: Hollywood Masculinity in the Reagan Era*. New Brunswick, NJ: Rutgers UP, 1994. Print.

Jenkins, Christopher. "One Drive, Two Deaths in Cormac McCarthy's *Child of God*." *Cormac McCarthy Journal* 13.1 (2015): 86–99. Print.

"Johnny Hardstaff." RSA *Films* [n.d.]. Web. 10 September 2014.

Jones, Chris. "Brilliant, but Hardly a Play." *Chicago Tribune* 29 May 2006. Web. 26 July 2014.

Jones, Malcolm Jr. "Brightening Western Star." *Newsweek* 123 (13 June 1994). 54. Print.

Jordan, Richard. "'Just Write' Says Successful Author." *University of Tennessee Daily Beacon* 28 January 1969. 6. Print.

Josephs, Allen. "The Quest for God in *The Road*." *The Cambridge Companion to Cormac McCarthy*. Ed. Steven Frye. New York: Cambridge UP, 2013. 133–148. Print.

Josyph, Peter. *Adventures in Reading Cormac McCarthy*. Lanham, MD: Scarecrow Press, 2010. Print.

———. *Cormac McCarthy's House*. Austin: U of Texas P. 2013. Print.

———. "Losing Home: A Conversation with Ted Tally about *All the Pretty Horses*." *Southern Quarterly* 40.1 (2001): 132–146. Print.

Jurgensen, John. "Hollywood's Favorite Cowboy." *Wall Street Journal* 20 November 2009. Web. 20 July 2014.

Kelley, Kevin. Personal interview. 3 March 2011.

Kelly, Christopher. "'The Road' One of the Worst Movies of the Year." *Contra Costa Times* [CA] 25 November 2009. Entertainment. Print.

King James Bible. *Bible Gateway*. Web. 2 July 2014.

Kirn, Walter. "'No Country for Old Men': Texas Noir." *New York Times* 18 July 2005: E1. Print.

Kitses, Jim. "Bloodred Horizons." *Sight and Sound* 11.3 (2001): 12–15. Print.

Knepper, Steven. "*The Counselor* and Tragic Recognition." *Cormac McCarthy Journal* 14.1 (2016): 37–54. Print.

Kriegsman, Alan. "Public TV's 'Visions' of Expanded Dramatic and Creative Horizons." *Washington Post* 16 January 1977. E3. Print.

Kroll, Justin. "Perez Has Appointment with 'Counselor.'" *Daily Variety* 30 July 2012. News 4. Print.

Kunsa, Ashley. "'Maps of the World in Its Becoming': Post-Apocalyptic Naming in Cormac McCarthy's *The Road*." *Journal of Modern Literature* 33.1 (2009): 57–74. Print.

Kushner, David. "Cormac McCarthy's Apocalypse." *Rolling Stone* 27 December 2007–10 January 2008. 43–53. Print.

Kwon, Lillian. "'The Road' as Outreach?" *Christian Post* 13 November 2009. Web. 2 July 2014.

Lacey, Liam. "Oscar Watch 2014: Will It Be Streep's Year Again?" *Globe and Mail* [Canada]. 1 March 2013. R1. Print.

Lane, Preston. Personal interview. 28 February 2011.

Leitch, Thomas. *Film Adaptation and Its Discontents: From Gone with the Wind to The Passion of the Christ*. Baltimore: Johns Hopkins UP, 2007. Print.

Lessing, Gotthold Ephraim. *Laocoön: An Essay on the Limits of Painting and Poetry*. Trans. Edward Allen McCormick. Baltimore: Johns Hopkins UP, 1984. Print.

Lewis, Hilary. "'The Counselor's' Michael Fassbender, John Leguizamo on Cormac McCarthy's First Screenplay." *Hollywood Reporter* 10 October 2013. Web. 1 September 2014.

Lilley, James. "Of Whales and Men: The Dynamics of Cormac McCarthy's Environmental Imagination." *Southern Quarterly* 38.2 (2000): 111–122. Print.

Longino, Bob. "At the Movies: 'Pretty Horses' Ends Up a Pretty Lame Western." *Atlanta Journal and Constitution* 22 December 2000. 16P. Print.

Luce, Dianne. "Cormac McCarthy and Albert Erskine: The Evolution of a Working Relationship." *Resources for American Literary Study* 35 (2012): 303–338. Print.

———. "Cormac McCarthy's First Screenplay: 'The Gardener's Son.'" *Perspectives on Cormac McCarthy*. Rev. ed. Ed. Edwin Arnold and Dianne Luce. Jackson: UP of Mississippi, 1999. 71–96. Print.

———. "Cormac McCarthy's *The Sunset Limited*: Dialogue of Life and Death (a Review of the Chicago Production)." *Cormac McCarthy Journal* 6 (2008): 13–21. Print.

———. "Hillcoat's *The Road* and the Repression of Ecological Tragedy." Roundtable paper for "McCarthy's *The Road*: Novel and Film." American Literature Association Symposium on American Fiction, 1890–Present. Savannah, GA, October 2010.

———. "John Grady Cole's Heroism in *All the Pretty Horses*." *Sacred Violence*. Vol. 2, *Cormac McCarthy's Western Novels*. 2nd ed. Ed. Wade Hall and Rick Wallach. El Paso: Texas Western P, 2002. 57–70. Print.

———. *Reading the World: Cormac McCarthy's Tennessee Period*. Columbia: U of South Carolina P, 2009. Print.

———. "The Road and the Matrix: The World as Tale in *The Crossing*." *Perspectives on Cormac McCarthy*. Ed. Edwin Arnold and Dianne Luce. Jackson: UP of Mississippi, 1999. 195–220. Print.

———. "'They aint the thing': Artifact and Hallucinated Recollection in Cormac McCarthy's Early Frame-Works." *Myth, Legend, Dust: Critical Responses to Cormac McCarthy*. Ed. Rick Wallach. Manchester: Manchester UP, 2000. 21–36. Print.

Lumenick, Lou. "This Guidance Not Suggested." *New York Post* 25 October 2013. 41. Print.

Lyman, Rick. "After Choppy Seas, a Film Nears Port." *New York Times* 23 December 2000. B11. Print.

Lyttleton, Oliver. "Review: James Franco's Tossed Off and Drab Cormac McCarthy Adaptation 'Child of God.'" *Indiewire, The Playlist* 29 July 2014. Web. 3 September 2014.

MacKenzie, Cameron. "A Song of Great Order: The Real in Cormac McCarthy's *The Crossing*." *Cormac McCarthy Journal* 13.1 (2015): 99–119. Print.

MacNab, Geoffrey. "Bleak but Moving Tale of the Apocalypse." *Independent* [London] 3 September 2009. News 6. Print.

Mangrum, Benjamin. "Democracy, Justice, and Tragedy in Cormac McCarthy's *No Country for Old Men*." *Religion and Literature* 43.3 (2011): 107–133. Print.

Marlowe, Christopher. *The Jew of Malta*. Ed. Paul Negri. Mineola, NY: Dover Thrift Editions, 2003. Print.

Marshall, Lee. "*Child of God*." *Screen Daily* 31 August 2013. Web. 3 September 2014.

Marx, Leo. *The Machine in the Garden: Technology and the Pastoral Ideal in America*. Oxford: Oxford UP, 1964. Print.

Maslin, Janet. "The Road through Hell, Paved with Desperation." *New York Times* 25 September 2006. Web. 27 July 2014.

McBride, Charlie. "Debating Life and Death in *The Sunset Limited*." *Galway Advertiser* 28 June 2007. Web. 26 July 2014.

McCarthy, Cormac. *All the Pretty Horses*. New York: Knopf, 1992. Print.

———. *Blood Meridian*. New York: Random House, 1985. Print.

———. *Child of God*. New York: Random House, 1973. Print.

———. *Cities of the Plain*. New York: Knopf, 1998. Print.

———. "Cities of the Plain." Unpublished shooting script. Cormac McCarthy Papers Box 70, Folder 3, Southwestern Writers Collection, Wittliff Collections, Texas State University, San Marcos.

———. *The Counselor*. New York: Vintage, 2013. Print.

———. *The Crossing*. New York: Knopf, 1994. Print.

———. *The Gardener's Son*. Hopewell, NJ: Ecco Press, 1996. Print.

———. *No Country for Old Men*. New York: Knopf, 2005. Print.

———. "No Country for Old Men." Unpublished screenplay. Cormac McCarthy Papers Box 79, Folder 5, Southwestern Writers Collection, Wittliff Collections, Texas State University, San Marcos.

———. *The Orchard Keeper*. New York: Random House, 1965. Print.

———. *The Road*. New York: Vintage, 2006. Print.

———. "Scenes of the Crime." *New Yorker* 10 and 17 June, 2013. 66–69. Print.

———. *The Stonemason*. Hopewell, NJ: Ecco Press, 1994. Print.

———. *The Sunset Limited*. New York: Vintage, 2006. Print.

———. *Suttree*. New York: Random House. 1979. Print.

———. "Whales and Men." Unpublished screenplay. Printout with no corrections. Cormac McCarthy Papers Box 97, Folder 5, Southwestern Writers Collection, Wittliff Collections, Texas State University, San Marcos.

McCarthy, Todd. "*All the Pretty Horses*." *Daily Variety* 13 December 2000. 12. Print.

———. "*No Country for Old Men*." *Variety* 18 May 2007. Web.

———. "*The Road*." *Daily Variety* 4 September 2009. Reviews 2. Print.

McClintock, Pamela. "CineEurope: Javier Bardem's Hairdo in 'The Counselor' Inspired by Brian Grazer's." *Hollywood Reporter* 26 June 2013. Web. 1 September 2014.

McCracken, Brett. "*The Road*." *Christianity Today* 25 November 2009. Web. 30 June 2014.

McGee, Celia. "Billy Bob Thornton's Rough Ride: Thornton Battles Rumor Mill on 'Pretty Horses.'" *Daily News* 20 December 2000. New York Now 47. Print.

McGrath, Charles. "At World's End, Honing a Father-Son Dynamic." *New York Times* 27 May 2008. E1. Print.

McSweeney, Terrence. "'Each Night Is Darker—Beyond Darkness': The Environmental and Spiritual Apocalypse of *The Road* (2009)." *Journal of Film and Video* 65.4 (2003): 42–58. Print.

Medina, Jeremy. "Cormac McCarthy's *Blood Meridian* Film Changes Directors." *Paste Magazine* 28 August 2008. Web. 19 September 2014.

Mitchell, Broadus. *William Gregg: Factory Master of the Old South*. Chapel Hill: U of North Carolina P, 1928. Print.

Montague, Kate. "Cormac McCarthy's Baroque Meridians." Paper presented at "Borders and Landscapes in the Works of Cormac McCarthy." Conference held at the University of Western Sydney, 23–25 July 2014.

Morrison, Gail Moore. "*All the Pretty Horses*: John Grady Cole's Expulsion from Paradise." *Perspectives on Cormac McCarthy*. 2nd ed. Ed. Edwin Arnold and Dianne Luce. Jackson: UP of Mississippi, 1999. 175–194. Print.

Morsberger, Robert E. "Steinbeck and the Stage." *The Short Novels of John Steinbeck*. Ed. Jackson J. Benson. Durham, NC: Duke UP, 1990. 271–294. Print.

Mundik, Petra. "'Striking the Fire out of the Rock': Gnostic Theology in Cormac McCarthy's *Blood Meridian*." *South Central Review* 26.3 (2009): 72–97. Print.

Murray, Rebecca. "Josh Brolin Discusses *No Country for Old Men*." *About.com, Hollywood Movies* 13 November 2007. Web.

Naglazas, Mark. "Road to McCarthy." *West Australian* [Perth] 28 January 2010. Web. 15 July 2014.

Naremore, James. "Introduction: Film and the Reign of Adaptation." *Film Adaptation*. Ed. James Naremore. New Brunswick, NJ: Rutgers UP, 2000. 1–18. Print.

Neale, Steve. "Prologue: Masculinity as Spectacle: Reflections on Men and Mainstream Cinema." *Screening the Male: Exploring Masculinities in Hollywood Cinema*. Ed. Steven Cohan and Ina Rae Hark. London: Routledge, 1993. 9–20. Print.

Neumaier, Joe. "Appeal Denied: Odd Script about Larcenous Lawyer Wastes Best Cast Money Can Buy." *Daily News* [NY] 25 October 2013. Now 41. Print.

"The New Classics." *Entertainment Weekly* 18 June 2007. Web. 27 July 2014.

Nietzsche, Friedrich. *The Birth of Tragedy: Out of the Spirit of Music*. Trans. Shaun Whiteside. New York: Penguin Classics, 1994. Print.

No Country for Old Men. Dir. Joel and Ethan Coen. Perf. Tommy Lee Jones, Javier Bardem, Josh Brolin. Paramount, 2007. DVD.

———. "The Making of *No Country for Old Men*." Special feature. Prod. Steven Kochones.

———. "Working with the Coens." Special feature.

"*No Country for Old Men* (2007)." Review. *Rotten Tomatoes* [n.d.]. Web. 30 July 2014.

O'Connor, John. "TV: WNET Showing Haunting 'Gardener's Son.'" *New York Times* 6 January 1977. Print.

Odam, Matthew, and Joe Gross. "Here Come the Prestige Films." *Austin American-Statesman* 6 September 2013. A360, T24. Print.

O'Hehir, Andrew. "Meet the Worst Movie Ever Made." *Salon.com* 26 October 2013. Web. 2 September 2014.

The Oprah Winfrey Show. 5 June 2007. CBS. Television.

Patch, Nick. "James Franco Wants to Buy Toronto 13-Year-Old's Fan Art." *Prince George Citizen* [British Columbia] 13 September 2011. Web. 1 September 2014.

Patterson, John. "We've Killed a Lot of Animals." *Guardian* 21 December 2007. Web. 25 June 2016.

Payne, Roger. *Among Whales.* New York: Scribner, 1995. Print.

Pearce, Richard. Foreword. *The Gardener's Son.* Hopewell, NJ: Ecco Press, 1996. v–vi. Print.

Peebles, Stacey. "Yuman Belief Systems and Cormac McCarthy's *Blood Meridian.*" *Texas Studies in Language and Literature* 45.2 (2003): 231–244. Print.

Peek, Wendy Chapman. "The Romance of Competence: Rethinking Masculinity in the Western." *Journal of Popular Film and Television* 30.4 (2003): 206–219. Print.

Peers, Martin, et al. "The Bidding Begins for Multimedia's Menagerie." *Variety* 12–18 June 1995. 4. Print.

Pendleton, Austin. "Austin in New York." 16 November 2006. Steppenwolf Theatre Company Blog. Web. 26 July 2014.

———. Personal interview. 7 August 2015.

Penhall, Joe. "Last Man Standing: What Cormac McCarthy Made of My Adaptation of *The Road.*" *Guardian* 4 January 2010. Web. 20 July 2014.

Petrikin, Chris. "Damon Astride 'Horses.'" *Daily Variety* 15 April 1998. News 1. Print.

———, and Dan Cox. "Col Lassos Followups to 'Horses.'" *Daily Variety* 28 April 1998. News 1. Print.

Phillips, Dana. "History and the Ugly Facts of Cormac McCarthy's *Blood Meridian.*" *Cormac McCarthy: New Directions.* Ed. James Lilley. Albuquerque: U of New Mexico P, 2002. 17–47. Print.

Plato. *The Republic of Plato.* Trans. Allan Bloom. 2nd ed. New York: Basic Books, 1968. Print.

Pols, Mary. "*The Counselor*: Hard-Boiled Hokum." *Time* 24 October 2013. Web. 2 September 2014.

Powers, Lindsay. "Samuel L. Jackson Is Highest-Grossing Actor of All Time." *Hollywood Reporter* 27 October 2011. Web.

Puig, Claudia. "Be Glad This Talky 'Counselor' Doesn't Charge By the Word: It's a Crime to Waste Such a Talented Cast in This Implausible Thriller." *USA Today* 25 October 2013. 2D. Print.

———. "'Child of God': Pray You Don't Have to See It." *USA Today* 31 July 2014. Web.

———. "'The Road' Traverses Bleak, Bold Terrain: Performances Put Film on Oscar Map." *USA Today* 25 November 2009. 3D. Print.

Pulver, Andrew. "Brad Pitt and Angelina Jolie Set to Reunite in Ridley Scott's 'The Counselor'." *Guardian* 13 April 2012. Web. 1 September 2014.

———. "Cameron Diaz Sounded 'Like Rihanna' on *The Counsellor*." *Guardian* 8 November 2013. Web. 1 September 2014.

———. "Penelope Cruz Set to Join Javier Bardem in *The Counselor*." *Guardian* 20 April 2012. Web. 1 September 2014.

Quirk, William. "'Minimalist Tragedy': Nietzschean Thought in McCarthy's *The Sunset Limited*." *Cormac McCarthy Journal* 8.1 (2010): 34–54. Print.

The Road. Dir. John Hillcoat. Perf. Viggo Mortensen, Kodi Smit-McPhee. 2929 Productions, 2009. DVD.

———. "The Making of *The Road*." Special feature.

Roberts, Monty. *The Man Who Listens to Horses*. New York: Random House, 1996. Print.

Roche, Mark W. "The Greatness and Limits of Hegel's Theory of Tragedy." *A Companion to Tragedy*. Ed. Rebecca Bushnell. Malden, MA: Blackwell, 2009. 51–67. Print.

Rothermel, Dennis. "Denial and Trepidation Awaiting What's Coming in the Coen Brothers' First Film Adaptation." *No Country for Old Men: From Novel to Film*. Ed. Lynnea Chapman King, Rick Wallach, and Jim Welsh. Lanham, MD: Scarecrow Press, 2009. 173–198. Print.

Ryan, Richard. "Galloping Fiction." *Christian Science Monitor* 11 June 1992. 13. Print.

Scott, A. O. "Father and Son Bond in Gloomy Aftermath of Disaster." *New York Times* 25 November 2009. C1. Print.

———. "He Found a Bundle of Money, and Now There's Hell to Pay." *New York Times* 9 November 2007. Web. 3 July 2014.

———. "Lost Souls Adrift across a Barren Mesa." *New York Times* 25 December 2000. E1. Print.

"Scott: I Love Counsellor's Drama." *Belfast Telegraph* 7 October 2013. Web. 1 September 2014.

Sedgwick, Eve Kosofsky. *Between Men: English Literature and Male Homosocial Desire*. New York: Columbia UP, 1985. Print.

Sepich, John. *Notes on Blood Meridian*. Rev. and exp. Austin: U of Texas P, 2008. Print.

Sexton, David. "Partners in Crime: Michael Fassbender and Penelope Cruz do their best as a couple caught in a drugs deal that goes bad, but the real villains of this misadventure are director Ridley Scott and writer Cormac McCarthy." *Evening Standard* [London] 15 November 2013. Features 44, 45. Print.

"She's Just a Daredevil Woman! Real Life Action Hero Doubles for Cameron Diaz and Nicole Kidman as One of Britain's Top Stuntwomen." *Daily Mail Online* 5 February 2014. Web. 2 September 2014.

Siegel, Tatiana. "Coens' New 'Men': Harrelson, Root." *Hollywood Reporter* 7 June 2006. Web.

———. "'Road' Trip for Theron." *Daily Variety* 15 January 2008. 1. Print.

Simonson, Robert. "NJ's McCarter Replaces *Stonemason* with *Cherry Orchard*." *Playbill* 14 October 1999. Web. 26 July 2014.

Slotkin, Richard. *Gunfighter Nation: The Myth of the Frontier in Twentieth-Century America*. Norman: U of Oklahoma P, 1998. Print.

Snyder, Phillip. "Cowboy Codes in Cormac McCarthy's Border Trilogy." *A Cormac McCarthy Companion: The Border Trilogy*. Ed. Edwin Arnold and Dianne Luce. Jackson: UP of Mississippi, 2001. 198–227. Print.

Sophocles. *The Three Theban Plays*. Trans. Bernard Knox. New York: Penguin, 2000. Print.

Spurgeon, Sara. "The Sacred Hunter and the Eucharist of the Wilderness: Mythic Reconstructions in *Blood Meridian*." *Cormac McCarthy: New Directions*. Ed. James Lilley. Albuquerque: U of New Mexico P, 2002. 75–102. Print.

Sragow, Michael. "'The Counselor' Is Guilty." *Orange County Register* 25 October 2013. Show M. Print.

Stam, Robert. "Introduction: The Theory and Practice of Adaptation." *Literature and Film: A Guide to the Theory and Practice of Film Adaptation*. Ed. Robert Stam and Alessandra Raengo. Malden, MA: Blackwell, 2005. 1–52. Print.

Strauss, Bob. "'Road' Blocks: Post-Apocalyptic Film Hits Some Rough Patches." *Daily News of Los Angeles* 27 November 2009. L1. Print.

Stuever, Hank. "All Aboard HBO's Theological Choo-Choo." *Washington Post* 12 February 2011. C8. Print.

The Sunset Limited. Dir. Tommy Lee Jones. Perf. Tommy Lee Jones, Samuel L. Jackson. HBO, 2011. DVD.

———. Commentary track. Perf. Tommy Lee Jones, Samuel L. Jackson, Cormac McCarthy.

———. "The Making of *The Sunset Limited*." Special feature.

"*The Sunset Limited*: Stellar Thesps Keep 'Limited' on Track." *Variety* 7 February 2011. Web. 3 July 2014.

Tally, Ted. "All the Pretty Horses" screenplay draft. 2 September 1993. Cormac McCarthy Papers Box 54, Folder 7, Southwestern Writers Collection, Wittliff Collections, Texas State University, San Marcos.

Taubin, Amy. "Blu-Ray Pick: The Counselor." *Film Comment*. Film Society of Lincoln Center, March/April 2014. Web. 2 September 2014.

Terrill, Tom. "Murder in Graniteville." *Toward a New South? Studies in Post–Civil War Southern Communities*. Ed. Orville Burton and Robert C. McMath Jr. Westport, CT: Greenwood Press, 1982. 193–222. Print.

Tesich, Steve. "Blood Meridian." 1995. Typescript. Southwestern Writers Collection, Wittliff Collections, Texas State University, San Marcos.

Thielman, Sam. "H'W'D Ponies Up with McCarthy." *Variety* 22 October 2007. Web. 19 September 2014.

Thompson, Anne. "'No Country' 'Tis of Three: Coens, Jones." *Hollywood Reporter* 2 February 2006. Web.

Thornton, Billy Bob, and Kinky Friedman. *The Billy Bob Tapes: A Cave Full of Ghosts*. New York: William Morrow, 2012. Print.

Tonkin, Boyd. "Cormac and the Camera." *Independent* [London] 13 November 2013. Web. 12 September 2014.

"The 2007 Pulitzer Prize Winners: Fiction." *Pulitzer.org* [n.d.]. Web. 29 September 2014.

"2013 Must-See Movies: This year's most-talked-about releases run the gamut from terrorism and alien invasions to tales of comic and real-life heroes." *Toronto Star* 4 January 2013. E1. Print.

Vancheri, Barbara. "'The Road' Leads to Pittsburgh." *Pittsburgh Post-Gazette* 16 January 2008. C1. Print.

Vernant, Jean-Pierre, and Pierre Vidal-Naquet. *Myth and Tragedy in Ancient Greece.* Trans. Janet Lloyd. Cambridge, MA: Zone Books, 1990. Print.

Vescio, Bryan. "Strangers in Everyland: *Suttree*, Huckleberry Finn, and Tragic Humanism." *Cormac McCarthy Journal* 4.1 (2005): 60–71. Print.

Wallace, Garry. "Meeting McCarthy." *Southern Quarterly* 30.4 (1992): 134–139. Print.

Wallace, Jennifer. *The Cambridge Introduction to Tragedy.* New York: Cambridge UP, 2007. Print.

Walters, Ben, and J. M. Tyree. "Cash and Carrion: Film of the Month: *No Country for Old Men*." *Sight and Sound* 18.2 (2008): 48–49. Print.

Warshow, Robert. "Movie Chronicle: The Westerner." *Film Theory and Criticism.* 6th ed. Ed. Leo Braudy and Marshall Cohen. New York: Oxford UP, 2004. 703–716. Print.

Wegner, John. "'Wars and Rumors of Wars' in Cormac McCarthy's Border Trilogy." *A Cormac McCarthy Companion: The Border Trilogy.* Ed. Edwin Arnold and Dianne Luce. Jackson: UP of Mississippi, 2001. 73–91. Print.

Weinraub, Bernard. "Mike Nichols Plans a Career Finale." *New York Times* 15 March 1993. C13. Print.

Weintraub, Steve. "Exclusive Interview with Writer/Director William Monahan for LONDON BOULEVARD." *Collider.com* 20 November 2010. Web. 19 September 2014.

Welsh, James. "Borderline Evil: The Dark Side of Byzantium in *No Country for Old Men*, Novel and Film." *No Country for Old Men: From Novel to Film.* Ed. Lynnea Chapman King, Rick Wallach, and James Welsh. Lanham, MD: Scarecrow Press, 2009. 73–85. Print.

West, Benjamin. "Personal Foul: Lester Ballard's Post-Concussion Syndrome." Paper presented at the American Literature Association conference, Boston, May 2015.

White, Christopher. "Dreaming the Border Trilogy: Cormac McCarthy and Narrative Creativity." *Cormac McCarthy Journal* 13.1 (2015): 120–141. Print.

Wielenberg, Erik. "God, Morality, and Meaning in Cormac McCarthy's *The Road*." *Cormac McCarthy Journal* 8.1 (2010): 1–19. Print.

Williams, David. "*Blood Meridian* and Classical Greek Thought." *Intertextual and Interdisciplinary Approaches to Cormac McCarthy.* Ed. Nicholas Monk. New York: Routledge, 2012. 6–23. Print.

Wittliff, Bill. Personal interview. 5 March 2014.

Woodward, Richard. "Cormac Country." *Vanity Fair* August 2005: 98, 100, 103–104. Print.

———. "Cormac McCarthy's Venomous Fiction." *New York Times* 19 April 1992. Web.

Yeats, William Butler. *The Collected Works of W. B. Yeats.* Vol. 1, *The Poems.* 2nd ed. Ed. Richard Finneran. New York: Scribner, 1997. Print.

Young, Julian. *The Philosophy of Tragedy: From Plato to Zizek*. New York: Cambridge UP, 2013. Print.

Zeitchik, Steven. "'Road' Might Not Be Done in Time for '08." *Hollywood Reporter* 16 October 2008. Web. 27 July 2014.

Zinoman, Jason. "A Debate of Souls, Torn Between Faith and Unbelief." *New York Times* 31 October 2006. Web. 26 July 2014.

Index

"Whales." *See* "Whales and Men"
   (screenplay)
"Whales and Men" (screenplay), 2, 9,
   55–59, 67, 73, 77–79, 85, 90, 107–108;
   and *The Crossing*, 7, 43, 56, 58; research
   for, 54. *See also* ecology
Wielenberg, Erik, 121
Wild Bunch, The, 42–43
Williams, David, 8, 44, 202
Winfrey, Oprah. See *Road, The* (novel):
   and *The Oprah Winfrey Show*
Wittliff, Bill, 41, 56

wolves. See *Crossing, The*
women, representations of, 6, 150–153,
   166, 178–190
Woodward, Richard, 8, 11, 13, 16–17,
   43–44, 98
Woolmer, Howard, 23, 31, 42, 45, 52, 54,
   73–76

Yeats, W. B., 61, 65–67
Young, Julian, 5, 8